# Database Technology:

# Nulls Considered Harmful

*The Problem of Missing Information*

C. J. Date

Published by:

115 Linda Vista, Sedona, AZ 86336 USA
https://www.TechnicsPub.com

Cover design by Lorena Molinari



First Printing 2024



Printed in the United States of America.

| | |
|---|---|
| ISBN, print ed. | 9781634624763 |
| ISBN, Kindle ed. | 9781634624770 |
| ISBN, PDF ed. | 9781634624824 |

*Wovon man nicht reden kann, darüber muss man schweigen.*
(Whereof one cannot speak, thereon one must remain silent.)

—Ludwig Wittgenstein:
*Tractatus Logico-Philosophicus* (1921)

Missing so much and so much

—Frances Cornford:
*To a Fat Lady Seen from the Train* (1910)

As we know, there are known knowns. There are things we know we know.
We also know there are known unknowns.
That is to say, we know there are some things we don't know.
But there are also unknown unknowns, the ones we don't know we don't know.

—Donald Rumsfeld:
*DoD news briefing* (2002)

If it was so, it might be; and if it were so, it would be;
but as it isn't, it ain't. That's logic.

—Lewis Carroll:
*Through the Looking-Glass and What Alice Found There* (1871)

Nothin' ain't worth nothin'

—Kris Kristofferson and Fred Foster:
*Me and Bobby McGee* (1969)

——— ♦♦♦♦♦ ———

***To all those friends and family who have helped***
***in so many ways during the tribulations of the last few years***

# About the Author

C. J. Date is an independent author, lecturer, researcher, and consultant, specializing in relational database technology. He is best known for his book *An Introduction to Database Systems* (8th ed., Addison-Wesley, 2004), which has sold around a million copies at the time of writing and is used by several hundred colleges and universities worldwide. He is also the author of numerous other books on database management, including most recently:

- From Morgan Kaufmann: *Time and Relational Theory: Temporal Databases in the Relational Model and SQL* (with Hugh Darwen and Nikos A. Lorentzos, 2014)

- From O'Reilly: *View Updating and Relational Theory: Solving the View Update Problem* (2013); *SQL and Relational Theory: How to Write Accurate SQL Code*, 3rd ed. (2015); *The **New** Relational Database Dictionary* (2016); *Type Inheritance and Relational Theory: Subtypes, Supertypes, and Substitutability* (2016)

- From Apress: *Database Design and Relational Theory: Normal Forms and All That Jazz*, 2nd ed. (2019)

- From Technics: *Logic and Relational Theory: Thoughts and Essays on Database Matters* (2020); *Fifty Years of Relational, and Other Database Writings: More Thoughts and Essays on Database Matters* (2020); *Stating the Obvious, and Other Database Writings: Still More Thoughts and Essays on Database Matters* (2020); *E. F. Codd and Relational Theory, Revised Edition: A Detailed Review and Analysis of Codd's Major Database Writings* (2021); *Database Dreaming, Volumes I and II: Relational Writings Revised and Revived* (2022); *On Cantor and the Transfinite* (2023); *Keys, Foreign Keys, and Relational Theory* (2023); *The Relational Model for Database Management Version 2 – A Critical Analysis* (2024)

Mr Date was inducted into the Computing Industry Hall of Fame in 2004. He enjoys a reputation that is second to none for his ability to explain complex technical subjects in a clear and understandable fashion.

# Contents

# Preface

A few months before I left my secondary school, when I was age 16 or so—and, let me add, somewhat against my own personal wishes—I was made a school prefect. This appointment meant among other things that I was entitled to mete out small punishments for minor crimes, typically infractions of school rules. In fact I almost never did anything of the kind, because I would have felt hopelessly hypocritical in imposing punishment for crimes that I'd been committing myself throughout most of my school years, and indeed probably continued to commit as a prefect. However, there was one prefectorial—if that's a word—task I couldn't avoid. Like other prefects, I was required to serve as form prefect for one of the junior forms. What this meant in practice was that I had to be present in "my" form room fifteen minutes or so before the start of the school day and keep the boys in order until the form master arrived. (The school was boys only, perhaps I should add.) And I recall just one occasion when I did in fact hand out a punishment in that capacity ... There was one extremely annoying small boy who kept pushing and pushing the boundaries—I forget exactly what it was he was doing, but in any case it doesn't matter now. Anyway, eventually reaching my limit, I said "OK, that's enough. You can write me an essay, and hand it in by the end of the week." Small boy: "An essay? What on?" Me: "Well, what would you like to write an essay on?" Small boy (very clever): "Nothing!" Me: "All right—give me an essay on nothing, two pages, by Friday." He did, too.

Of course, the irony is that *nullology*, the study of nothing, is in fact an extremely interesting subject, much more so than either I or the small boy could possibly have realized at the time.[1] It's certainly highly relevant to my own professional interest, which is database technology. What's more, there are arguments—well, loose ones—to the effect that the whole of mathematics is built out of nothing (or out of the empty set, at any rate). Cosmologists even believe the entire universe was created out of nothing. Clearly we're talking about a very nontrivial matter here! It's also one that I'm sure is much more complicated than most people think. Here's a quote that sums up the matter beautifully: "Nothing—nobody understands it. But then he would." (Anon? I got it from Martin Gardner.)

---

[1] *Nullology* is a neologism, of course. It was coined by an old friend of mine at IBM, Bob Engles, who defined it—very much tongue in cheek, I hasten to add—as "the study of nothing at all."

Be all that as it may, the small boy wrote only two pages on the subject—but now I've written a whole book. And if you feel, as you very well might feel, that just two pages are surely more than enough for such a topic, then what can I possibly say that will justify a whole book? Especially since the message of that book is going to be: Don't touch this stuff! It's dangerous!

Well, let me clarify what I've just said. This book isn't really about "nothing," as such, at all. Rather, it's about *nulls*—more specifically, about the use of nulls in the database context to represent the fact that some piece of information is missing for some reason. In other words, nulls don't really represent "nothing"; instead, they represent the fact that there's no definite information to be had (other than the definite information that there's no definite information, of course).

Now, as that deliberately convoluted sentence is meant to suggest, it can be quite difficult even just to talk about these matters clearly. What isn't difficult, though, is to make all kinds of bad jokes or puns in connection with them (though those jokes aren't always intended as such, I might add—but when they aren't, I'm not sure that doesn't make matters worse). To illustrate the point, here are the titles of a few writings on the subject. First a few of my own:

*Nothing to Worry About*
*NOT Is Not "Not"!*
*Nothing in Excess*
*Round and Round the Nullberry Bush*
*Null and Void*

Ed Boyno has given us:

*Nulls Ain't Nuthin'*

David McGoveran has contributed:

*Nothing from Nothing*
*Basic Logic: Nothing Compares 2 U*
*Can't Lose What You Never Had*

Hugh Darwen has proposed:

*The Null Before the Storm*

And a debate on the topic between Ted Codd and myself that appeared in *Database Programming & Design* 6, No. 10 (October 1993) had the title—chosen by the editor of that magazine, let me emphasize, not by either of us—

*Much Ado about Nothing*

A version of that debate appears as Appendix C of the present book. In the course of it, by the way, Codd makes the following absolutely priceless remark:

*Database management would be simpler if missing values didn't exist.*

I'm sorry to say I don't think he was joking.

Anyway, to paraphrase what I said earlier, the overall message of this book is that nulls are just bad news, and I hope you'll be persuaded of the truth of that message very early on in your reading. You might even have felt that way before ever you set eyes on this book; indeed, I rather hope you did. But I think the book can serve a useful purpose nevertheless. To be specific, I think it can act as a convenient summary of many of the pertinent arguments, both pro and con (but mostly con), and also perhaps as a sourcebook for some of the problems nulls can cause.

That said, perhaps I should elaborate briefly on my own position with respect to these matters. As I've indicated, nulls are proposed as a solution to the missing information problem. Now, that problem is a real problem, and an important one, too: Information can be missing for all kinds of reasons, as I'll show, and thus we definitely need a way of dealing with such matters in our formal database systems. Unfortunately, it's widely agreed—this isn't just my opinion—that *no fully satisfactory solution to that problem is known at this time*. What is known, though, is that nulls are a disastrously bad one! I mean, the cure (such as it is) is worse than the disease, as this book will make very plain, and as I hope you'll agree after reading it.

Of course, if nulls aren't the solution, then what is? After all, the problem is a real problem, as I've said. So the book includes not only a detailed critique of nulls as such, but also numerous practical suggestions for dealing with the problem—viz., missing information—that nulls are supposed to solve.

### *Suppliers and Parts*

You won't be surprised to learn that most if not all of the examples in this book make use of the familiar suppliers and parts database. That database contains three tables (more specifically, three base tables): namely, S (suppliers), P (parts), and SP (shipments of parts by suppliers). Here's a picture showing the usual sample values:

S

| SNO | SNAME | STATUS | CITY |
|---|---|---|---|
| S1 | Smith | 20 | London |
| S2 | Jones | 10 | Paris |
| S3 | Blake | 30 | Paris |
| S4 | Clark | 20 | London |
| S5 | Adams | 30 | Athens |

P

| PNO | PNAME | COLOR | WEIGHT | CITY |
|---|---|---|---|---|
| P1 | Nut | Red | 12.0 | London |
| P2 | Bolt | Green | 17.0 | Paris |
| P3 | Screw | Blue | 17.0 | Oslo |
| P4 | Screw | Red | 14.0 | London |
| P5 | Cam | Blue | 12.0 | Paris |
| P6 | Cog | Red | 19.0 | London |

SP

| SNO | PNO | QTY |
|---|---|---|
| S1 | P1 | 300 |
| S1 | P2 | 200 |
| S1 | P3 | 400 |
| S1 | P4 | 200 |
| S1 | P5 | 100 |
| S1 | P6 | 100 |
| S2 | P1 | 300 |
| S2 | P2 | 400 |
| S3 | P2 | 200 |
| S4 | P2 | 200 |
| S4 | P4 | 300 |
| S4 | P5 | 400 |

And here are SQL definitions for these tables:

```
CREATE TABLE S
  ( SNO    CHAR(5)      ,
    SNAME  VARCHAR(20)  ,
    STATUS INTEGER      ,
    CITY   VARCHAR(25)  ,
    UNIQUE ( SNO ) )    ;

CREATE TABLE P
  ( PNO    CHAR(6)              ,
    PNAME  VARCHAR(12)          ,
    WEIGHT FIXED DECIMAL(5,2)   ,
    COLOR  VARCHAR(10)          ,
    CITY   VARCHAR(25)          ,
    UNIQUE ( PNO ) )            ;
```

```
CREATE TABLE SP
  ( SNO CHAR(5)                                          ,
    PNO CHAR(6)                                          ,
    QTY INTEGER                                          ,
    UNIQUE ( SNO , PNO )                                 ,
    FOREIGN KEY ( SNO ) REFERENCES S ( SNO )             ,
    FOREIGN KEY ( PNO ) REFERENCES P ( PNO ) )           ;
```

Actually the precise definitions of these tables do vary somewhat from one book of mine to another (deliberately so, of course). In particular, it suits my purposes better in some books to make at least some of the columns be of some user defined type, instead of (as here) defining them all to be of some system defined type such as INTEGER. But the specifics of user defined types aren't particularly relevant to the principal theme of the present book, and so I judged it simpler, this time around, to use system defined types only.

I should mention too that in those other books I invariably specify NOT NULL for every column, but I haven't done so here because, of course, to do so would undermine the entire purpose of the book.

***Prerequisites***

My target audience is database professionals. Thus, I assume you're somewhat familiar with both the relational model and the SQL language. However, I don't think it'll hurt if I review a few technical matters here briefly.

First of all, I hope and assume you're thoroughly familiar with terms and concepts such as *database management system* (DBMS), *relation*, *attribute*, *tuple* (rhymes with "couple," and short for *n*-tuple), *key*, *foreign key*, and *SQL*, as well as *projection*, *join*, *union*, and all of the other usual operators of the relational algebra. But let me say a few words regarding the terms *relation*, *attribute*, and *tuple* in particular. Those terms are, of course, the relational analogs of the SQL terms *table*, *column*, and *row*, respectively—but as I hope you know, there are some significant logical differences in each case. I'm not going to go into detail on those logical differences here; I'll just say that, given the fact that those differences do exist, I find it unfortunate that so much of the database community talks in terms of tables, columns, and rows instead of relations, attributes, and tuples. But precisely because it does, I decided, somewhat against my better judgment, to do the same in the present book (most of the time, at any rate, though not exclusively).

All of that said, however, let me at least give a few basic (and fairly formal) definitions for the record:

**Definition (type):** A named, and in practice finite, set of values; not to be confused with the internal or physical representation of the values in question, which is an implementation issue. Every value, every variable, every attribute, every read-only operator, every parameter, and every expression is of some type. *Note:* Types are also referred to, especially in the relational context, as *domains*.

**Definition (heading):** A *heading* $H$ is a set, the elements of which are *attributes*. Let $H$ have cardinality $n$ ($n \geq 0$);[2] then the value $n$ is the *degree* of $H$. A heading of degree zero is *nullary*, a heading of degree one is *unary*, a heading of degree two is *binary*, ..., and more generally a heading of degree $n$ is *n-ary*. Each attribute in $H$ is of the form $<A_j,T_j>$ ($1 \leq j \leq n$), where $A_j$ is the *attribute name* and $T_j$ is the corresponding *type name*, and the attribute names $A_j$ are all distinct.

**Definition (tuple):** Let heading $H$ be of degree $n$. For each attribute $<A_j,T_j>$ in $H$, define a *component* of the form $<A_j,T_j,V_j>$, where the *attribute value* $V_j$ is a value of type $T_j$. The set—call it $T$—of all $n$ components so defined is a *tuple value* (or just a *tuple* for short) over the attributes of $H$. $H$ is the *tuple heading* (or just the heading for short) for $T$; the degree and attributes of $H$ are, respectively, the degree and attributes of $T$; and the *type* of $T$ is TUPLE $H$.

**Definition (body):** Given a heading $H$, a *body* $B$ conforming to $H$ is a set of $m$ tuples ($m \geq 0$), each with heading $H$. The value $m$ is the *cardinality* of $B$.

**Definition (relation):** Let $H$ be a heading, and let $B$ be a body conforming to $H$. The pair $<H,B>$—call it $R$—is a *relation value* (or just a *relation* for short) over the attributes of $H$. $H$ is the *relation heading* (or just the heading for short) for $R$; the degree and attributes of $H$ and the cardinality of $B$ are, respectively, the degree, attributes, and cardinality of $R$; and the *type* of $R$ is RELATION $H$.

---

[2] The cardinality of a set is the number of elements (or *members*) it contains. See the definition of *body*, following.

These definitions are, of course, all expressed in relational terms (*relation*, *attribute*, *tuple*, etc.). Translating them into corresponding SQL terms—if such terms even exist, I suppose I have to add, because I'm not sure they always do—I'll leave as an exercise. However, please note that I'll be assuming throughout this book, where it makes any difference, that you're reasonably familiar with the foregoing definitions and understand them.

There's one more term I'd also like you to understand, even though I won't be using it at all in the body of the book, and that's the term *relation variable*, abbreviated *relvar*. To elaborate: What all too many people call either "tables" or "relations"—meaning by that term constructs in the database—are indeed variables. After all, their value certainly changes over time as INSERT, DELETE, and UPDATE operations are performed on them, and "changing over time" is exactly what makes them variables. In fact, *not* distinguishing clearly between relation values and relation variables—or table values and table variables, in SQL—has led to an immense amount of confusion in the past, and continues to do so to this day. In our book on *The Third Manifesto*,[3] therefore, Hugh Darwen and I decided to face up to this problem right at the outset. To be specific, we framed our remarks in that book in terms of relation values when it really was relation values that we meant, and in terms of relation variables when it really was relation variables that we meant, and we abided by that discipline rigorously (indeed, 100%). But we also introduced two abbreviations: We allowed "relation value" to be abbreviated to just *relation* (exactly as we allow, e.g., "integer value" to be abbreviated to just *integer*), and we allowed "relation variable" to be abbreviated to a new term, *relvar*.

Unfortunately, however, neither the database community in general (Ted Codd included), nor the SQL community in particular, has ever really picked up on the foregoing terminology. As a consequence, you need to be aware that references in database writings to relations (or tables) must often be understood as meaning relation (or table) variables specifically, not relation (or table) values. Rightly or wrongly, therefore, I decided when I was working on this book (a) to stay with the terminology that will be more familiar to most of my intended readers, and thus (b) to leave it up to you to decide for yourself when the word *relation* (or more usually *table*) means what it says and when it doesn't. Sorry about that; but the fault isn't entirely mine.

---

[3] *Databases, Types, and the Relational Model: The Third Manifesto*, 3rd ed. (Addison-Wesley, 2007). *Note:* For the record, that book contains a precise and formal definition of the relational model—as indeed many other books of mine do also (see, e.g., *SQL and Relational Theory*, 3rd ed., O'Reilly, 2015). Please refer to any of those books if you need further relational specifics.

### *Structure of the Book*

As you can see, this book consists of the present preface—which should definitely not be skipped, by the way—followed by eight detailed chapters, together with two brief appendixes and an index. A few specifics regarding the chapters as such:

- Chapter 1 lays the groundwork by providing a detailed overview of conventional two-valued logic, 2VL (which is, of course, what the relational model is founded on).

- Chapters 2-5 are the heart of the book: They explain Codd's proposed extensions to the relational model—extensions based on nulls and three-valued logic, 3VL, that is, and intended to address the missing information problem—and demonstrate in detail what's wrong with them and why they don't solve the problem they were meant to solve.

- Chapter 6 deals with some of the additional problems—problems, that is, over and above the ones described in Chapters 2-5—that are introduced by the language SQL.

- Chapters 7 and 8 then describe various practical approaches to the missing information problem, approaches that stay firmly in the realm of 2VL and don't involve any such suspect notions as nulls or 3VL at all.

Now, I must make it very clear that almost nothing in the book is new. I've written about these matters before, many times; in fact, a review of my own files shows that I've published well over twenty papers on the subject (some of them with coauthors). But many of those papers are hard to find, and in any case they're widely scattered; thus, I thought it would be helpful—I mean, it would serve a useful purpose—to bring all of the material together in one place, and consolidate and organize it properly, and edit out the worst of the overlaps, and also (sad to say) take the opportunity to correct a few errors. So that's what I've tried to do, and this book is the result.

Regarding that result, though, I must make it clear that I make no claim of completeness. I've tried to be thorough, and accurate, and systematic, but (to repeat) the treatment is still almost certainly incomplete. But that's because I frankly doubt whether any treatment of the subject could ever be fairly described as complete. The problems are endless!—the problems, I mean, that nulls and 3VL can give rise to. All I've done, and all I claim to have done, is provide a kind of compendium of the *kinds* of problems nulls and 3VL can cause. However, I sincerely hope that such a compendium can at least serve as sufficient warning to achieve my overriding goal, which is this: I'd like to ensure that if, despite everything I have to say on the subject, you decide to go ahead and use nulls and 3VL after all, then at least you'll be doing so with your eyes wide open.

I'd like to say something else. To repeat, the material isn't new—but it doesn't seem to be very widely understood (not if the available evidence is anything to go by, at any rate). Certainly the material doesn't seem to be discussed very much in the database literature in general. In fact, I'm not aware of any other publication that's devoted to the topic or covers it as extensively as this book does. To say it again, therefore, I hope the book can serve a useful purpose.

### *References*

The following publications—all of them by Codd—are the ones of most direct relevance to the subject matter of this book in general:

- E. F. Codd: "Extending the Database Relational Model to Capture More Meaning," *ACM Transactions on Database Systems 4*, No. 4 (December 1979)

Codd was, of course, the inventor of the original relational model, back in the late 1960s and early 1970s. Thus, the primary purpose of the foregoing paper, written some ten years subsequently, was to introduce an extended version of the original model, which (the extended version, that is) Codd referred to as *RM/T*. Before it gets into RM/T as such, however, the paper reviews the original model as Codd saw it at the time, and that review includes for the first time a fairly detailed discussion of nulls and 3VL. So 1979 was when he added nulls and 3VL to his original model, by which time it had survived without them for a good ten years.

For brevity I'll refer to the foregoing paper in what follows as *Codd's 1979 paper*, or sometimes as just *the 1979 paper* if it's clear from context which particular paper I have in mind.

- E. F. Codd: "Missing Information (Applicable and Inapplicable) in Relational Databases," *ACM SIGMOD Record 15*, No. 4 (December 1986)

This paper was the first of Codd's writings to be devoted to the subject of missing information exclusively.[4] I won't have much to say about it in what follows—not as such, at any rate—because it was subsequently incorporated more or less verbatim into Codd's book *The Relational Model for Database Management Version 2* (see the next reference). I note for the record, though, that this paper was also the first of Codd's writings to explicitly endorse not just three- but four-valued logic (4VL).

- E. F. Codd: *The Relational Model for Database Management Version 2* (Addison-Wesley, 1990)

Of course, Codd's overall aim in this book wasn't just to describe a way of dealing with missing information; rather, it was to give a complete description of his "new, improved" version of the relational model, which he called RM/V2. But RM/V2 includes as an integral component support for both 3VL and 4VL (and two kinds of nulls accordingly), and in fact references to those extended logics permeate his entire book.

I'll refer to this book in what follows as *Codd's RM/V2 book* or just as *the RM/V2 book*—though perhaps I should make it clear that almost all of those references appear in just one chapter, Chapter 5. Also, you might be interested to know that one of my own books consists of a detailed review of the RM/V2 book, viz., *The Relational Model for Database Management Version 2 – A Critical Review* (Technics, 2024).

### *Closing Remarks*

Let me finish up these prefatory remarks with a word about my title for this book. As you're doubtless aware, the phrase "considered harmful" has become something of a cliché in computing circles. It was originally used in the heading of a letter from E. W. Dijkstra in *Communications of the ACM 11*, No. 3 (March 1968):

---

[4] It's true that he'd touched on these matters in his earlier articles in *Computerworld*—"Is Your DBMS Really Relational?", October 14th, 1985; "Does Your DBMS Run by the Rules?", October 21st, 1985—but that article was hardly very formal, and in any case nulls and 3VL weren't the primary topic.

*GO TO Considered Harmful*

This was the famous letter in which Dijkstra argued that (to quote) "the **go to** statement should be abolished from all 'higher level' programming languages." Some considerable time later, in *Communications of the ACM 30*, No. 3 (March 1987), a response was published from Frank Rubin, with the heading:

*"GO TO Considered Harmful" Considered Harmful*

This letter in turn was followed a couple of months later in the same journal by a correspondence involving various writers, published under the heading

*"'GO TO Considered Harmful' Considered Harmful" Considered Harmful?*

The next move is up to you.

C. J. Date
*Morristown, Vermont*
*2024*

# Chapter 1

# Two–Valued Logic

This chapter consists of a brief review and overview of some simple ideas from conventional logic (which is to say, conventional two-valued logic, with its two truth values TRUE and FALSE). You're probably familiar with most of these matters already. In fact, I hope you are.

## PROPOSITIONS

Here are some examples of natural language statements:

1. The Sun is a star.

2. Neptune is a star.

3. Venus is a planet.

4. Venus has at least two moons.

Each of these statements is, obviously enough, either true or false, unequivocally; in fact, of course, Statements 1 and 3 are true and Statements 2 and 4 are false. More to the point, each is an example of what logicians call a *proposition.* Here's a definition:

> **Definition (proposition):** A declarative statement, expressed in natural language or perhaps in some more formal notation, that's unequivocally either true or false.

Equivalently, a proposition is a statement that evaluates to either TRUE or FALSE, where TRUE and FALSE are literals of type truth value (Boolean literals, in other words). *Caveat:* It's a common mistake to think of propositions as necessarily being true. As the examples indicate, however, such is not the case. A false proposition is still a proposition, just as much as a true one is.

At the risk of confusing you, let me now say that I've already told you something that isn't entirely accurate. To be specific: Let *P* be a declarative statement in the sense of the foregoing definition; in other words, let *P* be a statement that's unequivocally either true or false. Then the corresponding proposition isn't really *P* as such—rather, it's the *assertion made by P* (in other words, it's what *P means*). For example, consider these two statements:

- The Sun is a star.

- Le soleil est une étoile.

Clearly there are two different statements here; equally clearly, though, they both represent the same proposition. In other words, there's a difference between (a) a proposition as such and (b) the syntactic or linguistic form in which that proposition happens to be expressed. In practice, however, it's normal to ignore such distinctions in informal discourse (and indeed in more formal discourse as well, much of the time); and for the rest of this book, I will. But you should at least keep them in the back of your mind, as it were.

Now, given some initial set of propositions, further propositions can be obtained by applying certain *connectives* (also known as *logical operators*) such as NOT, OR, and AND to the ones in that given set. I'll have more to say about connectives in general later in this chapter, but I'm sure the three I've just mentioned are already familiar to you. For the record, though, let me spell out the semantics of those three here. Let *P* and *Q* be arbitrary propositions. Then:

- NOT *P* is true if and only if *P* is false.

- *P* OR *Q* is true if and only if at least one of *P* and *Q* is true.

- *P* AND *Q* is true if and only if *P* and *Q* are both true.

A couple more definitions:

**Definition (simple proposition):** A proposition that involves no connectives.

**Definition (compound, or composite, proposition):** A proposition that's not simple; equivalently, a proposition that involves at least one connective.

Here are a couple of examples of compound propositions:

5. The Sun is a star or Neptune is a star.

6. (Venus is a planet and Neptune is a star) and (the Sun is a star).

Of these two, Statement 5 is true and Statement 6 is false. *Note:* I've used parentheses in Statement 6 in order to make the meaning—also known as the *intended interpretation*—absolutely clear. Parentheses can be used in this way wherever they seem necessary; in practice, however, we typically introduce certain *precedence rules* for the connectives, in order to reduce the number of parentheses that might otherwise be needed. But I'm not aiming for 100% completeness in my treatment of purely syntactic matters in this book, so I won't bother to define any such rules here; instead, I'll just use parentheses whenever I think they might be necessary in order to make my intended meaning clear.

## QUANTIFICATION

My next example, Statement 7, illustrates several further points:

7. Some planets in the Solar System have rings.

Note first that this statement certainly does represent a valid proposition; I mean, certainly it's either true or false, unequivocally. (In fact, of course, it's true.) But I'd like to analyze it a little more carefully. In order to do that, let me first give a more precise version of the statement (a more precise way, that is, of saying the same thing):

7. There exists at least one planet—call it *X*—in the Solar System such that *X* has rings.

Current orthodox opinion has it that the Solar System contains just eight planets: viz., Mercury, Venus, Earth, Mars, Jupiter, Saturn, Uranus, and Neptune

(Pluto is no longer considered a planet as such but merely a "dwarf planet").[1] That being so, Statement 7 is clearly equivalent to, and can be thought of as being shorthand for, the following compound proposition (I deliberately switch now to a different font)—

```
7. Mercury has rings  OR
   Venus   has rings  OR
   Earth   has rings  OR
   Mars    has rings  OR
   Jupiter has rings  OR
   Saturn  has rings  OR
   Uranus  has rings  OR
   Neptune has rings
```

—or, more simply and more succinctly, "*X* has rings, where *X* is one of {Mercury, Venus, ..., Neptune}." In this latter formulation, the symbol *X* denotes a *range variable*—specifically, one whose range is the set of eight planets, or in other words a variable whose legal values are precisely the values in that range.[2]

The important point about range variables as far as we're concerned is that they're not variables in the ordinary programming language sense; rather, they're variables in the sense of logic. In particular, their names are effectively arbitrary. For example, we could replace all occurrences of the name *X* in Statement 7 by a different name, say *Y*, thus—

7. There exists at least one planet—call it *Y*—in the Solar System such that *Y* has rings.

—without changing the meaning of the statement in any way whatsoever.

Now let me focus on the first few words of what I described as that "more precise way" of formulating the statement:

There exists at least one planet—call it *X*—in the Solar System such that ...

---

[1] To quote Wikipedia: "A dwarf planet is a small planetary-mass object that is in direct orbit around the Sun, massive enough to be gravitationally rounded, but [not massive enough] to achieve orbital dominance like the eight classical planets of the Solar System. The prototypical dwarf planet is Pluto, which for decades was regarded as a planet before the 'dwarf' concept was adopted in 2006."

[2] I note in passing that *X* here isn't just a range variable, it's also what logicians called a *bound* variable (it's "bound" by the expression "There exists at least one planet—call it *X*").

These words together constitute a *quantification*. In practice, we would normally replace them by the much more succinct formulation (and now I switch to that different font again)

```
EXISTS X
```

—along with additional text, which I'll omit until further notice, that defines what the pertinent range is. The keyword EXISTS denotes a *quantifier* (the *existential* quantifier, to be precise),[3] and the complete *quantified expression* would thus more typically look something like this:

```
EXISTS X ( X has rings )
```

For more on quantification in general, see the section after next. For now, let me just point out explicitly something I hope you've realized for yourself anyway: namely, that the text in parentheses here ("*X* has rings") does *not* represent a proposition—it isn't unequivocally either true or false—because it contains a reference to a variable, *X*.

## PREDICATES

Consider now the following statements:

8. The Sun is a *K*.

9. *L* is a star.

10. *M* is a planet.

11. *M* has at least *N* moons.

These statements aren't unequivocally either true or false; by definition, therefore, they're not propositions. Instead, they might be regarded as *generalized* or *parameterized* propositions, or in other words as *predicates*. (In

---

[3] In general, to *quantify* something is to say how many of that something there are. In the case of the existential quantfier EXISTS, the "how many" in question is *at least one*. But there are other quantifiers as well in addition to EXISTS, as we'll soon see. *Note:* The existential quantifier is typically represented in logic texts by the symbol ∃ (a backward uppercase E).

fact, of course, they're generalized or parameterized versions of Statements 1-4, respectively, from the section before last.) Replacing the parameters by actual values, or *arguments* (which is to say, *instantiating* the predicates), has the effect of converting those predicates into propositions as such. For example, we can instantiate the predicate in Statement 8 by replacing the parameter *K* by some value. If we replace *K* by "star," we obtain the true proposition "The Sun is a star"; if we replace *K* by "planet," we obtain the false proposition "The Sun is a planet."

Statements 9 and 10 resemble Statement 8 in that they too each involve just a single parameter. Statement 11, however ("*M* has at least *N* moons") has two, viz., *M* and *N*. If we replace both of those parameters by arguments, we obtain a proposition once again—for example:

> Mars has at least two moons.

But suppose we replace just one of the parameters, perhaps as here:

> Mars has at least *N* moons.

This statement isn't a proposition—we can't say it's unequivocally true or false—because it still involves a parameter. In fact, of course, it's another predicate. More terminology:

- A predicate with exactly *r* parameters ($r \geq 0$) is said to be an *r*-place predicate. For example, "*M* has at least *N* moons" is a two-place predicate.

- If *P* is an *r*-place predicate, and if we replace *s* of *P*'s parameters ($r \geq s \geq 0$) by arguments, we obtain an ($r-s$)-place predicate. For example, given the two-place predicate "*M* has at least *N* moons," if we replace the parameter *M* by the argument Mars but don't replace the parameter *N* by anything, we obtain the one-place predicate "Mars has at least *N* moons." Likewise, if we replace the parameter *N* by the argument two but don't replace the parameter *M* by anything, we obtain the one-place predicate "*M* has at least two moons."

- If we replace *all* of the parameters of a given predicate by arguments, we obtain a 0-place predicate. For example, given the two-place predicate

"*M* has at least *N* moons," if we replace *M* by Mars and *N* by two, we obtain the 0-place predicate "Mars has at least two moons."

- But a 0-place predicate is just a proposition! So a proposition is in fact a special case of a predicate (it's the special case where the number of parameters is zero). To put it another way, all propositions are predicates, but "most" predicates aren't propositions.

## MORE ON QUANTIFICATION

As we've just seen, therefore, one way of obtaining a propositon from a predicate is by *fully instantiating* it (in other words, by replacing all of its parameters by arguments). But there's another way too, and that's by using quantification. Again consider Statement 11 ("*M* has at least *N* moons"). If we apply existential quantification to the parameter *M*, we obtain

```
EXISTS M ( M has at least N moons)
```

("there exists a planet *M* such that *M* has at least *N* moons"). If we apply it to *N*, we obtain

```
EXISTS N ( M has at least N moons)
```

("there exists an integer *N* such that planet *M* has at least *N* moons"). Each of these is still a predicate—a one-place predicate, to be precise—and not a proposition, because each of them still involves a parameter. But we could if we like go on to quantify over the remaining parameter as well in each case, to obtain the following results:

```
EXISTS N ( EXISTS M ( M has at least N moons) )

EXISTS M ( EXISTS N ( M has at least N moons) )
```

Both of these statements say the same thing: namely, that there exist a planet *M* and an integer *N* such that *M* has at least *N* moons. This statement *is* unequivocally either true or false—it's true if there does indeed exist at least one planet with at least one moon, and false otherwise. (I'm assuming here, reasonably enough, that the minimum permitted value for the range variable *N* is one.) By definition, therefore, these statements are propositions (the same proposition in both cases, in fact). So to sum up:

- If *P* is an *r*-place predicate, and if we quantify over *s* of *P*'s parameters ($r \geq s \geq 0$), we obtain an ($r$–$s$)-place predicate.

- If $s = r$, the result is a 0-place predicate, or in other words a proposition.

So that's the existential quantifier. As I'm sure you know, however, there's another quantifier in common use as well: viz., the *universal* quantifier FORALL ("for all" or "for every").[4] Here's an example of a statement (a false one, as it happens) involving universal quantification:

12. Every planet has a moon.

Or a little more formally:

```
FORALL X ( X has a moon )
```

Of course, the range variable *X* here ranges over the set of eight planets once again. Thus, Statement 12 is clearly equivalent to, and can be thought of as being shorthand for, the following compound proposition—

```
12. Mercury has a moon   AND
    Venus   has a moon   AND
    Earth   has a moon   AND
    Mars    has a moon   AND
    Jupiter has a moon   AND
    Saturn  has a moon   AND
    Uranus  has a moon   AND
    Neptune has a moon
```

—or, more simply and more succinctly, "Every *X* in the set {Mercury, Venus, ..., Neptune} has a moon."

Here's another example:

13. Every planet revolves around a star.

---

[4] The universal quantifier is typically represented in logic texts by the symbol ∀ (an upside down uppercase A).

Formally:

```
FORALL X ( EXISTS Y ( X revolves around Y ) )
```

*X* in this example ranges over the set of all planets—not just the ones in our own Solar System, let's assume—and *Y* ranges over the set of all stars. What this example illustrates once again, therefore, is the notion that in the quantified expression

```
Q X ( exp )
```

(where *Q* is a quantifier, *X* is a range variable, and *exp* is an expression involving zero or more references to *X*), that expression *exp* might itself be a quantified expression in turn. And so on, recursively, to any depth.

One last point to close this section. Here again is Statement 13:

```
FORALL X ( EXISTS Y ( X revolves around Y ) )
```

What this proposition means is: Every planet revolves around a star. But suppose we switch the quantifiers, thus:

```
EXISTS Y ( FORALL X ( X revolves around Y ) )
```

What this revised proposition means is: There exists a star such that every planet revolves around it (which is clearly false, of course). In other words, *changing the order of the quantifiers has changed the meaning*. So it's very important to get the order right! In general, in fact, given a sequence of like quantifiers—either all EXISTS or all FORALL—then the order doesn't matter (as we saw, at least in the case of EXISTS, near the beginning of this section); but with unlike quantifiers, the order matters very much.

## WE DON'T NEED BOTH QUANTIFIERS

Having introduced the two quantifiers (EXISTS and FORALL), I now have to tell you that we don't actually need them both. Why not? Because each can be defined in terms of the other, thanks to the following identity:

```
FORALL X ( exp ) ≡ NOT ( EXISTS X ( NOT ( exp ) ) )
```

(The symbol "≡" here is the equivalence symbol; it can be read as "is logically equivalent to" or "has the same truth value as" or "is logically identical to") Here's an example: The natural language statements "Everyone is mortal" (i.e., all persons are mortal) and "No one is immortal" (i.e., no person is not mortal) both say the same thing. More formally:

```
14.  FORALL X ( X is mortal )
                         ≡ NOT ( EXISTS X ( NOT ( X is mortal ) ) )
```

What's more, Statement 15 below says exactly the same thing as Statement 14, though the equivalence is perhaps not immediately obvious:

```
15.  EXISTS X ( NOT ( X is mortal ) )
                         ≡ NOT ( FORALL X ( X is mortal ) )
```

In fact we can *prove*, formally, that Statements 14 and 15 both say the same thing. Here's how. Start with Statement 15, but invert it to interchange the expressions on the two sides of the "≡" symbol (this is legal, because $P \equiv Q$ and $Q \equiv P$ are equivalent):

```
     NOT ( FORALL X ( X is mortal ) )
                         ≡ EXISTS X ( NOT ( X is mortal ) )
```

Now negate both sides (this is legal, because $P \equiv Q$ and NOT ($P$) ≡ NOT ($Q$) are equivalent):

```
     NOT ( NOT ( FORALL X ( X is mortal ) ) )
                         ≡ NOT ( EXISTS X ( NOT ( X is mortal ) ) )
```

Finally, simplify the expression on the left side by dropping the two NOTs and corresponding parentheses (this is legal, because NOT (NOT ($P$)) is equivalent to just $P$):

```
     FORALL X ( X is mortal )
                         ≡ NOT ( EXISTS X ( NOT ( X is mortal ) ) )
```

And this result is Statement 14. QED.

So, to repeat, we don't need both EXISTS and FORALL. But it's very convenient to have both in practice, because some predicates and propositions are "more naturally" expressed in terms of EXISTS and others in terms of

FORALL. I'll illustrate this point using SQL and the suppliers and parts database.

Consider the query "Get suppliers who supply all parts." A formulation of this query using conventional logic would look something like this:

```
SX WHERE FORALL PX ( EXISTS SPX ( SX.SNO = SPX.SNO AND
                                  SPX.PNO = PX.PNO ) )
```

(SX, SPX, and PX here are range variables ranging over the suppliers table, the shipments table, and the parts table, respectively.)

SQL, however, supports only EXISTS, not FORALL.[5] As a consequence, the query can be expressed in SQL only much more awkwardly, perhaps something like this:

```
SELECT SX.*
FROM   S AS SX
WHERE  NOT EXISTS
     ( SELECT PX.*
       FROM   P AS PX
       WHERE  NOT EXISTS
            ( SELECT SPX.*
              FROM   SP AS SPX
              WHERE  SX.SNO = SPX.SNO
              AND    SPX.PNO = PX.PNO ) )
```

(loosely, "get suppliers where there doesn't exist a part they don't supply"). Well, single negation can be difficult, as we all know; but double negation is much worse.

I'll have more to say about the foregoing example in the section after next.

## OTHER QUANTIFIERS

*This section is mostly just by way of an aside. You can skip it on a first reading.*

---

[5] In fact it doesn't really support EXISTS either—at least, not as a quantifier as such. Instead, it supports a computational function, or operator, by that name. Here's a definition: The SQL EXISTS function takes a table *T* as its sole argument and returns FALSE if *T* is empty, TRUE otherwise. This sleight of hand works (kind of) because if *X* is a range variable ranging over the rows of table *T*, then the quantifier EXISTS *X* does indeed return FALSE if *T* is empty and TRUE otherwise. Note, however, that (as a moment's thought will show) it's not possible to play the same kind of trick with FORALL, which is why SQL doesn't support FORALL. PS: I say "as a moment's thought will show," but I do recommend that you take that moment and convince yourself that "the same kind of trick" indeed can't be made to work for FORALL.

The most important quantifiers in practice are, of course, the ones I've been discussing, viz., EXISTS and FORALL; indeed, it's quite rare to hear other quantifiers even mentioned. But others are certainly possible. There's no a priori reason, for example, why we shouldn't allow quantifiers of the form

```
there are at least three X's such that
```

or

```
a majority of X's are such that
```

or

```
an odd number of X's are such that
```

(and so on). One fairly important special case is

```
there exists exactly one X such that
```

I'll use the keyword UNIQUE for this one. Here are a couple of examples:

- `UNIQUE X ( X is a moon of Earth )`

  *Meaning:* Earth has exactly one moon (true).

- `UNIQUE X ( planet X has intelligent life )`

  *Meaning:* Exactly one planet has intelligent life. I'll let you decide for yourself what the truth value of this one is!

## RANGE VARIABLES

It's time to take care of an issue I've been ducking so far: namely, if *X* is a range variable, how do we know—come to that, how does the system know—what *X*'s legal values are? Clearly, what we need is some kind of declarative mechanism that will let us define not just range variables as such, but their corresponding ranges in particular.

Actually I've already shown how this issue is handled in SQL. Here again are the first two lines from the SQL example in the section "We Don't Need Both Quantifiers":

```
SELECT SX.*
FROM   S AS SX
```

The specification "S AS SX" in the FROM clause effectively defines SX to be a range variable that ranges over the tuples of the suppliers relation—or over the rows of the suppliers table, rather, since we're talking SQL here. In other words, the legal values of SX are precisely the rows of that table.

Unfortunately, a small complication now enters the picture. The fact is, range variable definitions in SQL are often implicit (with the consequence that some users might not realize that such things even exist).[6] For example, here's an alternative formulation in SQL—in practice, a more likely one—of the query "Get suppliers who supply all parts":

```
SELECT S.*
FROM   S
WHERE  NOT EXISTS
     ( SELECT P.*
       FROM   P
       WHERE  NOT EXISTS
            ( SELECT SP.*
              FROM   SP
              WHERE  S.SNO = SP.SNO
              AND    SP.PNO = P.PNO ) )
```

But what needs to be clearly understood about this formulation is that in the final (third) WHERE clause—

```
WHERE  S.SNO = SP.SNO
AND    SP.PNO = P.PNO
```

—those appearances of the names S and SP and P do *not* refer to the tables with those names! Rather, they refer to *range variables* that have, implicitly, been given the same names as the tables they range over. For example, the opening two lines—

---

[6] Such things as range variables, I mean. The picture is complicated still further by SQL's own terminology in this area, which has to do with something it calls "correlation names," I'll have more to say about this terminological issue in a few moments.

```
SELECT S.*
FROM   S
```

—must be clearly understood as being shorthand for the following:

```
SELECT S.*
FROM   S AS S
```

(italics and boldface added for emphasis). And that specification "S AS S" must be understood in turn as defining a range variable called S—that's the "AS S" portion—that ranges over the table with that same name S.[7]

As an aside, let me add the following. First of all, the foregoing explanation is completely accurate—but it uses my own terminology, which is *not* the terminology that SQL itself uses. In order to explain this point, first let me repeat the opening two lines from the original version of the example:

```
SELECT SX.*
FROM   S AS SX
```

The point, then, is this: The name "SX" here is an example of what official SQL literature refers to, not as the name of a range variable as such—in fact, "range variable" isn't a SQL term at all[8]—but rather as a *correlation name*. But there's no SQL construct called a "correlation"! So what exactly do such names name? And how exactly does SQL explain how the corresponding mechanism works?

Well, be all that as it may, my own clear preference is to introduce explicit range variable definitions, in the form of separate, independent statements. Here for example is how I'd prefer to formulate the foregoing query (the formulation is the same as before, of course, except that now—at last!—I'm including the necessary range variable definitions):

```
SX  RANGES OVER S  ;
SPX RANGES OVER SP ;
PX  RANGES OVER P  ;

SX WHERE FORALL PX ( EXISTS SPX ( SX.SNO = SPX.SNO AND
                                  SPX.PNO = PX.PNO ) )
```

---

[7] Every time I try to explain this point I'm reminded of something an old friend of mine in IBM once said to me in connection with this very issue: "You mathematicians are all the same—you spend hours agonizing over things that are perfectly obvious to everyone else." PS: The friend was Bob Engles, already mentioned in the preface as inventor of the term *nullology*.

[8] At least, it wasn't when SQL was first defined. It was added later, though, but only in a halfhearted kind of way, and "correlation name" still seems to be the preferred term.

## CONNECTIVES

The terms *connective* and *logical operator* are used interchangeably to refer to certain truth valued operators: specifically, ones that (a) take as input either exactly one truth value (monadic operators) or exactly two truth values (dyadic operators) and (b) produce as output just a single truth value. Here's a definition:

> **Definition (connective):** A read-only monadic or dyadic logical operator. There are exactly 20 connectives in two-valued logic, four monadic and 16 dyadic, corresponding directly to the four possible monadic and 16 possible dyadic truth tables (see below).

Using *t* and *f* denote the truth values TRUE and FALSE, respectively, here then are those truth tables. First the monadics:

| | |
|---|---|
| t | t |
| f | t |

| | |
|---|---|
| t | t |
| f | f |

| NOT | |
|---|---|
| t | f |
| f | t |

| | |
|---|---|
| t | f |
| f | f |

And now the dyadics:

| | t | f |
|---|---|---|
| t | t | t |
| f | t | t |

| IF | t | f |
|---|---|---|
| t | t | f |
| f | t | t |

| NAND | t | f |
|---|---|---|
| t | f | t |
| f | t | t |

| | t | f |
|---|---|---|
| t | f | f |
| f | t | t |

| OR | t | f |
|---|---|---|
| t | t | t |
| f | t | f |

| | t | f |
|---|---|---|
| t | t | f |
| f | t | f |

| XOR | t | f |
|---|---|---|
| t | f | t |
| f | t | f |

| | t | f |
|---|---|---|
| t | f | f |
| f | t | f |

| | t | f |
|---|---|---|
| t | t | t |
| f | f | t |

| IFF | t | f |
|---|---|---|
| t | t | f |
| f | f | t |

| | t | f |
|---|---|---|
| t | f | t |
| f | f | t |

| NOR | t | f |
|---|---|---|
| t | f | f |
| f | f | t |

| | t | f |
|---|---|---|
| t | t | t |
| f | f | f |

| AND | t | f |
|---|---|---|
| t | t | f |
| f | f | f |

| | t | f |
|---|---|---|
| t | f | t |
| f | f | f |

| | t | f |
|---|---|---|
| t | f | f |
| f | f | f |

Points arising:

- The connectives most frequently encountered in practice are, of course, NOT (*negation*), OR (*disjunction*), AND (*conjunction*), IF (*implication*, often represented by the symbol "⇒"), and IFF (*equivalence*, also called "if and only if," often represented by the symbol "≡").
  
  *Note:* A number of different symbols and/or common names, or keywords, are used in the literature to denote individual connectives (not just the ones mentioned here, but certain others as well). A few of those names are mentioned in the bullet item immediately following. Note, however, that most connectives don't have common names at all.

- Other named connectives include NAND, NOR, and XOR (i.e., exclusive OR; by convention, the unqualified term OR is always taken to mean inclusive OR specifically).

- Of the various dyadic connectives with explicit names, only IF has a truth table that's not symmetric about the diagonal (the diagonal from top left to bottom right, that is). That table is meant to be read as follows. Let operands *P* and *Q* have truth values as indicated down the left side of the table and across the top, respectively; then the expression IF *P* THEN *Q* has truth value as indicated in the body of the table. Analogous remarks apply to all of the asymmetric connectives (and to the symmetric ones too, of course, but in those cases it makes no difference as to which operand is which).

I note before going any further that the dyadic tables can also be drawn in a different style, one that more closely resembles that of the monadic ones. Here are a few examples:

| OR | | |
|---|---|---|
| t | t | t |
| t | f | f |
| f | t | t |
| f | f | t |

| AND | | |
|---|---|---|
| t | t | t |
| t | f | f |
| f | t | f |
| f | f | f |

| IF | | |
|---|---|---|
| t | t | t |
| t | f | f |
| f | t | t |
| f | f | t |

| IFF | | |
|---|---|---|
| t | t | t |
| t | f | f |
| f | t | f |
| f | f | t |

Neither style is more correct than the other—it's just that sometimes one is more convenient, sometimes the other is.

Now, it should be clear from all of the above that the various connectives aren't all primitive—some can be defined in terms of others. For example, the proposition

```
IF P THEN Q
```

is logically equivalent to the proposition

```
( NOT P ) OR Q
```

—in other words, it's false if and only if *P* is true and *Q* is false, as you can see from the truth table for IF. As a matter of fact, *all possible* monadic and dyadic connectives can be expressed in terms of suitable combinations of NOT and either AND or OR![9] Here's a proof:

- First of all, it's easy to see from De Morgan's Laws—see the next section—that we don't need both AND and OR. To be specific:

```
P AND Q  ≡  NOT ( NOT ( P ) OR NOT ( Q ) )
```

and

```
P OR Q  ≡  NOT ( NOT ( P ) AND NOT ( Q ) )
```

These equivalences are easily established by means of truth tables. Here for example is a proof of the first one (I refer to certain columns here by their left to right numeric position for space reasons):

| *P* | *Q* | P AND Q | NOT *P* | NOT *Q* | 4 OR 5 | NOT 6 | 3 ≡ 7 |
|---|---|---|---|---|---|---|---|
| *t* | *t* | *t* | *f* | *f* | *f* | *t* | *t* |
| *t* | *f* | *f* | *f* | *t* | *t* | *f* | *t* |
| *f* | *t* | *f* | *t* | *f* | *t* | *f* | *t* |
| *f* | *f* | *f* | *t* | *t* | *t* | *f* | *t* |

[9] Conventional two-valued logic, 2VL (which certainly supports NOT, OR, and AND) is thus *truth functionally complete*. In general, a logic is truth functionally complete if and only if every possible connective can be defined in terms of the given ones. Truth functional completeness is an extremely important property; a logic without it would be like an arithmetic that was missing certain operations (the operation of addition, say) and would thus be of extremely limited utility.

Since the last column, column 8, contains nothing but *t* (TRUE) in every position, the claimed equivalence is shown, and it follows that AND can be defined in terms of NOT and OR. *Exercise:* Make sure you understand the foregoing argument before reading any further.

A similar proof—exercise for the reader!—can be used to show that OR can be defined in terms of NOT and AND. Thus, each of AND and OR can be defined in terms of the other and NOT, and it follows that we can freely use both AND and OR in what follows.

- Now consider the monadic connectives (i.e., the ones involving just a single proposition *P*). Let the connective under consideration be denoted *c*(*P*). Then the four possibilities are as follows:

```
c(P)   ≡  P                      /* identity      */
c(P)   ≡  NOT ( P )              /* NOT           */
c(P)   ≡  P OR NOT ( P )         /* always TRUE   */
c(P)   ≡  P AND NOT ( P )        /* always FALSE */
```

- Now consider the dyadic connectives (i.e., the ones involving two propositions, *P* and *Q*). Let the connective under consideration be denoted *c*(*P*,*Q*). Then the 16 possibilities are as follows:

```
c(P,Q)   ≡   P
c(P,Q)   ≡   Q
c(P,Q)   ≡   NOT ( P )
c(P,Q)   ≡   NOT ( Q )
c(P,Q)   ≡   P AND Q
c(P,Q)   ≡   P OR Q
c(P,Q)   ≡   P AND NOT ( Q )
c(P,Q)   ≡   P OR NOT ( Q )
c(P,Q)   ≡   NOT ( p ) AND Q
c(P,Q)   ≡   NOT ( P ) OR q
c(P,Q)   ≡   NOT ( P ) AND NOT ( Q )
c(P,Q)   ≡   NOT ( P ) OR NOT ( Q )
c(P,Q)   ≡   P AND NOT ( P ) AND Q AND NOT ( Q )
c(P,Q)   ≡   P OR NOT ( P ) OR Q OR NOT ( Q )
c(P,Q)   ≡   ( NOT ( P ) OR Q ) AND ( NOT ( Q ) OR P )
c(P,Q)   ≡   ( NOT ( P ) AND Q ) OR ( NOT ( Q ) AND P )
```

QED.

Perhaps even more remarkably, all 20 of the foregoing connectives can in fact be expressed in terms of just one primitive. Can you find it? (*Pause here to let you think about this question.*)

——— ♦♦♦♦♦ ———

*Answer:* Actually there are two such primitives, NOR and NAND, sometimes denoted by a down arrow, "↓" (the *Peirce arrow*) and a vertical bar, "|" (the *Sheffer stroke*), respectively.[10] Here are the truth tables:

| NOR | *t* | *f* |
|---|---|---|
| *t* | *f* | *f* |
| *t* | *f* | *t* |

| NAND | *t* | *f* |
|---|---|---|
| *t* | *f* | *t* |
| *f* | *t* | *t* |

As these truth tables suggest, $P \downarrow Q$ ("*P* NOR *Q*") is equivalent to NOT (*P* OR *Q*) and $P|Q$ ("*P* NAND *Q*") is equivalent to NOT (*P* AND *Q*). In what follows, I'll concentrate on NOR (I'll leave NAND to you).

Observe first that this connective can helpfully be thought of as "neither nor" ("neither the first operand nor the second is true"). I now show how to define NOT, OR, and AND in terms of this operator:

$$\text{NOT } ( P ) \equiv P \downarrow P$$
$$P \text{ AND } Q \equiv ( P \downarrow P ) \downarrow ( Q \downarrow Q )$$
$$P \text{ OR } Q \equiv ( P \downarrow Q ) \downarrow ( P \downarrow Q )$$

For example, let's take a closer look at the case of *P* AND *Q*:

| *P* | *Q* | $P \downarrow P$ | $Q \downarrow Q$ | $(P \downarrow P) \downarrow (Q \downarrow Q)$ |
|---|---|---|---|---|
| *t* | *t* | *f* | *f* | *t* |
| *t* | *f* | *f* | *t* | *f* |
| *f* | *t* | *t* | *f* | *f* |
| *f* | *f* | *t* | *t* | *f* |

This truth table shows that $(P \downarrow Q) \downarrow (Q \downarrow Q)$ is equivalent to *P* AND *Q*, because its first, second, and final columns are identical to the corresponding columns in the truth table for AND. The other two cases can be demonstrated similarly. Thus, NOT, OR, and AND can all be expressed in terms of NOR alone. And since we've already seen that all 20 connectives can all be expressed in terms of NOT, OR, and AND, the overall conclusion follows. QED.

---

[10] In my book *An Introduction to Database Systems*, 8th ed. (Addison-Wesley, 2004), I said the Sheffer stroke corresponded to NOR, not NAND. I don't accept full responsibility for this mistake, however!—the logic text I was working from at the time got it wrong, too.

## CONTRADICTIONS AND TAUTOLOGIES

A *contradiction* in logic is an expression that's guaranteed to evaluate to FALSE, regardless of the values of any variables that might be involved in that expression. Here are some examples (*P* here is any truth valued expression):

```
P AND NOT ( P )

P IFF NOT ( P )

P AND FALSE

FALSE
```

By contrast, a *tautology* in logic—and let me note immediately that tautologies are much more important in practice than contradictions[11]—is an expression that's guaranteed to evaluate to TRUE, regardless of the values of any variables that might be involved. Here are some examples:

```
P OR NOT ( P )

P IFF P

P AND TRUE

TRUE
```

And here are a couple of particularly important ones ("De Morgan's Laws"; *Q* here, like *P*, is any truth valued expression):

```
NOT ( P AND Q ) ≡ ( NOT P ) OR  ( NOT Q )

NOT ( P OR  Q ) ≡ ( NOT P ) AND ( NOT Q )
```

These two aren't just tautologies, they're *identities*—they state, in effect, that certain truth valued expression are equivalent, in the sense that they both have the same truth value. Identities are particularly important in the database context in the process known as *query rewrite*: the process, that is, of transforming some given expression into another expression that's logically equivalent to the given one, but we hope will perform better. Query rewrite can

---

[11] Of course, *X* is a tautology if and only if NOT (*X*) is a contradiction.

be done either by the user or—much more important (?)—by the system optimizer.

Now, we can, of course, write down on paper any logical expression we like. Here are a few examples (some of which are simplified versions of ones we've already seen, while others are new). I've numbered them for purposes of subsequent reference.

1. `IF P THEN Q`
2. `IF ( P AND Q ) THEN P`
3. `IF P THEN ( P OR Q )`
4. `P OR NOT P`
5. `P IFF ( NOT ( NOT P ) )`
6. `( P IFF Q ) IFF ( ( IF P THEN Q ) AND ( IF Q THEN P ) )`
7. `P AND NOT P`

Clearly, just writing a given expression down on paper isn't the same as saying the expression in question is a tautology. In order to say a given expression *is* a tautology, we need another symbol, "⊨" ("it is the case that"). To express the fact that Example 2 above is a tautology, for example (which it clearly is—check the truth tables if you're not sure), we would write:

```
⊨ IF ( P AND Q ) THEN P
```

As you can easily verify, Examples 2-6 above are all tautologies; of these, however, only Examples 5 and 6 are identities (i.e., tautologies of the form *X* IFF *Y*, or $X \equiv Y$). By contrast, Example 7 is a contradiction—the only one in the set, as it happens.

*Terminology*: The operator "⊨" ("it is the case that," referred to by the name *double right turnstile*) is an example of a *metalogical* operator, because it enables us to make logical statements, or metastatements, about logic itself. Other metalogical operators do exist, but they're beyond the scope of this book.

## DEFINITIONS

To close this preliminary chapter, here for purposes of future reference are definitions, in alphabetical order, for some of the concepts introduced in previous sections. The definitions are deliberately not always very rigorous.

**Definition (bound variable):** Within a predicate, a variable that's quantified. For example, the variable *X* is bound in the predicate EXISTS *X* (*P*(*X*)).

**Definition (connective):** A read-only monadic or dyadic logical operator. There are exactly 20 connectives in conventional two-valued logic, four monadic and 16 dyadic, corresponding directly to the four possible monadic and 16 possible dyadic truth tables.

**Definition (existential quantifier)**: Let *P*(*X*) be a predicate with sole parameter *X*; then EXISTS *X* (*P*(*X*)) is a proposition, and it means "There exists at least one argument *A* that can be substituted for *X* such that *P*(*A*) is true." In this example, EXISTS *X* is an existential quantifier, and *X* is an existentially quantified range (or bound) variable. Points arising:

- Some writers refer to EXISTS by itself (i.e., as opposed to EXISTS *X*) as the existential quantifier; indeed, I'll probably do the same myself in what follows. The literature is not consistent on this point.

- If $A_1$, $A_2$, ..., $A_n$ are all of the possible arguments in the foregoing example, then EXISTS *X* (*P*(*x*)) is equivalent to

  ```
  FALSE OR P(A1) OR P(A2) OR ... OR P(An)
  ```

  Note that this expression evaluates to FALSE if the variable *X* has an empty range.

**Definition (free variable):** A parameter.

**Definition (instantiation)**: Loosely, the process, or the result of the process, of replacing the arguments of a predicate by parameters. More precisely, let *P* have *r* parameters (i.e., let *P* be an *r*-place predicate). Then we can instantiate *P* by substituting arguments for any number *s* of its parameters ($0 \leq s \leq r$), thereby obtaining an ($r-s$)-place predicate. If $s = r$, the instantiation is said to be full (and the term *instantiation*, unqualified, is usually taken to mean full instantiation specifically, unless the context demands otherwise); otherwise it's said to be partial. Full instantiation of a predicate yields a proposition.

**Definition (parameter):** Within a predicate, a variable that's not bound (i.e., not quantified). *Note:* In conventional logic texts, parameters are more usually referred to as *free variables*.

**Definition (predicate):** A truth valued function; a parameterized or generalized proposition. *Note:* Strictly speaking, however, if *P* is a truth valued function, then the corresponding predicate isn't really *P* as such—rather, it's the meaning of *P*, or in other words what *P* denotes.

**Definition (proposition):** A 0-place predicate; a predicate with no parameters; a statement that's unequivocally either true or false. *Note:* Strictly speaking, however, if *P* is a truth valued statement (and if *P* has no parameters), then the corresponding proposition isn't really *P* as such—rather, it's the meaning of *P*, or in other words what *P* denotes.

**Definition (range variable):** A variable that "ranges over" some set of values (typically the set of tuples in some relation, in the database context) and can appear either bound or free in logical expressions.

**Definition (universal quantifier**): Let *P*(*X*) be a predicate with sole parameter *X*; then FORALL *X* (*P*(*X*)) is a proposition, and it means "For all possible arguments *A* that can be substituted for *X*, *P*(*A*) is true." In this example, FORALL *X* is a universal quantifier, and *X* is a universally quantified range (or bound) variable. Points arising:

- Some writers refer to FORALL by itself (i.e., as opposed to FORALL *X*) as the quantifier; indeed, I'll probably do the same myself in what follows. The literature is not consistent on this point.

- If $A_1$, $A_2$, ..., $A_n$ are all of the possible arguments in the foregoing example, then FORALL X (*P*(*X*)) is equivalent to

```
TRUE AND P(A1) AND P(A2) AND ... AND P(An)
```

Note that this expression evaluates to TRUE if the variable *X* has an empty range.

### *Table Predicates*

There are two further terms I need to define, terms I haven't used in this chapter prior to this point, but ones I'm going to need later on. The first is *table predicate*:

**Definition (table predicate):** Let *T* be a (relational) table. Then the table predicate for *T* is the predicate that represents the user understood meaning of *T*. If *T* has *n* columns, that predicate will be *n*-adic—it will have one parameter for each column of *T*, and no others.

*Note:* In accordance with *The Closed World Assumption* (see the next subsection below), *T* will contain, at any given time, all and only those rows that correspond to instantiations of the table predicate for *T* that evaluate to TRUE at that time. Observe, therefore, that if a given row *R* could appear in table *T* but doesn't (at some given time), then the interpretation is: The instantiation corresponding to *R* of the table predicate for *T* is FALSE (at that given time).

For example, the predicate for the suppliers table S is:

*Supplier SNO is under contract, is named SNAME, has status STATUS, and is located in city CITY.*

Well, let me immediately elaborate on what I've just said! That italicized predicate is certainly the one I'll be assuming elsewhere in this book to be the one for table S. However, it would really be more accurate to say the predicate is rather:

*We know that*—or (perhaps better) *We believe that—supplier SNO is under contract, is named SNAME, has status STATUS, and is located in city CITY.*

The point is, there can't be any guarantee that the database truly reflects the state of affairs that exists in the real world—all it can do is reflect what users tell it. And what users tell it will reflect their beliefs about the real world, not necessarily the real world per se. Note in particular, therefore, that if a certain row, say (S6,Gomez,30,Madrid), fails to appear in table S, the accurate interpretation is *not* as follows:

> *It's not the case that supplier S6 is under contract, is named Gomez, has status 30, and is located in city Madrid.*

Rather, it's as follows:

> *It's not the case that we know that*—or, more colloquially and more simply, just *We don't know whether—supplier S6 is under contract, is named Gomez, has status 30, and is located in city Madrid.*

Of course, it's customary to ignore such refinements in informal contexts, but perhaps it ought not to be.

### *The Closed World Assumption*

The other term I still need to define (or concept I need to explain, rather) is *The Closed World Assumption* (CWA for short):

> **Definition (*Closed World Assumption*):** Loosely, the assumption that everything stated or implied by the database is true and everything else is false. More precisely, let table *T* have predicate *P* (see the previous subsection). Then *The Closed World Assumption* says that:
>
> a. If row *R* appears in *T* at a given time, then the instantiation of *P* corresponding to *R* is assumed to be true at that time.
>
> b. Conversely, if row *R* could appear in *T* at a given time but doesn't, then the instantiation of *P* corresponding to *R* is assumed to be false at that time.

In other words, row *R* appears in table *T* at a given time *if and only if* it satisfies the predicate for *T* at that time (in other words, if and only if the corresponding instantiation of the predicate for *T* is a true proposition). What's more, it follows that (a) if proposition *Q* is represented by a row that appears in some table that can be derived from the tables in the database at some given time, then (b) proposition *Q* is true at that time (which is why the phrase "or implied" appears in the original CWA definition).

Here are some examples. First, the row (S1,P1,300) currently appears in the shipments table SP (see the sample values in the preface), and we can therefore assume that it's currently the case that supplier S1 supplies part P1 in quantity 300. By contrast, the row (S5,P6,250) doesn't currently appear, though presumably it could; we can therefore assume that it's currently not the case that supplier S5 supplies part P6 in quantity 250.

As for an example of implied information, the supplier number S3 currently appears in the projection of table SP on {SNO}; we can therefore assume that it's currently the case that supplier S3 supplies some part in some quantity. By contrast, the supplier number S5 doesn't currently appear in that projection, though presumably it could; we can therefore assume that it's currently not the case that supplier S5 supplies any part in any quantity.

I'll have quite a lot more to say about *The Closed World Assumption* in Chapters 7 and 8.

# Chapter 2

# Three–Valued Logic: The Basics

Now I turn my attention to three-valued logic and related matters. This chapter is concerned mostly just with setting the scene.

## AN INTRODUCTORY EXAMPLE

Conventional logic deals with exactly two truth values, TRUE and FALSE, and for that reason is often referred to more specifically as two-valued logic (2VL for short). Sometimes, however, we have to deal with propositions—at least, let's call them propositions for the time being, though whether they really deserve to be referred to as such is a question in itself—whose truth value we don't know. In the case of the suppliers and parts database, for example, we might want to enter information into the parts table P regarding a particular part (P7, say) whose color we don't know. Let's examine this example a little more carefully:

- First of all, we obviously can't insert a row into table P saying that part P7 is, say, blue, because rows in tables in a relational database are supposed to represent "true facts"—more precisely, true propositions—and we don't know whether the proposition "Part P7 is blue" is true or not. In other words, if we did insert such a row into the table, then we'd effectively be asserting that a certain proposition is true even though we can't say for certain that it is; in fact, it might be false. Thus, if we did insert such a row, we might even be accused of lying.

- Of course, we can't insert a row into table P saying that part P7 is any other specific color, either (orange, green, whatever), for exactly analogous reasons.

In his 1979 paper "Extending the Database Relational Model to Capture More Meaning," therefore, Codd proposed a mechanism for dealing with this kind of situation.[1] More precisely, he proposed a construct called a *null*, which

a. Is definitely not a value as such; instead, it's a kind of placeholder for a value, the value in question being missing for some reason. Note, therefore, that the term *null value* (much heard in SQL contexts in particular) is highly misleading; in fact, it's a contradiction in terms, and in my opinion should never be used.

b. Is allowed to appear at any row and column intersection within any database table, barring integrity constraints to the contrary.

c. Has the interpretation *value unknown*.

Well ... right away I think I need to interrupt myself. All I'm trying to do in the present chapter is introduce some of the basic ideas surrounding the general concept of null. Unfortunately, however, this whole subject is extremely difficult to explain clearly, because almost everything anyone says—almost everything anyone *can* say—by way of explanation turns out on closer examination to just make no sense. In fact, if you think carefully enough about some of the statements I've already made in this chapter by way of "explanation"—including, incidentally, all three of a., b., and c. above—I believe you'll find they don't really stand up to proper critical analysis. But I have to start somewhere! I won't achieve the objectives I have in mind for this book if right at the outset I just throw up my hands and say "It's all nonsense, anyway"—even though it is. Until further notice, therefore, I'm afraid we're simply going to have to suspend disbelief, as it were, and pretend that nulls can be made to make sense after all.

So let's soldier on. In accordance with Codd's nulls scheme, then, we might insert a row for part P7 into table P that looks like this (the color is

---

[1] The paper was published in *ACM Transactions on Database Systems 4*, No. 4 (December 1979). As noted in the preface, I'll refer to it from this point forward just as *Codd's 1979 paper*.

*A note on chronology:* While it's true that Codd didn't add nulls to the relational model *formally* until 1979, the fact is that they'd already been implemented a few years previously in the IBM Research prototype System R—see M. M. Astrahan et al., "System R: Relational Approach to Database Management," *ACM Transactions on Database Systems 1*, No. 2 (June 1976). But then again, Codd had written a paper as far back as 1971 ("A Data Base Sublanguage Founded on the Relational Calculus," IBM Research Report RJ893, July 26th, 1971) in which he gave a brief example showing that he was already thinking—though perhaps not in any great depth—about such matters before the System R project even began. So exactly who it was that invented nulls as we've come to know and love them, and exactly when that happened, are matters that at this distance aren't entirely clear. Maybe it was a joint effort.

unknown, but the name, weight, and city are—let's assume—all known and have the values shown):

| PNO | PNAME | COLOR | WEIGHT | CITY |
|---|---|---|---|---|
| P7 | Bolt | *null* | 17.0 | Madrid |

Suppose, therefore, that this row has indeed been inserted, and table P thus now looks like this:

P

| PNO | PNAME | COLOR | WEIGHT | CITY |
|---|---|---|---|---|
| P1 | Nut | Red | 12.0 | London |
| P2 | Bolt | Green | 17.0 | Paris |
| P3 | Screw | Blue | 17.0 | Oslo |
| P4 | Screw | Red | 14.0 | London |
| P5 | Cam | Blue | 12.0 | Paris |
| P6 | Cog | Red | 19.0 | London |
| P7 | Bolt | *null* | 17.0 | Madrid |

Then the question arises: How do nulls behave when we try to use them in some way—if we try to do comparisons on them, for example? Well, consider the query "Get all blue parts," which might be formulated thus:[2]

```
P WHERE COLOR = 'Blue'
```

Now, the comparison in the WHERE clause here is clearly satisfied by the rows for parts P3 and P5 and not by the ones for parts P1, P2, P4, or P6. But what about the one for part P7? Here's how I believe Codd would answer this question (but I must make it clear that the wording that follows is mine, not Codd's):

- For part P7, the comparison in question becomes, in effect,

  ```
  COLOR = null
  ```

[2] A more precise formulation would be PX WHERE PX.COLOR = 'Blue', where PX is a range variable ranging over the rows of the parts table P. As in SQL, however, let's agree to adopt some "obvious" syntax rules that make simpler formulations like the one shown legitimate. Though I feel compelled to add that, as I've had occasion to remark elsewhere, *obvious* is possibly the most dangerous word in mathematics.

- Such a comparison evaluates, not to true and not to false, but to *unknown* ("the third truth value"), *even if the color is null. Note:* For definiteness, I'll assume from this point forward that the system supports Boolean literals TRUE, FALSE, and UNKNOWN accordingly.

- The truth valued expression in the WHERE clause in the query under consideration thus evaluates to UNKNOWN for part P7. Of course, it's precisely that WHERE clause that controls which rows appear in the result of the query overall; and in such a context, UNKNOWN gets treated as—in effect, it gets implicitly converted, or *coerced*, to—FALSE, with the result that the row in question is rejected. In the example, therefore, the row for part P7 doesn't appear in the final result.

So that's the basic idea: Nulls lead to the need for a third truth value, and hence for a three-valued logic (3VL for short). Here then are the 3VL truth tables for the connectives NOT, OR, and AND (using *t*, *u*, and *f* to stand for TRUE, UNKNOWN, and FALSE, respectively):

| NOT | |
|---|---|
| t | f |
| u | u |
| f | t |

| OR | t | u | f |
|---|---|---|---|
| t | t | t | t |
| u | t | u | u |
| f | t | u | f |

| AND | t | u | f |
|---|---|---|---|
| t | t | u | f |
| u | u | u | f |
| f | f | f | f |

The tables for OR and AND are, I think, reasonable enough—at least, let's agree as much for present purposes—but the one for NOT needs a little more explanation. According to that table, NOT UNKNOWN is still UNKNOWN. Now, this state of affairs might seem a little counterintuitive (in natural language, "not unknown" surely means "known"), but in fact it does make a kind of sense. For example, if we don't know the color for part P7, then we don't know that it's blue, and we don't know that it's not blue, either. (Or at any rate that's what the 3VL scheme assumes. In the real world it might be the case that even if we don't know what color the part is exactly, we might at least know it's not blue. But the 3VL scheme isn't fine grained enough to be able to deal with more complex situations like this one.)

## A MORE SEARCHING EXAMPLE

I turn now to a more searching example, this time involving the suppliers table, table S. Suppose that table looks like this (i.e., suppose the city is unknown for suppliers S2, S4, and S5):

| SNO | SNAME | STATUS | CITY |
|---|---|---|---|
| S1 | Smith | 20 | London |
| S2 | Jones | 10 | *null* |
| S3 | Blake | 30 | Paris |
| S4 | Clark | 20 | *null* |
| S5 | Adams | 30 | *null* |

Now consider the following expression (or query, if you prefer):

```
S WHERE CITY = 'London'
```

In accordance with the explanations in the previous section, this expression will evaluate to a table of just one row:

| SNO | SNAME | STATUS | CITY |
|---|---|---|---|
| S1 | Smith | 20 | London |

For brevity, let's agree to refer to this result, a trifle sloppily, as "just S1." Of course, the reason why the result is just S1 is that S1 is the only supplier for whom the condition in the WHERE clause evaluates to TRUE. But that's a problem right there! As we know, that condition actually has three possible values—TRUE, UNKNOWN, and FALSE—but as we saw in the previous section, UNKNOWN gets coerced to FALSE in this context, and so the WHERE clause overall has only two possible results, not three. In other words, the system has produced *definite output from indefinite input* (or so it might be argued, at any rate). Here in brief is one possible consequence of this state of affairs:

- Suppose the user does know that S4, say, is currently represented in the input table (viz., table S).

- However, S4 is clearly not represented in the output table (the result).

- So the user might reasonably conclude that S4 isn't in London.

But this conclusion is wrong. So has the system lied to us?

Well, maybe not. What the user needs to understand is that the expression

```
S WHERE CITY = 'London'
```

*doesn't* represent the query "Get suppliers in London"—rather, it represents the query "Get suppliers *known to be* in London." Further, that "known to be" refers to the *system*'s knowledge, not the user's; that is, a still more accurate interpretation of the query would be "Get suppliers known *to the system* to be in London." Thus, the conclusion to be drawn from the fact that S4 doesn't appear in the result isn't that S4 isn't in London; rather, it's that S4 isn't *known to the system to be* in London. So no, the system hasn't exactly lied to us after all. But it's a very fine distinction, isn't it! Indeed, it's a distinction that's likely to escape most users (or so it seems to me, at any rate); certainly it's one that never gets very much attention in practice. Do you feel comfortable knowing that society at large is busy building literally thousands of major practical applications on the basis of databases where such fine distinctions are of such crucial significance?

Let me repeat the message of the preceding paragraph in different words, because it's important. The overriding point is this: While the two conditions "location is London" and "location isn't London" are mutually exclusive and exhaust the full range of possibilities in the real world, the database doesn't contain the real world—rather, it contains *the system's knowledge of* the real world. And in the case at hand there are three possibilities, not two, regarding that knowledge—"location is known to be London," "location is known not to be London," and "location is unknown." And we obviously can't ask the system questions about the real world, we can only ask it about its knowledge of the real world, as represented by the data in the database. Thus, the counterintuitive nature—or what 3VL advocates might call the *alleged* counterintuitive nature—of the foregoing example derives from a confusion over levels: The user is thinking at the level of the real world, but the system is thinking at the level of its knowledge of that real world.

Now, if the foregoing were the only kind of difficulty arising in connection with 3VL and its counterintuitive nature, I don't think there'd be much of a problem—it would just be a matter of absorbing and understanding, and taking to heart, the substance of the preceding paragraphs. Unfortunately, however, matters don't stop there, as I'll now proceed to show.

### *More on Table Predicates*

What's the predicate for table S? The obvious answer to this question, and indeed the one I gave near the end of the previous chapter, is as follows:

> *Supplier SNO is under contract, is named SNAME, has status STATUS, and is located in city CITY.*

Actually this entire statement should really be preceded by "We believe that" or "The system knows that" or some other such qualifying phrase, but let's agree to overlook this point for the moment in the interest of simplicity. What's much more to the point for present purposes is that the statement fails to take nulls into account. Let's suppose, then (again for simplicity, but only for the moment), that column CITY permits nulls, but no other column does. Then the predicate will have to look more like this:

> *Supplier SNO is under contract, is named SNAME, has status STATUS, and either is located in city CITY or has a location that's unknown.*

Now suppose, perhaps a little more realistically, that nulls can appear in every column of table S except for column SNO.[3] Then the predicate becomes:

> *Supplier SNO is under contract, either is named SNAME or has a name that's unknown, either has status STATUS or has a status that's unknown, and either is located in city CITY or has a location that's unknown.*

Well, I think you'll agree that such a predicate is pretty clumsy, to say the least. Do we *really* want users to have to deal with such complexity, or have to think in such cumbersome terms? Personally, I don't think so. But I'll leave it at that for now; I'll come back to the point, and discuss it in detail, in Chapter 8.

---

[3] Why do I exclude column SNO here, do you think?

### *The Example Continued*

Here's another query against the suppliers table as shown near the beginning of this section:

```
S WHERE CITY ≠ 'London'
```

An analysis similar to that in connection with the previous example (S WHERE CITY = 'London') applies here also, and the result is just S3.

What about this one (a combination of the previous two)?—

```
S WHERE CITY = 'London' OR CITY ≠ 'London'
```

The result is S1 and S3, the union of the previous two results. But wait a minute—surely the condition in the WHERE clause here is a tautology, isn't it? Surely every supplier is either in London or not in London! So shouldn't the result be all suppliers (S1, S2, S3, S4, S5)?

Well, no, it shouldn't; once again the query expression doesn't quite mean what it looks as if it means. To be specific, it doesn't mean "Get suppliers either in or not in London"—rather, it means "Get suppliers either *known to be* in London or *known not to be* in London." In other words, once again we're talking about the logical difference between reality as such, on the one hand, and the system's knowledge of reality on the other.

Let me spell out the foregoing argument in detail (apologies for the repetition, but the point is important—indeed, fundamentally so). In the real world, there are just two possibilities:

1. The supplier is in London.

2. The supplier isn't in London.

As far as the system is concerned, however, there are three possibilities, not two:

1. The supplier is known to be in London.

2. The supplier isn't known to be in London.

3. The supplier's location isn't known at all.

Another fine distinction, then (and all of the previous remarks regarding such a situation apply once again).

It follows from the foregoing that the truth valued expression

```
CITY = 'London' OR CITY ≠ 'London'
```

isn't a tautology after all. Or rather: It *is* a tautology in 2VL, but not in 3VL—and of course 3VL is what we're dealing with here.

To generalize from this example, let *P* be some arbitrary truth valued expression. In 2VL, then, the expression

```
( P ) OR ( NOT ( P ) ) )
```

is a tautology. By contrast, the analogous tautology in 3VL is this (italics and boldface added for emphasis):

```
( P ) OR ( NOT ( P ) ) ) OR ( MAYBE ( P ) )
```

Note that MAYBE! MAYBE is another 3VL monadic connective, like NOT.[4] Here's the truth table:

| MAYBE | |
|---|---|
| *t* | *f* |
| *u* | *t* |
| *f* | *f* |

As this table shows, MAYBE returns TRUE if its argument is UNKNOWN and FALSE otherwise. Loosely speaking, therefore, we might say that whereas the purpose of NOT is to convert a FALSE into a TRUE, the purpose of MAYBE is to convert an UNKNOWN into a TRUE.

I'll have more to say about MAYBE in the next section. For now, let me just say a word about contradictions. Recall that in 2VL the expression

```
( P ) AND ( NOT ( P ) )
```

---

[4] I'm departing slightly from Codd's scheme here; Codd's scheme doesn't include a MAYBE connective as such—instead, it includes a MAYBE option, or *qualifier*, on "queries" (i.e., table expressions, not Boolean expressions). It also includes "maybe" versions of some—not all— of the relational algebra operators (see the section "Relational Algebra," later in this chapter).

is a contradiction. The 3VL analog (slightly tricky, this one!) is

```
( P ) AND ( NOT ( P ) ) AND ( NOT ( MAYBE ( P ) ) )
```

(If you need to convince yourself that this latter is correct, try writing out the truth table.)

I still haven't finished with the suppliers table from the beginning of this section. Here's yet another query on that table:

```
S WHERE CITY = CITY
```

The result is S1 and S3. Remarks similar to those concerning the previous example apply to this one also, because (of course)

```
CITY = CITY
```

is a tautology in 2VL but not in 3VL (in particular, it fails to yield TRUE in 3VL if CITY is null). But there's another point to be made here. The fact that an expression of the form $X = X$ isn't a tautology in 3VL constitutes a violation of an absolutely fundamental logical principle: namely, the principle known as *The First Axiom of Equality*, which states that $X = X$ is true for all $X$. In my opinion, this state of affairs, all by itself, should be sufficient to show that to embrace nulls and 3VL is to set out on a rocky and dangerous path, one where not all difficulties can be foreseen and the final destination is, to say the least, uncertain (I almost wrote "unknown"). You have been warned.

## THE MAYBE OPERATOR

You might have noticed that, so far, I haven't considered the question—at least, not explicitly—of how we might go about retrieving the rows from table S where the CITY column contains a null. Well, we do at least know that the following won't do the trick:

```
S WHERE CITY = NULL
```

Why not? Because as noted previously, the expression CITY = NULL *always* evaluates to UNKNOWN, even for a row in which the CITY column does indeed contain a null. That UNKNOWN then gets coerced to FALSE, and the net effect is that the result is empty (i.e., contains no rows at all).

The following formulation, by contrast, will do what's required:

```
S WHERE MAYBE ( CITY = 'London' )
```

*Explanation:*

- For rows where the CITY column contains the value London, the condition in parentheses evaluates to TRUE, and the MAYBE operator then (in effect) coerces that TRUE to a FALSE.

- For rows where the CITY column contains a value other than London (but not a null, because of course null isn't a value at all), the condition in parentheses evaluates to FALSE, which the MAYBE operator then leaves unchanged (equivalently, it coerces it to itself).

- For rows where the CITY column contains a null, the condition in parentheses evaluates to UNKNOWN, and the MAYBE operator then coerces that UNKNOWN to a TRUE.

The net effect is that just those rows are retrieved for which the CITY column contains a null.

But did you notice one odd thing about the foregoing explanation? The fact is, the final result would have been exactly the same if the condition in parentheses had been

```
CITY = 'Paris'
```

or

```
CITY = 'Athens'
```

or indeed

```
CITY = 'xyz'
```

for absolutely any '*xyz*' whatsoever (just so long as it's a legitimate value for column CITY, of course). In other words, the actual value ('London' or 'Paris' or ...) in terms of which we choose to formulate the query is utterly irrelevant.

Maybe—I choose my words carefully—that's why, in SQL, there's a special "null testing" operator called IS NULL. In SQL, we can write

```
SELECT *
FROM   S
WHERE  CITY IS NULL
```

(CITY IS NULL, observe, not CITY = NULL, because *nothing* is equal to null, not even null itself) to retrieve just the rows for which the CITY column contains a null. Here's the truth table for IS NULL (*V* here denotes an arbitrary scalar value):

| | IS NULL |
|---|---|
| NULL | *t* |
| *V* | *f* |

I should add that SQL supports IS NOT NULL also; the expression *exp* IS NOT NULL where *exp* is a scalar expression, is defined as you would expect to be logically equivalent to NOT (*exp* IS NULL), which returns TRUE if *exp* evaluates to either TRUE or FALSE and to FALSE otherwise.

On the third hand (I switch now to a different example) ... Suppose we're given a table EMP (employees) with columns ENO (employee number), JOB, DOB (date of birth), SALARY, and perhaps others; and suppose we want to retrieve employee numbers for employees for whom it might be the case, but is neither definitely known to be the case nor definitely known not to be the case, that (a) they're programmers, and (b) they were born prior to January 18th, 1992, and (c) they have a salary less than $80,000. Here then is one possible formulation (SQL style, but using the MAYBE operator):

```
SELECT ENO
FROM   EMP
WHERE  MAYBE
     ( JOB = 'Programmer' AND
       DOB < DATE '1992-01-18' AND
       SALARY < 80000 )
```

Here by contrast is an actual SQL formulation, using not MAYBE but the IS NULL operator:

```
SELECT   ENO
FROM     EMP
WHERE  ( JOB IS NULL AND
         DOB < DATE '1992-01-18' AND
         SALARY < 80000 )
OR     ( JOB = 'Programmer' AND
         DOB IS NULL AND
         SALARY < 80000 )
OR     ( JOB = 'Programmer' AND
         DOB < DATE '1992-01-18' AND
         SALARY IS NULL )
OR     ( JOB IS NULL AND
         DOB IS NULL AND
         SALARY < 80000 )
OR     ( JOB = 'Programmer' AND
         DOB IS NULL AND
         SALARY IS NULL )
OR     ( JOB IS NULL AND
         DOB < DATE '1992-01-18' AND
         SALARY IS NULL )
OR     ( JOB IS NULL AND
         DOB IS NULL AND
         SALARY IS NULL )
```

I conclude that support for the MAYBE operator is desirable (if nulls and 3VL are supported at all, that is, which I don't actually think they should be).

PS: Actually, the SQL standard does support an operator, IS UNKNOWN, that could be used to advantage in connection with queries like the one just discussed. Here first is the corresponding truth table:

| | IS UNKNOWN |
|---|---|
| *t* | *f* |
| *u* | *t* |
| *f* | *f* |

In other words, IS UNKNOWN is basically just the MAYBE operator as previously discussed. So the SQL query under consideration could alternatively (and more simply) be expressed as follows:

```
SELECT   ENO
FROM     EMP
WHERE  ( JOB = 'Programmer' AND
         DOB < DATE '1992-01-18' AND
         SALARY < 50000 ) IS UNKNOWN
```

However, I don't know whether any SQL products (as opposed to the standard as such) actually support IS UNKNOWN at the time of writing.

For completeness I note that the SQL standard also supports the operators IS TRUE and IS FALSE, as well as negated versions of all three (IS NOT TRUE, IS NOT FALSE, IS NOT UNKNOWN). Here are the truth tables:

| | IS TRUE | IS UNKNOWN | IS FALSE |
|---|---|---|---|
| *t* | *t* | *f* | *f* |
| *u* | *f* | *t* | *f* |
| *f* | *f* | *f* | *t* |

| | IS NOT TRUE | IS NOT UNKNOWN | IS NOT FALSE |
|---|---|---|---|
| *t* | *f* | *t* | *t* |
| *u* | *t* | *f* | *t* |
| *f* | *t* | *t* | *f* |

I feel obliged to point out, though, that these operators bring more problems along in their wake (were you surprised?). For example, the expressions

```
NOT ( X )
```

and

```
( X ) IS NOT TRUE
```

look as if they should be equivalent, but they're not—if X is UNKNOWN, the first gives UNKNOWN, the second gives TRUE.[5]

On the other hand, I note that SQL's IS NOT FALSE in particular might actually be more useful on occasion than 3VL's MAYBE operator. Suppose employee Donald has just come down with measles, and we want to identify all employees who've either definitely been in contact with Donald or might have been. Using MAYBE, this query will have to look something like this:

```
SELECT   ENO
FROM     EMP
WHERE          ( EMP has been in contact with Donald )
OR       MAYBE ( EMP has been in contact with Donald )
```

---

[5] An analogous issue arises in connection with natural language. Let *X* be a variable of type BOOLEAN. Then the natural language statements—note the lowercase "is" in each—*X is not TRUE* and *X is NOT TRUE* aren't equivalent! The first means the value of *X* is either FALSE or UNKNOWN. The second means the value of *X* is FALSE. What do you conclude from this state of affairs?

But using IS NOT FALSE it looks like this:

```
SELECT  ENO
FROM    EMP
WHERE ( EMP in contact with Donald ) IS NOT FALSE
```

In other words, IS NOT FALSE saves us from having to write out the expression in parentheses twice—which could be a significant practical benefit, both from a human factors point of view and a performance point of view, if that expression is complex.

## OPERATIONS INVOLVING NULLS

Here then is a list of the operators we've discussed in this chapter so far:

- The equality comparison operator "="
- The logical operators NOT, OR, AND, and MAYBE
- The SQL operators IS NULL and IS NOT NULL
- The SQL operators IS TRUE, IS NOT TRUE, etc.

What follows is a more thorough treatment of 3VL operators in general.

### *Scalar Comparisons*

Let *theta* denote any of the scalar comparison operators "=", "≠", "<", "≤", ">", and "≥", and let *X* and *Y* denote scalar values such that

```
X theta Y
```

is a syntactically valid expression. What does that expression evaluate to if either *X* or *Y* "evaluates to null," or if they both do?[6] Since by definition null

---

[6] Of course, if *X* and *Y* do denote *values* as stated, then they can't possibly "evaluate to" null, since as explained earlier the whole point about null is that it's not a value. Indeed, the very phrase "evaluate to null" is a contradiction in terms. To repeat something I said earlier, it's just about impossible to talk about this stuff coherently, because none of it really makes sense. Again, however, let's just soldier on.

represents *value unknown*, we define the result in every case to be, not TRUE or FALSE, but rather "the third truth value" UNKNOWN.

By the way, let me now point out—indeed, let me emphasize—that UNKNOWN isn't the same as "unknown" (if you see what I mean). Let *exp* be some expression (possibly just a simple variable reference). Then:

- If we say the value of *exp* is unknown, we mean we don't know what the value of *exp* is. For example, we don't know what the value of the expression $X + 1$ is, if we don't know the value of $X$.

- By contrast, if we say the value of *exp* is UNKNOWN, then:

    a. First, *exp* must be, specifically, a Boolean or truth-valued expression, because only such expressions can possibly have UNKNOWN as their value. To put it another way, UNKNOWN is a value of type Boolean (and yes, it is indeed a *value*—to repeat, it's "the third truth value").

    b. Second, what we mean when we say the value of *exp* is UNKNOWN is that we do know what the value of *exp* is—it's that "third truth value," UNKNOWN.

To repeat a point already made in footnote 5, there are rich possibilities for confusion in this field.

### *Testing for Null*

We also need an operator, which I'll call IS_NULL, for testing whether a given scalar expression "evaluates to null." IS_NULL takes an arbitrary scalar expression as its argument and returns TRUE if that argument evaluates to null, FALSE otherwise.[7] Thus, e.g., the expression

```
IS_NULL ( COLOR )
```

returns TRUE if COLOR is null and FALSE otherwise.

---

[7] From now on I'll drop those quotation marks from phrases such as "evaluates to null," because I know how irritating they can be. But please understand that, conceptually, they should always be there.

*Note:* Of course, IS_NULL is basically just a slightly different spelling for SQL's IS NULL operator. Or is it? Well, I'm not in a position to be able to answer this question quite yet. I'll come back it in Chapter 6.

### *Set Membership*

Let set *Y* contain elements $Y_1$, $Y_2$, ..., $Y_n$ and no others. Then the expression

```
X IN Y
```

is defined to be shorthand for, and thus logically equivalent to, the expression

$$\text{FALSE OR } X = Y_1 \text{ OR } X = Y_2 \text{ OR } \ldots \text{ OR } X = Y_n$$

Observe that this latter expression evaluates to:

- FALSE if *Y* is empty
- UNKNOWN if *Y* is nonempty but *Yi* is null for all *i* ($i = 1, 2, \ldots, n$)
- TRUE otherwise

*X* NOT IN *Y* is defined to be logically equivalent to NOT (*X* IN *Y*).

### *Other Scalar Operations*

Let *alpha* denote any dyadic (infix) scalar operator that's not a comparison operator—e.g., "+", "–", "×", "| |" (string concatenation), etc.—and let *X* and *Y* denote scalar values such that

```
X alpha Y
```

is a valid expression. (I assume infix notation here purely for definiteness.) What does that expression evaluate to if either *X* or *Y* evaluates to null, or if they both do? Since by definition null represents "value unknown," we define the result in every case to be null, rather than some definite known value.[8]

---

[8] Of course, various anomalies arise here instantly, much like the one I referred to earlier as a violation of *The First Axiom of Equality* (viz., that $X = X$ is true for all *X*). One obvious one is this: Let *X* be of some numeric type; then $X - X$ should be zero. But it won't be, if *X* is null.

Monadic (prefix) operators are treated analogously. For example, let *X* be of some numeric type. Then +*X* and −*X* are valid expressions; and if *X* evaluates to null, then those expressions do so too.

## QUANTIFIERS

The existential and universal quantifiers are still defined the way they always were—namely, as iterated OR and iterated AND, respectively—but let me spell out the definitions for the record. Let set *Y* contain elements $Y_1$, $Y_2$, ..., $Y_n$ and no others; let *X* be a range variable whose range is *Y*; and let *P* be a predicate. Then the expression

```
EXISTS X ( P ( X ) )
```

is defined to be shorthand for, and thus logically equivalent to, the expression

```
FALSE OR P ( Y1 ) OR P ( Y2 ) OR ... OR P ( Yn )
```

Analogously, the expression

```
FORALL X ( P ( X ) )
```

is defined to be shorthand for, and thus logically equivalent to, the expression

```
TRUE AND P ( Y1 ) AND P ( Y2 ) AND ... AND P ( Yn )
```

Note in particular, therefore, that if (again) *X* ranges over *Y*, then the following is a tautology:

```
( Z IN Y ) ≡ ( EXISTS X ( X = Z ) )
```

## RELATIONAL ALGEBRA

In his 1979 paper—i.e., the paper in which he introduced the concept of nulls and their associated three-valued logic—Codd also considered the implications of these concepts for the operators of the relational algebra. In this section I give a brief summary of what he had to say in this connection (though I choose to use my own terminology here and there in preference to Codd's).

### *Restriction*

Restriction as such remains unchanged, inasmuch as it returns just those rows for which the specified Boolean expression evaluates to TRUE. However, Codd also proposed an additional operator, a "maybe" version of restriction, which returns just those rows for which the specified Boolean expression evaluates to UNKNOWN instead of TRUE. I'll have more to say about this new operator in a few moments.

### *Projection*

Projection also remains unchanged, with the following crucial exception:

- Even though the comparison null = null returns UNKNOWN, two nulls are nevertheless considered to be equal to one another in the context of projection (i.e., for the purposes of eliminating duplicates to produce the final result).

How does Codd explain—or explain away, I might rather say—this very obvious inconsistency? *Answer:* He doesn't. Not as far as I'm concerned, at any rate. What he does say (rather airily, it seems to me, and without anything by way of substantial justification) is this:

> This identification of one null value [*sic*] with another may appear to be in contradiction with our assignment of truth value [UNKNOWN] to the test [null = null]. However, [equality testing] for duplicate removal is an operation at a lower level of detail than equality testing in the evaluation of retrieval conditions. Hence, it is possible to adopt a different rule.

*Your comments here.*

### *Cartesian Product*

Cartesian product (or just product for short) remains unchanged.

### *Join*

Here I'm afraid we run into a significant terminological issue. Let me elaborate:

- My own very strong preference is always to use the unqualified term *join* to mean the natural join specifically (unless the context demands otherwise, of course), and that's what I'll do in the present book from this point forward. Why? Because natural join is far and away the most important "flavor" of join, both in theory and in practice.

- In his 1979 paper, by contrast, when he gets to the join operator (in the section in which he discusses nulls and 3VL, I mean), Codd talks exclusively in terms of what he calls the *theta* join (where *theta* stands for any of the usual scalar comparison operators "=", "≠", "<", and so on). In fact, he doesn't even mention natural join, as such, in that section at all!

Now, theta join isn't a primitive operator (it's defined to be a restriction of a Cartesian product), and so there's no need to say any more about it here.[9] By contrast, there certainly is more to be said about natural join—but that discussion would be a little out of place in the present context, and I'll defer it to the next chapter.

***Division***

Like theta join, division isn't a primitive operator (it can be defined in terms of projection, Cartesian product, and projection), so I won't bother to discuss it further here.

***Union, Intersection, and Difference***

These operators remains unchanged, except for the fact that, as with projection, two nulls are considered to be equal to one another for duplicate elimination purposes. My criticisms of this state of affairs in the case of projection (see above) apply here also.

---

[9] Except perhaps to note that (as with restriction) Codd additionally proposed a "maybe" version of this operator, which joins rows for which the join condition evaluates to UNKNOWN instead of TRUE.

### *MAYBE Operators*

The 1979 paper also defines "maybe" versions of restrict, theta join, and divide.[10] Since I omitted consideration of "regular" (or "true") theta join and divide in previous subsections, however, I'll do the same for their "maybe" counterparts here. As for "maybe restrict," it differs from the normal—i.e., "true"—restrict operator in that it returns those rows for which the specified Boolean expression evaluates to UNKNOWN instead of TRUE. In other words (and to invent some syntax on the fly), the expression

```
MAYBE_RESTRICT T WHERE bx
```

(where *T* is a table and *bx* is a Boolean expression) is logically equivalent to the expression

```
RESTRICT T WHERE MAYBE ( bx )
```

In fact, Codd would have had no need for his "maybe" algebraic operators at all, nor for his MAYBE qualifier on expressions, if only he'd defined the MAYBE logical operator (and allowed it to be used fully orthogonally, of course)—but he didn't. Of course, I'm assuming here that we do actually want to support 3VL, which I don't in fact believe. But if we're to do it at all, then I do think we should do it right, and doing it right includes supporting the MAYBE operator.

### *Outer Operators*

In that same 1979 paper Codd additionally proposes "outer" versions of certain of the foregoing operators: to be specific, theta join (also natural join), union, intersection, and difference. I'll defer detailed discussion of these new operators to Chapter 5—except to note that, presumably, the regular versions should therefore be referred to as "inner" operators, though Codd never uses any such term.

---

[10] Why do you think he omitted "maybe" versions of other operators—union, for example? If you think about this question for a few moments, I believe you'll come to realize there are still further difficulties with nulls and 3VL, difficulties I haven't attempted to describe in detail anywhere in this book.

## NULL ROWS AND TABLES

If nulls are placeholders for values, they must clearly be allowed to appear wherever values can appear. So where can values appear? Well, one obvious answer to this question, in the relational context, is "at column positions within rows within tables"; thus, nulls must obviously be allowed to appear in such positions (barring integrity constraints to the contrary), as of course we already know. And that obvious answer is the one invariably assumed throughout Codd's writings on the subject, and indeed throughout most other people's writings on the subject as well.

Let me now point out, however, that the foregoing answer is incomplete. To be specific, there are at least two further places, in a relational context, where values can appear:

- *Rows within tables:* At any given time, a row within a table is a value—specifically, a row value.

- *Tables as such:* At any given time, a table as such is a value—specifically, a table value.

Any complete proposal for using nulls as placeholders for values thus needs to deal with the possibility of *null rows* and *null tables* accordingly.

Now, Codd never mentioned either of these possibilities at all, as far as I'm aware (certainly not in any of his published writings, at any rate). SQL, by contrast, does have some vague notion of null rows (but not, I think, null tables); however, I don't believe that notion was ever taken seriously or properly thought through, though of course I could be wrong. Anyway, I don't intend to discuss these issues in detail in this book, because it's not my aim to present an exhaustive treatment of the subject.[11] However, I do want to make a few specific points:

- We already know, of course, that if we're to accept the idea of nulls and 3VL at all, then we must allow rows to contain a null component, or in fact any number of such components. A row might even contain *nothing but* such components—i.e., have all of its components null. Please note

---

[11] After all, if it turns out—and in my opinion it does—that nulls and three-valued logic have implications for simple scalars that just can't be tolerated, then there's no point in even considering their implications for rows and tables. At least, not in any great detail.

carefully, however, that such a row (i.e., a row of all nulls) is still not itself a "null row"! A null row as such is a whole different concept.[12]

- We also have to allow tables to contain both (a) rows in which any or all components are null and (b) null rows. Please note, however, that a table that contains nothing but (a) rows containing nothing but nulls, and/or (b) null rows, isn't itself a "null table." A null table as such is a whole different concept.[13]

- More generally, of course, we have to allow sets to contain null elements. Please note, however, that a set that contains nothing but null elements isn't itself a null set. A null set as such is a whole different concept.

- Recall now that according to Codd, nulls—"scalar" nulls, at any rate—are considered as duplicates of one another for duplicate elimination purposes (i.e., in projection, union, and so on), despite the fact that the expression NULL = NULL doesn't evaluate to TRUE. We can extend this idea to rows as follows. Let $X$ and $Y$ be rows of the same type,[14] and let corresponding components of $X$ and $Y$ be $(X_1,Y_1)$, $(X_2,Y_2)$, ..., $(X_n,Y_n)$. Then $X$ and $Y$ are duplicates of one another if and only if, for all $i$ ($i = 1, 2, ..., n$), $X_i$ and $Y_i$ are duplicates of one another—i.e., either $X_i = Y_i$, or $X_i$ and $Y_i$ are both null.

- We can extend the ideas of the previous bullet item to tables and thereby define what it means for two tables to be duplicates of one another. Rather meanly, though, I'll leave the details as an exercise.

Well, you're probably thinking by this time that I can't be serious—this stuff is surely getting much too complicated, and in fact completely out of hand.

---

[12] It's also one that SQL gets itself into a terrible muddle over. See the section "IS NOT NULL vs. NOT IS NULL" in Chapter 6 or, for a much more extensive discussion of the subject, Chapter 1 ("Equality") of my book *Stating the Obvious, and Other Database Writings* (Technics, 2020).

[13] I'm tempted to add at this point that if you're not confused by now, then you're not thinking clearly. (In other words, if you're not confused, you're confused: IF NOT *P* THEN *P*. What do you think we should conclude from this state of affairs?)

[14] Codd would say rather that the rows in question have to be "union compatible," but I prefer to replace this very ad hoc notion by the much more carefully thought out notions of *row type* and *table type* (or tuple type and relation type, rather). See, e.g., my book *SQL and Relational Theory*, 3rd ed. (O'Reilly, 2015) for further discussion.

And I won't argue with you! All I'm trying to do is spell out some of the logical consequences—some of the ideas we apparently have to buy into—if we accept this whole business of nulls and 3VL in the first place. However, let me get back to something I'm very serious about indeed:

- A row with at least one null component doesn't represent a valid tuple. (I'll elaborate on this point in Chapter 5.)
- A table that contains at least one such row doesn't represent a valid relation.
- Thus, **nulls break the relational model!** (Apologies for shouting, but the message is so crucial.)

Let me repeat: If the database contains any nulls, we're not dealing with the relational model any more. This point is so important, I want to say it one more time, in more formal relational terms:

- A "domain" (or type) that contains a null isn't a domain.
- A "tuple" with an attribute defined on such a "domain" (or type) isn't a tuple.
- A "relation" that contains such a "tuple" isn't a relation.

So the entire edifice collapses, and *all bets are off*. I find it very hard to understand why Codd would want to destroy his beautiful relational model by adding nulls and 3VL to it, but that, in effect, is exactly what he did.

## THE END (FOR NOW)

This brings us to the end of our preliminary investigation into 3VL and related matters. In the next chapter I plan to explore in greater detail some of the consequences of the ideas we've covered thus far. For now, I'd just like to leave you with the following thought:

- First, there's no question that the missing information problem is a real and important problem: Information in the real world is often missing for some reason, and users, and/or would-be users, are very well aware of that fact.

- Second, SQL has nulls.

Taken together, these points allow SQL product vendors to say, in effect, to prospective customers: "Missing information? Don't worry about it! We have *nulls*!" And the customer thinks: "Well, great—that sounds good." And, indeed, nulls do sound good; more specifically, they do look like a solution to the missing information problem—at first.[15] It's only when you really poke into them, as we've started to do in this chapter (but *only* started, let me stress), that the problems begin to emerge, and you begin to realize that the apparent attractiveness of nulls is specious, and superficial, and indeed unwarranted. Unfortunately, however, that realization could easily come a little bit too late as far as the customer is concerned. I mean, it's entirely possible that:

- The customer has signed on the dotted line and purchased and installed the system.

- Databases have been built with nulls in them, and applications against those databases have been built as well.

- The customer is fully committed to those databases and those applications.

- And now it's all just too late to go back.

My message, then—what I'm trying to achieve with this book—is this: I want to warn the reader of the problems that nulls can cause, and the magnitude of those problems, in an attempt to persuade the said reader to avoid nulls like the plague they are. Personally, I wouldn't touch them with a ten foot pole.

---

[15] As David Maier puts it in his book *The Theory of Relational Databases* (Computer Science Press, 1983): "It all makes sense if you squint a little and don't think too hard."

# Chapter 3

# Three–Valued Logic: Some Logical Consequences

In the previous chapter I explained the basic ideas behind nulls and three-valued logic, 3VL. Now I'd like to go on and examine some logical consequences of those ideas.

## TRAPS FOR THE UNWARY

I'll start by reviewing a few items that in most cases I did at least touch on in Chapter 2 but would now like to elaborate on, somewhat. The items in question have to do with states of affairs, and/or logical inferences, that are obviously and intuitively valid in 2VL but aren't necessarily so in 3VL. In other words, they're traps for the unwary: traps that can lead to mistakes—mistakes of several different kinds, in fact, and ones that can be made by the user or the system, and quite possibly both.

### *X = X Doesn't Necessarily Yield TRUE*

As noted in the previous chapter, 3VL thus violates *The First Axiom of Equality* (viz., that *X* = *X* for all *X*). Frankly, I believe this state of affairs all by itself should be sufficient to cause us, or indeed anyone, to question the wisdom of going down the 3VL path. But me elaborate briefly. After all, equality is clearly of fundamental importance, and so it might help to give a precise definition of it here:[1]

---

[1] The definition that follows is based on one in the book *Databases, Types, and the Relational Model: The Third Manifesto*, 3rd ed. (Addison-Wesley, 2007), by Hugh Darwen and myself. Of course, it's a 2VL definition; and therefore talks exlusively about equality of *values*—so let me renind you yet one more time that nulls aren't values.

**Definition (equality):** Loosely, two values are equal if and only if they're one and the same value. More precisely, let $V_1$ and $V_2$ be values. Then $V_1 = V_2$ yields TRUE if and only if:

a. $V_1$ and $V_2$ are of the same type, $T$; and

b. *Op* is an operator with a parameter $P$; and

c. $P$ is such that the argument corresponding to $P$ in some invocation of *Op* is allowed to be of type $T$; and

d. For all such operators *Op*, two successful invocations of *Op* that are identical in all respects except that the argument corresponding to $P$ is $V_1$ in one invocation and $V_2$ in the other are indistinguishable in their effect.

Incidentally, it's worth noting that SQL manages to violate the foregoing definition in numerous ways—and that's even if we ignore the effects of 3VL, which (of course) only makes matters worse. In fact, I suggest you try you making a detailed list of such SQL violations. It's a salutary exercise! I won't try to give such a list here, but I will at least make a few general (and pertinent) observations.[2] In SQL, the "=" operator:

1. Sometimes gives TRUE when the comparands are definitely distinct

2. Sometimes gives TRUE when the comparands are probably distinct

3. Sometimes has user defined, and hence arbitrary, semantics

4. Isn't supported at all for (a) tables, (b) certain user defined types, (c) the system defined type XML, and—at least in some products—(d) certain other system defined types as well

Finally, let me remind you also that if $X$ is of a type for which subtraction makes sense, one consequence of all of the above is that $X - X$ doesn't

---

[2] The observations in question are taken from Chapter 1 ("Equality") of my book *Stating the Obvious, and Other Database Writings* (Technics, 2020). *Note:* The scond of them does have to do with 3VL, but the other three don't.

necessarily yield zero. Note the implications of such a state of affairs for the "query rewrite" process in particular.

### *X < X Doesn't Necessarily Yield FALSE*

I'm assuming here, of course, that *X* is of a type for which the comparison operator "<" is defined, for otherwise the comparison "*X* < *X*" will fail on a type error. (By contrast, the equality operator "=" is—in fact, must be—defined for *every* type,[3] so the comparison "*X* = *X*" is always legal, with semantics as defined in the previous subsection.)

### *S ⊆ S Doesn't Necessarily Yield TRUE*

*S* here denotes a set, and "⊆" denotes the set comparison operator *is included in* or *is a subset of.* Now, in 2VL, such operators are defined as follows:

> **Definition (set inclusion, etc.):** Set $S_1$ is included in—i.e., is a subset of—set $S_2$ ("$S_1 \subseteq S_2$") if and only if every element of $S_1$ is also an element of $S_2$; moreover, set $S_2$ includes—i.e., is a superset of—set $S_1$ ("$S_2 \supseteq S_1$") if and only if $S_1 \subseteq S_2$. Set $S_1$ is equal to set $S_2$ ("$S_1 = S_2$") if and only if each includes the other. Observe that every set is both a subset and a superset of itself;[4] observe also that every set includes the empty set.
>
> *Note:* The term *containment* is sometimes used as a synonym for inclusion in the foregoing sense, but this usage is generally deprecated—better to say of a set that it *contains* its elements but *includes* its subsets.

To put the foregoing a little more formally, if $X_1$ and $X_2$ range over $S_1$ and $S_2$, respectively, then

```
( S1 ⊆ S2 ) ≝ FORALL X1 ( EXISTS X2 ( X2 = X1 ) )
```

*Note:* The symbol "≝" here means "is defined as."

---

[3] Not in SQL, though, as we saw on the previous page.

[4] If $S_1$ is a subset of $S_2$ and $S_1 \neq S_2$, then $S_1$ is a *proper* subset of (or is *properly* included in) $S_2$, and $S_2$ is a *proper* superset of (or *properly* includes) $S_1$.

But now suppose we're in the realm of 3VL, and suppose further that (a) $S_1$ and $S_2$ are the same set, $S$ say, and (b) some element $X_i$ of that set $S$ is null.[5] Then there's no element $X$ of $S$ such that $X = X_i$—not even element $X_i$ itself! Thus, that set $S$ isn't included in itself. Of course, we can't say it *isn't* included in itself, either. Nor can we say it's equal to itself! In such a case, therefore, the expressions $S \subseteq S$, $S \supseteq S$, and $S = S$ must all presumably yield UNKNOWN.

Incidentally, note that now we have a situation in which something—here, the set $S$—isn't equal to itself, and yet the something in question isn't null. (Why isn't it null? Because a set certainly isn't itself considered to be null just because it happens to contain a null element. See the section "Rows and Tables" in the previous chapter.)

### *P OR NOT P Doesn't Necessarily Yield TRUE*

In other words, *P* OR NOT *P* isn't a tautology (where *P* is a proposition, of course). I discussed this one in detail in the previous chapter. However, I also raised the question in that chapter of whether a statement should actually be regarded as a proposition at all if there's a possibility that it might have truth value UNKNOWN, given that propositions in general are supposed to evaluate to either TRUE or FALSE unequivocally.

Well, for the purposes of this book, at least, I'm going to set a stake in the ground and answer that question in the affirmative. That is, I'm going to assume the following definition:

> **Definition (3VL proposition):** A declarative statement, expressed in natural language or perhaps in some more formal notation, that evaluates unequivocally to TRUE or UNKNOWN or FALSE, regardless of the values of any free variables (i.e., parameters) involved.

### *T JOIN T Doesn't Necessarily Yield T*

*T* here is a table, of course, and JOIN means the natural join specifically. Now, when I mentioned natural join in the previous chapter, I deliberately didn't get into a lot of detail regarding exactly what I meant by that term (i.e., "natural join")—but now I need to. Here then are my preferred definitions. First, we need to know what it means for two tables to be *joinable*:

---

[5] But does this stipulation even make sense (i.e., that a set might contain a null element)? In Chapter 2 I assumed it does; however, see the next section for further discussion of this issue.

**Definition (joinable):** Tables $T_1$ and $T_2$ are joinable if and only if columns with the same name are of the same type.

For example, the suppliers table S and the shipments table SP have exactly one column with the same name (viz., SNO, "supplier number"), and that column is of the same type in both cases. The tables are therefore joinable. *Note:* As another example, the same goes for the supplier table S and the parts table P, because they too have just one column with the same name (viz., CITY), and again that column is of the same type in both cases.

**Definition (natural join, or just "join" for short):** Let tables $T_1$ and $T_2$ be joinable. Then the expression

```
T1 JOIN T2
```

denotes the natural join of $T_1$ and $T_2$, and it returns the table with heading the set theory union of the headings of $T_1$ and $T_2$ and body the set of all rows *R* such that *R* is the set theory union of a row from $T_1$ and a row from $T_2$.[6]

For example, the expression S JOIN SP denotes the natural join of S and SP. That join has a heading consisting of columns SNO, SNAME, STATUS, CITY, PNO, and QTY,[7] and the result, given our usual sample values, looks like this (not all rows shown):

| SNO | SNAME | STATUS | CITY | PNO | QTY |
|---|---|---|---|---|---|
| S1 | Smith | 20 | London | P1 | 300 |
| S1 | Smith | 20 | London | P2 | 200 |
| S1 | Smith | 20 | London | P3 | 400 |
| .. | ..... | .. | ...... | .. | ... |
| S4 | Clark | 20 | London | P4 | 300 |
| S4 | Clark | 20 | London | P5 | 400 |

[6] Note how this definition relies on the fact that rows—or at any rate tuples—are sets, and so too are headings (and bodies). PS: Refer to the preface if you need to refresh your memory regarding the meanings of the terms *heading* and *body* in a relational context.

[7] Not neessarily in that order, of course!—headings are *sets*, and thus have no ordering to their elements.

In other words (and very loosely!): The body of the result consists of all rows of the form (*sno,sn,st,sc,pno,q*) such that the row (*sno,sn,st,sc*) appears in S and the row (*sno,pno,q*) appears in SP.

Now, it follows from all of the above that, at least in 2VL, *T* JOIN *T* reduces to simply *T*. But not in 3VL, if *T* contains any nulls! (Why not, exactly?) In other words, it's a little as if, in 3VL, we're dealing with an arithmetic where 1 × 1 isn't equal to 1. I'll pause here for a moment to let you think about some of the implications of this state of affairs.

PS: Oddly enough, no analogous situation arises in connection with union or intersection; that is, the expressions *T* UNION *T* and *T* INTERSECT *T* do both reduce to just *T*, even in 3VL. But that's because for those operators—as in the case of projection, as we saw in the previous chapter—two nulls are defined to be equal to one another after all! I really think Codd should have made his mind up once and for all on this fundamental question: Are two nulls equal, or aren't they? So far as I'm aware, however, that's something he never did.

### *Intersection Is No Longer a Special Case of Natural Join*

This state of affairs is an immediate consequence of (a) the fact that, as just indicated, two nulls are considered equal for the purposes of INTERSECT, but at the same time (b) they aren't considered equal for the purposes of JOIN. Let me elaborate briefly. In 2VL, intersection *is* a special case of natural join (a property, by the way, that could be of interest to the optimizer); to be specific, it's the special case in which the two given tables both have the same heading. But the situation is different in 3VL. I'll leave it as an exercise for you to construct an example to illustrate the difference, if you're interested.

I note in passing that Cartesian product too is a special case of natural join in 2VL; it's the special case in which the two given tables have no column names in common. In contrast to the situation with respect to intersection, however, this state of affairs continues to hold in 3VL, as well as in 2VL. Again I'll leave it as an exercise to construct an example to illustrate the point.

## CAN A SET CONTAIN A NULL?

Now we come to a very fundamental question that I touched on but deliberately didn't discuss in detail in either the previous section or the previous chapter: viz., *can a set can contain a null?*

Well, if the answer to this question is no, the whole nulls and 3VL exercise would be rather pointless, wouldn't it. I mean, it would imply among other things that tuples (rows, if you prefer) couldn't contain nulls—recall once again that tuples are sets—and so there'd be no way to get nulls into the database in the first place. So we have to assume that the answer is yes, a set can indeed contain a null. (In fact, of course, I've been assuming as much at numerous points in both the previous section and the previous chapter, as I'm sure you must have noticed.)

In any case, Codd himself certainly assumed the answer was yes, because in his 1979 paper he explicitly discusses the question of the truth value of the expression $\{\omega\} \subseteq X$, where $\omega$ (omega) denotes a null, "$\subseteq$" denotes set inclusion, and $X$ denotes a nonempty set. (An equivalent expression is $\omega \in X$, where "$\in$" denotes set membership; it can be pronounced *is a member of*, or *is an element of*, or simply *in* or *is in*.) Here's Codd's text:

> With regard to set membership $\in$ and set inclusion $\subseteq$, we assign the truth value $\omega$ to the expressions: $\omega \in S$ and $\{\omega\} \subseteq S$, whenever $S$ is a nonempty unary relation (even if $S$ does contain a null value [*sic*]).

*Note:* This extract can be criticized on a number of grounds, but I don't want to get sidetracked at this point. I'll come back to those criticisms at the end of this section.

If a set can indeed contain a null, however, then numerous further questions arise—questions, by the way, that for the most part I've never even seen 3VL advocates raise, let alone answer:

- The expression NULL $\in X$ will always return UNKNOWN for any nonempty set $X$, regardless of whether $X$ does actually contain a null. So we'll need a new operator such as CONTAINS_A_NULL ($X$) to test whether a given set $X$ does in fact contain a null. (Does SQL support such an operator?)

- The expression $V \in X$ will always return either TRUE or UNKNOWN, never FALSE, for any value $V$ if set $X$ does in fact contain a null; so we'll need a new operator such as DOES_NOT_CONTAIN ($X$,$V$) to test whether a given set $X$ that does contain a null does *not* contain some specified value $V$. (Again, does SQL support such an operator?)

- Note in particular the implications of the previous point for checking that a value that's proposed for assignment to some variable is of the same type as that variable. Let the value and type in question be *V* and *T*, respectively. Since a type is basically just a set of values, in 2VL the required type checking is equivalent to checking simply that the expression $V \in T$ evaluates to TRUE. In 3VL, however, it looks as if we'll need a new operator such as DOES_CONTAIN (*T*,*V*) to test whether a given set that might or might not contain a null does at any rate contain the specified value *V*. (Once again, does SQL support such an operator?)

  Here's a question for you to think about: Are the following expressions logically equivalent?—

  ```
  DOES_NOT_CONTAIN ( T , V )

  NOT ( DOES_CONTAIN ( T , V ) )
  ```

  (Yes, you really do have to ask questions like this in 3VL.)

- In view of the previous point and others like it, it might be easier just to insist that types (equivalently, domains) can't contain nulls. But then a relation that contains a null—more precisely, a relation that contains a tuple that contains a null, or if you prefer a table that contains a row that contains a null—won't be a subset of the Cartesian product of its underlying domains, thus violating Codd's original definition of a relation.

  *Note:* A nulls advocate might claim that the foregoing assertion is specious and is due to what Codd calls, in his RM/V2 book (see Chapter 5), a "value oriented misinterpretation": If table EMP includes a row saying "Joe's salary is null," then that null isn't a value as such, it's merely a placeholder for a value; in other words, presumably there does exist some value *V* that actually is Joe's salary, and if we were to replace that null by that value *V* (and replace all other nulls in table EMP in similar fashion), then what results *would* be a subset of the Cartesian product of the pertinent domains. But even if we accept this counterargument in the case of "value unknown" nulls, it doesn't seem to be valid for other kinds of nulls; consider, for example, the "value inapplicable" null.[8]

---

[8] Of course, the possibility that there might be further kinds of nulls takes us beyond the realm of 3VL as such anyway. See Chapter 5 for further discussion.

- If a set can contain a null, then as previously noted the expression $X \subseteq X$ will return UNKNOWN, not TRUE, if *X* does in fact contain a null. So we'll need some more extensions, linguistic and otherwise, in addition to the ones already sketched above. First, we'll need an appropriately extended definition of what it means for one set to be included in another. Second, we'll need a new operator in order to test whether one set is indeed included in another according to that extended definition.

- In particular, if $S_1$ and $S_2$ are, respectively, the sets {1,2} and {1,2,NULL}, then the comparison $S_1 = S_2$ will presumably return UNKNOWN. (Loosely speaking, if the null is a placeholder for either 1 or 2, the sets will be equal, but if it's a placeholder for some other value, then they won't be.) All right; but what if $S_1$ and $S_2$ are, respectively, the sets {1,2} and {1,2,3,NULL}? Then there's no way they can possibly be equal, and the comparison $S_1 = S_2$ should thus surely return FALSE. But does it? *Answer:* I don't know—I've never seen 3VL advocates even mention this question—but if I were a betting man I'd bet on *no*.

- A related point: What's the cardinality of the set {1,2,NULL}? More generally, what's the cardinality of any set that contains a null? Is it null—i.e., unknown—also? (But note, however, that the cardinality of such a set isn't *completely* unknown; e.g., the cardinality of the set {1,2,NULL} is unknown, certainly, but it must be either two or three. Such considerations lead us into another problem, however, one that I've referred to elsewhere as the "distinguished nulls" problem.[9] I omit further discussion here.)
  Related question: Can a set contain two nulls?

- I've said that a set that contains a null isn't the same as a null set—but maybe that's wrong. In fact, suppose it is; suppose that a set that contains a null is itself simply null. In other words, that set apparently contains itself as a member! Are you there, Bertrand Russell?

Finally, I return as promised to that quote from Codd's 1979 paper, which I repeat here for convenience:

---

[9] E.g., in Chapter 15 ("Null Values [*sic*] in Database Management") of my book *Relational Database: Selected Writings* (Addison-Wesley, 1986).

With regard to set membership ∈ and set inclusion ⊆, we assign the truth value ω to the expressions: ω ∈ *S* and {ω} ⊆ *S*, whenever *S* is a nonempty unary relation (even if *S* does contain a null value [*sic*]).

As noted earlier, this extract can be criticized on a number of grounds. Here are some of them.

- First of all, note the appearance of the phrase *null value*, a phrase that (as explained in Chapter 2) is actually a contradiction in terms and makes no sense. (Actually, Codd's 1979 paper—the paper from which the extract is taken—uses that phrase not once but many times, over and over again.)

  *Full disclosure:* I used that same phrase myself in certain early writings (see, e.g., footnote 9 on the previous page)—but that was when I was still very much under Codd's influence, and still taking everything he said as gospel truth and not to be questioned.

- Next, consider this text from the second line of the quoted text:

  ... {ω} ⊆ *S*, whenever *S* is a nonempty unary relation.

  A couple of points here:

  1. If *S* is a relation (or table) as stated, then it's a set of rows (or its body is, at least). So for the expression "{ω} ⊆ *S*" to make sense—in fact, for it to be syntactically well formed in the first place—the expression "{ω}" must denote a set of rows, and hence the expression "ω" must denote a row. But it doesn't: It denotes a null, and the 1979 paper assumes throughout (albeit tacitly, I think I need to add) that nulls can appear only where scalars are permitted, not rows.

  2. Ignoring the previous point for simplicity, the fact that *S* is explicitly stated to be nonempty suggests rather strongly that if it were empty, then the expression "{ω} ⊆ *S*" would evaluate not to ω but to FALSE. If so, however, then this position is logically very similar to the one outlined earlier, to the effect that the comparison

     ```
     { 1 , 2 } = { 1 , 2 , 3 , NULL }
     ```

     should also, but presumably doesn't, evaluate to FALSE (?).

But the biggest problem with the extract as quoted is the suggestion that "the third truth value" UNKNOWN should be represented by ω, or in other words by null ("we assign the truth value ω to [certain truth-valued expressions whose value isn't known]"). Indeed, the following extract from the 1979 paper appears just prior to the one quoted earlier (boldface added):

> [What] is the truth value of *x* = *y* if *x* or *y* or both are null? An appropriate result in each of these cases is the unknown truth value, rather than true or false. Accordingly, we adopt a three-valued logic for use in extracting data from databases that may contain null values. **We use the same symbol "ω" to denote the unknown truth value**, because truth values can be stored in databases and we want the treatment of all unknown or null values to be uniform.

Well, I'm sorry, but this position seems to me to reflect nothing but confusion—rather massive confusion at that—on Codd's part. Let me spell the argument out very carefully, one step at a time:[10]

- Let *X* be a Boolean variable (i.e., a variable of type BOOLEAN, or in other words a variable whose permitted values are truth values).

- In a 3VL system, then, the possible values of *X* are TRUE, UNKNOWN, and FALSE.

- If we say "*X* is UNKNOWN," we mean the value of *X* is the truth value UNKNOWN.

- But if we say "*X* is unknown," we mean, of course, that we don't know the value of *X*.

In other words, UNKNOWN is not "unknown"!—there's a logical difference between the two concepts. And to condense and paraphrase some text from the book *Databases, Types, and the Relational Model: The Third Manifesto*, 3rd ed. (Addison-Wesley, 2007), by Hugh Darwen and myself:

---

[10] The problem this argument illustrates was discussed briefly in the section "Operations Involving Nulls" (subsection "Scalar Comparisons") in the previous chapter.

> As Wittgenstein once observed, *all logical differences are big differences*. And one interesting corollary of this maxim is that *all logical mistakes are big mistakes*. Because, of course, a mistake is a difference—a difference between what's right and what's wrong.

In my view, confusing UNKNOWN and "unknown" is a logical mistake. Do we really want to go down this path?

## WRONG ANSWERS

Considerations such as those discussed in this chapter so far have at least one very important practical consequence, viz.:

> *A 3VL system can deliver wrong answers.*

What exactly do I mean by "wrong answers" here? I mean: A 3VL system is capable of producing answers that are (of course) correct as far as the logic is concerned, but are *not* correct in the real world. In other words, *3VL does not match reality*—it doesn't behave the way the world behaves. And that, in my opinion, is why 3VL isn't useful for the purpose at hand (i.e., dealing with missing information). In fact, not only is it not useful, I'd say it's positively dangerous.

Let's look at a concrete example. Here's a sample set of values for a hugely simplified version of the suppliers and parts database:

S

| SNO | CITY |
|---|---|
| S1 | London |

P

| PNO | CITY |
|---|---|
| P1 | *null* |

Consider now the (admittedly highly contrived) query "Get (SNO,PNO) pairs such that *either* the supplier and part cities are different *or* the part city isn't Paris (or both)":

```
( S.SNO , P.PNO ) WHERE S.CITY ≠ P.CITY OR P.CITY ≠ 'Paris'
```

Now let's focus on just the Boolean expression in the WHERE clause:

```
S.CITY ≠ P.CITY OR P.CITY ≠ 'Paris'
```

For the only data we have, this expression becomes

```
'London' ≠ NULL OR NULL ≠ 'Paris'
```

which reduces to

```
UNKNOWN OR UNKNOWN
```

which reduces in turn to just UNKNOWN. That UNKNOWN then gets coerced to FALSE, and the net effect is that nothing is retrieved.

But now let's think about the example a little more carefully. First of all, part P1 certainly does have a city, because all parts have a city—it's just that in the case at hand we don't know what that city is. In other words, that null means *city unknown*, and it's serving as a placeholder for some real city. Let *X* be the city in question. Then:

- Either *X* is Paris or it isn't.

- If *X* is Paris, then the Boolean expression

  ```
  'London' ≠ NULL OR NULL ≠ 'Paris'
  ```

  becomes

  ```
  'London' ≠ 'Paris' OR 'Paris' ≠ 'Paris'
  ```

  which reduces to

  ```
  TRUE OR FALSE
  ```

  which reduces to TRUE.

- If *X* isn't Paris, then the Boolean expression

  ```
  'London' ≠ NULL OR NULL ≠ 'Paris'
  ```

  becomes

  ```
  'London' ≠ X OR X ≠ 'Paris'
  ```

which reduces to

```
'London' ≠ X OR TRUE
```

because *X* isn't Paris, which again reduces to TRUE.

Either way, then, TRUE is the right answer! But 3VL says UNKNOWN is the right answer (and that UNKNOWN then gets coerced to FALSE). So, under 3VL, the query has produced the wrong answer—and that's a real problem. In my opinion, in fact, it's a complete showstopper.

Just to hammer the point home, here's an even more trivial example (more trivial, that is, than the one we've just finished discussing). Assume the same sample values as above, and consider this expression:

```
P WHERE CITY = CITY
```

Surely this expression should return all parts (actually just P1, given the specified sample values). But given those sample values, what it will actually return is an empty result: in other words, another wrong answer.

*Note:* The reason I didn't lead with this simpler example is because in a way I think it's actually *too* simple—too simple, I mean, to have the impact I think is needed to drive the "wrong answer" message home.

## IMPLICATION, EQUIVALENCE, AND EXPRESSION TRANSFORMATION

I gave the following 3VL truth tables for NOT, OR, and AND in the previous chapter:

| NOT | |
|---|---|
| *t* | *f* |
| *u* | *u* |
| *f* | *t* |

| OR | *t* | *u* | *f* |
|---|---|---|---|
| *t* | *t* | *t* | *t* |
| *u* | *t* | *u* | *u* |
| *f* | *t* | *u* | *f* |

| AND | *t* | *u* | *f* |
|---|---|---|---|
| *t* | *t* | *u* | *f* |
| *u* | *u* | *u* | *f* |
| *f* | *f* | *f* | *f* |

As we know from Chapter 1, however, there are other connectives in addition to these three. Two particularly important ones, at least in 2VL, are IF (implication) and IFF (equivalence). So what do IF and IFF look like in 3VL?

Now, this is an important question, and I'll have more to say about it in a few moments, also in Chapter 4. Unfortunately, it's one that Codd never answered in any of his published writings;[11] so the best we can do is just make some educated guesses.

First of all, then, let's suppose that IF and IFF are defined the way they are in 2VL. In other words, let's suppose that:

a. *Implication:* IF *P* THEN *Q* is defined as (NOT *P*) OR *Q*.

b. *Equivalence:* *P* IFF *Q* (alternatively, *P* ≡ *Q*) is defined as (IF *P* THEN *Q*) AND (IF *Q* THEN *P*).

The corresponding truth tables will then look like this:

| IF | *t* | *u* | *f* |
|---|---|---|---|
| *t* | *t* | *u* | *f* |
| *u* | *t* | *u* | *u* |
| *f* | *t* | *t* | *t* |

| IFF | *t* | *u* | *f* |
|---|---|---|---|
| *t* | *t* | *u* | *f* |
| *u* | *u* | *u* | *u* |
| *f* | *f* | *u* | *t* |

(*Exercise:* Check these.)

Here now are some consequences of the foregoing definitions.

- *Implication (IF):* IF *P* THEN *P* is certainly a tautology in natural language. For example, "If it's raining then it's raining" is certainly a true statement. And IF *P* THEN *P* is a tautology in 2VL also; for example,

```
IF CITY = 'London' THEN CITY = 'London'
```

  is certainly true as well, in 2VL. But in 3VL, with implication as defined above, this latter statement is *not* a tautology! If CITY is null, then CITY = 'London' evaluates to UNKNOWN, and the expression overall becomes

```
IF UNKNOWN THEN UNKNOWN
```

  which, as the truth table shows, reduces to UNKNOWN, not TRUE.

[11] SQL never answers it either, incidentally.

- *Equivalence (IFF):* *P* IFF *P* is certainly a tautology in natural language. For example, "It's raining if and only if it's raining" is certainly a true statement. And *P* IFF *P* is a tautology in 2VL also; for example,

  ```
  CITY = 'London' IFF CITY = 'London'
  ```

  is certainly true as well, in 2VL. But in 3VL, with equivalence as defined above, this latter statement is *not* a tautology! If CITY is null, then CITY = 'London' evaluates to UNKNOWN, and the expression overall becomes

  ```
  UNKNOWN IFF UNKNOWN
  ```

  which, as the truth table shows, again reduces to UNKNOWN and not to TRUE.

What these examples show, therefore, is that—at least with IF and IFF as defined above—statements that are tautologies in 2VL aren't necessarily tautologies in 3VL. (Similarly, statements that are contradictions in 2VL aren't necessarily contradictions in 3VL, of course.) These are serious problems! Why are they serious? *Answer:* Because they can lead to mistakes—mistakes, that is, on the part of the user or the system or both. How so? Well, to elaborate briefly:

- One of the things that both users and systems do—users in formulating expressions, systems in optimizing those expressions—is what's called *expression transformation* or, more colloquially, *query rewrite*. (I touched on this issue earlier in this chapter, also in Chapter 1.) The general idea is this: Given some relational expression *X* (typically representing some query), it's desirable to replace *X* by some other expression *Y* such that (a) *X* and *Y* are semantically equivalent, so they'll both produce the same result when evaluated, but (b) there are reasons to believe that *Y* will perform better, sometimes dramatically better, than *X*.

- No matter whether it's carried out by the user or the system, that process of replacing *X* by *Y* fundamentally relies on the validity of certain logical implications and logical equivalences. Those implications and equivalences in turn rely even more fundamentally on certain *identities* or *tautologies*: for example, the one that says that if *P* is true, and if *P* implies *Q* is also true, then *Q* must be true as well. Here's the standard example: If (a) it's true that I have no money, and if (b) it's also true that if I have no money then I'll have to wash dishes, then (c) it's true that—and it can safely be concluded that—I'll have to wash dishes.

- As we've seen, however, tautologies in 2VL aren't necessarily tautologies in 3VL. Thus, if a given transformation relies on a given 2VL tautology, then that transformation won't be valid in a 3VL system if that 2VL tautology isn't a 3VL tautology as well. And if some transformation isn't valid, then of course the transformed expression will, in general, produce the wrong answer.[12]

Now, I've already said the transformations I'm talking about can be carried out either by the user or by the system, but I think the point could do with a little more emphasis. To be specific:

- *Users:* Users can make mistakes in formulating the query in the first place, because logical inferences—inferences applied as part the user's thought process, I mean—that seem intuitively valid, and indeed are valid in 2VL, aren't necessarily valid in the system in question. (Assuming, of course, that the system in question is an implementation of 3VL—which, perhaps I should stress, SQL systems in particular supposedly are.)

- *System:* The system can make mistakes too, of course. Moreover, there's some relevant history here. I don't want to get into too much detail for fear of lawsuits, but essentially what happened was this. A certain DBMS, call it Product X, was built and marketed before SQL became a standard, and it supported 2VL only. Then SQL did become a standard, and the decision was made for obvious commercial reasons that Product X must now support the standard—which meant supporting SQL's brand of 3VL in particular. Well, what should have happened at this point was that every expression transformation that Product X was designed to carry out should have been reexamined to ensure that the transformation in question was still valid now the system was operating in a 3VL world. But that examination process didn't happen—at least, it certainly didn't happen 100%—and Product X was thus now producing wrong answers.

---

[12] Perhap I should rather say: It'll produce the right answer, but to the wrong question.

The following points are related to the foregoing but are worth calling out explicitly:

- First, we certainly have a right to require of any given 3VL implementation that (unlike Product X!) it never make any incorrect transformations. Unfortunately, however, there seem to be strictly fewer valid tautologies in 3VL than there are in 2VL—which means, loosely speaking, that 3VL is less optimizable than 2VL, and hence that performance overall in a 3VL system will never be as good as it can be in a 2VL system.

- Second, similar remarks apply to *n*-valued logics in general. That is, for any $n > 1$, there'll always be fewer tautologies in an $(n+1)$-valued logic than there are in an *n*-valued logic, and performance in an $(n+1)$-valued logic system will therefore never be as good, in general, as performance in an *n*-valued logic system. To put it another way, $(n+1)$-valued logic will always be less optimizable than *n*-valued logic.[13]

## WRONG ANSWERS bis

It's time to look at another concrete example: an even simpler one, in fact, than the one we discussed a couple of sections back.[14] The following picture shows sample values, in outline, for a simple database concerning departments and employees:

DEPT

| DNO | ...... |
|---|---|
| D2 | ...... |

EMP

| ENO | DNO | ...... |
|---|---|---|
| E1 | *null* | ...... |

Consider now the Boolean expression

```
DEPT.DNO = EMP.DNO AND EMP.DNO = 'D1'
```

[13] By the way, this point isn't purely academic, because in his RM/V2 book Codd actually proposed that DBMSs should be based on 4VL, not just 3VL. I'll have more to say on this latter in Chapter 5.

[14] Given the focus in the previous section on implication and equivalence in particular, I originally intended to give an example here that made use of those operators, but decided on reflection to make do with an even simpler one.

which, given the only data we have, reduces to

```
'D2' = NULL AND NULL = 'D1'
```

This expression in turn reduces to

```
UNKNOWN AND UNKNOWN
```

which reduces finally to just UNKNOWN.

Now, that original Boolean expression could be part of a query, of course. Here's an example of such a query, expressed just for a change in SQL:

```
SELECT ENO
FROM   DEPT , EMP
WHERE  NOT ( DEPT.DNO = EMP.DNO AND EMP.DNO = 'D1' )
```

Well, the expression in parentheses here evaluates to UNKNOWN, as we've seen. NOT (UNKNOWN) then returns UNKNOWN; that UNKNOWN in turn gets coerced to FALSE; and the final result is that nothing is retrieved (i.e., the result is empty). However, a "good" optimizer—this is the point at which this example differs in kind from the ones a couple of sections back—will notice that the expression in parentheses takes the form

```
A = B AND B = C
```

It will then infer that

```
A = C
```

(because equality is transitive). And so it will go on to extend the original expression in parentheses accordingly, so that it takes the form

```
A = B AND B = C AND A = C
```

(boldface for emphasis). The modified query thus looks like this:

```
SELECT ENO
FROM   DEPT , EMP
WHERE  NOT ( DEPT.DNO = EMP.DNO AND EMP.DNO = 'D1'
                               AND DEPT.DNO = 'D1' )
```

(boldface for emphasis again).

Before going any further, I'd like to stress the point that the foregoing trick—if I might be permitted to use such a term without sounding pejorative—would be perfectly legitimate, and often a good tactic, if we were in the realm of 2VL. But of course we aren't, we're in the realm of 3VL instead. So what actually happens in the example is this:

- The modified Boolean expression effectively becomes

  ```
  UNKNOWN AND UNKNOWN AND FALSE
  ```

  which reduces to just FALSE.

- The overall query thus effectively becomes

  ```
  SELECT ENO
  FROM   DEPT , EMP
  WHERE  NOT ( FALSE )
  ```

  or in other words

  ```
  SELECT ENO
  FROM   DEPT , EMP
  WHERE  TRUE
  ```

  and therefore returns the employee number E1. (More precisely, it returns a table of one column and one row, containing just that employee number E1.)

In other words, the query returns E1 if it's "optimized" and not if it isn't.

So what do we learn from this example? Well, first of all, it reinforces something we already know: viz., that tautologies in 2VL aren't necessarily tautologies in 3VL. Just to spell it out, the specific 2VL tautology we're talking about here is as follows:

$$\models ( A = B \text{ AND } B = C ) \equiv ( A = B \text{ AND } B = C \text{ AND } A = C )$$

Second, the example therefore also reinforces the point that if we're attempting to build a 3VL system, we need to be sure that every expression transformation performed by that system is valid in 3VL: even if—perhaps especially if—the expression transformation in question is "obviously" valid in

2VL.[15] The transformation performed in the example is valid in 2VL but not in 3VL; thus, performing it in a 3VL system has the effect of changing the semantics of the expression overall.

Third, the previous point applies most particularly in the special case when the 3VL system in question is actually an upgraded version of some earlier 2VL system.

Fourth ... well, I've said the transformation is invalid, and I've implied therefore that what we've been talking about is basically just an optimizer bug. But is it? Let's consider the example once again, a little more carefully this time:

- That null in the DNO column of the EMP row for employee E1 in table EMP means "value unknown." In other words, employee E1 is certainly in some department; we just don't know which department it is.

- That department either is or is not department D1.

- Now, the Boolean expression in parentheses in the original query was as follows:

```
DEPT.DNO = EMP.DNO AND EMP.DNO = 'D1'
```

- If the actual department for employee E1 is D1, this expression reduces (for the only data we have) to

```
'D2' = 'D1' AND 'D1' = 'D1'
```

  which reduces in turn to FALSE, because 'D2' = 'D1' is false.

- Alternatively, if the actual department for employee E1 is D*n* for some *n* other than 1, the expression reduces to

```
DEPT.DNO = 'Dn' AND 'Dn' = 'D1'
```

  which again reduces in turn to FALSE, because 'D*n*' = 'D1' is false.

---

[15] Actually this observation could and should be generalized by (a) replacing "2VL" by "*n*VL" and "3VL" by "(*n*+1)VL" and then (b) making it clear that the sentence that results is valid for all $n > 1$.

- Either way, then, FALSE is the right answer!

To spell it out, then: 3VL says UNKNOWN is the right answer, but reality says FALSE is (and the "optimized" version of the query did in fact produce the right answer after all—but that was a fluke, in a way, because the optimization as such certainly wasn't valid).[16] Once again, we see that 3VL doesn't match reality. In fact, let me state the matter more forcefully:

***If you have nulls in your database, you're getting wrong answers.***

---

[16] But would it have made any difference—and if so, what difference exactly—if {DNO} in table EMP were a foreign key referencing {DNO} in table DEPT?

# Chapter 4

# Three–Valued Logic: Some Questions of Intuition

*Caveat: Some of the arguments in this chapter are a little tricky, and I don't think you need worry if you don't follow them all, at least on a first reading. The fact is, this topic* **is** *very tricky, and to tell the truth I can't even swear that the arguments are all absolutely correct in every last detail. But the very fact that I feel I have to say that is exactly the point!—or a large part of the point, at any rate. Intuition can be extremely misleading in matters involving three-valued logic.*

The following picture shows a sample value for a slightly revised version of the suppliers and parts database. The revision consists in (a) adding a "shipment number" column, SPNO, to the shipments table SP, and then (b) making {SPNO} the primary key for that table. (The main reason for that revision is merely to avoid violating the so called *entity integrity rule*, which prohibits nulls in primary key columns. It's not important in the larger scheme of things.)

S

| SNO | SNAME | STATUS | CITY |
|---|---|---|---|
| S1 | Smith | 20 | London |
| S2 | Jones | 10 | Paris |
| S3 | Blake | 30 | Paris |
| S4 | Clark | 20 | *null* |

SP

| SPNO | SNO | PNO | QTY |
|---|---|---|---|
| SP1 | S1 | P1 | 300 |
| SP2 | S2 | P2 | 200 |
| SP3 | S3 | *null* | 400 |

*Note:* I omit the parts table P from the picture because it's not relevant to the sample queries I want to discuss (and I'll refer to this simplified database in what follows as "suppliers and shipments" accordingly). Note too, incidentally, that the revision to table SP has the additional effect of allowing that table to contain two or more rows with the same supplier number and same part number, though none of my examples will actually do as much.

## QUERY Q1

Here now is a simple expression, or query ("Query Q1"), involving the suppliers and shipments database:

```
S WHERE NOT EXISTS SP ( SP.SNO = S.SNO AND SP.PNO = 'P2' )
```

The question is: What does Query Q1 mean? I'd like you to think about that question for a moment or two before reading any further.

Well, I presume your response, or at least your initial response, to that question was something like this:

> Get suppliers who don't supply part P2.

Or perhaps a more stilted version of the same thing, such as:

> Get suppliers such that there doesn't exist a shipment showing they supply part P2.

And I imagine some such answer is what 99% of people would naturally give (apologies for the hyperbole here, but you know what I mean).

However, let me now point out that the foregoing answer can't possibly be correct, despite the fact that (as I've said) it's the one that most people would surely give. Why can't it be correct? *Answer:* Because it talks about *reality*—it has to do with what's true in the real world—and the database doesn't contain reality, it contains only the *system's knowledge* of reality, as I explained at some length in Chapter 2.

All right, then. So does the correct answer perhaps look like this?—

a. Get suppliers who are *not known* to supply part P2 (i.e., they might supply part P2, but the system doesn't definitely know whether they do or not).

Or this?—

b. Get suppliers who are *known not* to supply part P2 (i.e., they're definitely known not to supply part P2).

Or possibly even this?—

c. Get suppliers who are either not known or known not to supply part P2 (the union of a. and b.).

Before going any further, perhaps I should admit that I'm being just a little unfair here, because I haven't yet spelled out the semantics of EXISTS in the context of 3VL. Recall from Chapter 1, however, that EXISTS can be thought of, at least in 2VL, as just a repeated OR. That is, the expression

```
EXISTS X ( P ( X ) )
```

is effectively equivalent to, and thus shorthand for, the expression

```
FALSE OR P ( X1 ) OR P ( X2 ) OR ... OR P ( Xn )
```

where $X_1$, $X_2$, ..., $X_n$ are all of the values that the range variable *X* can possibly take. In other words:

- If there exists at least one such $X_i$ such that $P(X_i)$ is true ($i = 1, 2, ..., n$), then EXISTS *X* (*P*(*X*)) is true.

- If every $X_i$ is such that $P(X_i)$ is false ($i = 1, 2, ..., n$), then EXISTS *X* (*P*(*X*)) is false. In particular, EXISTS *X* (*P*(*X*)) is false if the set $\{X_1, X_2, ..., X_n\}$ is empty.

- If (a) there exists no $X_i$ such that $P(X_i)$ is true but (b) there does exist at least one $X_i$ such that $P(X_i)$ is unknown ($i = 1, 2, ..., n$), then EXISTS *X* (*P*(*X*)) is unknown.

Now let's get back to the original question ("What does Query Q1 mean?"). The possible interpretations, to repeat, were:

a. Get suppliers who are not known to supply part P2.

b. Get suppliers who are known not to supply part P2.

c. Get suppliers who are either not known or known not to supply part P2.

*Note:* If you're having difficulties over the difference between a. and b. here (more specifically, over the difference between *not known* and *known not*), thinking about the exactly parallel difference between the following two statements might help:

a′. I don't know if you have measles.

b′. I know you don't have measles.

All right; so how *exactly* do interpretations a. and b. differ? In order to answer this question, let's consider what the system knows. Here repeated for convenience are the sample data values:

S

| SNO | SNAME | STATUS | CITY |
|---|---|---|---|
| S1 | Smith | 20 | London |
| S2 | Jones | 10 | Paris |
| S3 | Blake | 30 | Paris |
| S4 | Clark | 20 | *null* |

SP

| SPNO | SNO | PNO | QTY |
|---|---|---|---|
| SP1 | S1 | P1 | 300 |
| SP2 | S2 | P2 | 200 |
| SP3 | S3 | *null* | 400 |

Now, regarding the question of which suppliers supply part P2—well, let's consider each of the four suppliers in turn. Here then is what the system knows:

1. It knows that supplier S1 definitely doesn't supply part P2. *Note:* I'll elaborate on this point below.

2. It knows that supplier S2 definitely does supply part P2.

3. It doesn't know whether supplier S3 supplies part P2 or not.

4. It knows that supplier S4 definitely doesn't supply part P2; in fact, it knows that supplier S4 doesn't supply any parts at all.

Now let me elaborate as promised on the first point above: namely, that the system knows that S1 doesn't supply P2. In making this claim, I'm appealing to *The Closed World Assumption* (CWA), which (as you'll recall) I discussed briefly at the end of Chapter 1. The CWA is a vitally important principle in the database context. Just to remind you, what it says, in effect, is as follows:

- If a given row appears in a given table, then it represents something that's known to be a "true fact." More precisely, it represents a proposition—an instantiation of the pertinent table predicate, of course—that's known to be true.

- Conversely, if a given row could appear in a given table but doesn't, then it represents something that's known not to be a "true fact." More precisely, it represents a proposition—an instantiation of the pertinent table predicate again—that's known to be false.

Thus, since there's no row for S1 and P2 (and also no row for S1 and an unknown part number) in table SP, we're entitled to interpret that state of affairs as meaning that "S1 supplies P2" is known not to be true.

I'll leave it as an exercise for you to determine how the CWA justifies the claims I made with respect to suppliers S2, S3, and S4. Here let me just note that I'll have quite a lot more to say about the CWA in Chapter 7.[1]

Now let's get back to Query Q1. Given what the system knows (the four numbered points above), it should I hope be clear that:

- If interpretation a. (the "not known" interpretation) is the correct one, the result should be S3.

- If interpretation b. (the "known not" interpretation) is the correct one, the result should be S1 and S4.

- If interpretation c. (the "not known or known not" interpretation) is correct, the result should be S1, S3, and S4.

---

[1] Actually, there are those who would argue that, in a world that embraces 3VL, *The Closed World Assumption* should be replaced by *The Open World Assumption* (OWA), which says that if a given row could appear in some given table but doesn't, then the corresponding proposition isn't false but unknown. I'll revisit this point in Chapter 7.

So let's "play computer"—i.e., let's now consider, for each supplier in turn, exactly how the overall query expression is evaluated:

1. For supplier S1, the expression in the WHERE clause becomes

```
NOT ( EXISTS SP ( SP.SNO = 'S1' AND SP.PNO = 'P2' ) )
```

   which evaluates to NOT FALSE (i.e., TRUE), since there doesn't exist an SP row for S1 and P2. So supplier S1 does appear in the result.

2. For supplier S2, the expression in the WHERE clause becomes

```
NOT ( EXISTS SP ( SP.SNO = 'S2' AND SP.PNO = 'P2' ) )
```

   which evaluates to NOT TRUE (i.e., FALSE), since there does exist an SP row for S2 and P2. So supplier S2 doesn't appear in the result.

3. For supplier S3, the expression in the WHERE clause becomes

```
NOT ( EXISTS SP ( SP.SNO = 'S3' AND SP.PNO = 'P2' ) )
```

   which evaluates to NOT UNKNOWN (i.e., UNKNOWN), since (a) there doesn't exist an SP row for S3 and P2 but (b) there *does* exist an SP row for S3 in which PNO is null. So for S3 the overall expression effectively becomes

```
S WHERE UNKNOWN
```

   That UNKNOWN then gets coerced to FALSE, and so supplier S3 doesn't appear in the result.

4. For supplier S4, the expression in the WHERE clause becomes

```
NOT ( EXISTS SP ( SP.SNO = 'S4' AND SP.PNO = 'P2' ) )
```

   which evaluates to NOT FALSE (i.e., TRUE), since there doesn't exist an SP row for S4 and P2 (actually, of course, there don't exist any SP rows for S4 at all). So supplier S4 does appear in the result.

So the final result is S1 and S4. *Conclusion:* Interpretations a. and c. are definitely incorrect; the correct one is interpretation b.("known not").

As an aside, I note that we could simplify Query Q1 slightly by using IN instead of EXISTS. Just to remind you from Chapter 2, IN is basically the *set membership* or *containment* operator: The expression *V* IN *Z* means "The value *V* is a member of, or is contained in, the set *Z*." But of course IN can be defined in terms of EXISTS. To be specific, *V* IN *Z* is equivalent to the following: There exists an element *Y* of *Z* such that *V* = *Y*. Thus, we could if we wanted rewrite Query Q1 like this—

```
S WHERE NOT ( S.SNO IN ( SP.SNO WHERE SP.PNO = 'P2' ) )
```

—or equivalently (but simplifying slightly) like this:

```
S WHERE S.SNO NOT IN ( SP.SNO WHERE SP.PNO = 'P2' )
```

So a minor syntactic simplification would indeed be possible. The semantics, however, would remain exactly as they were before.

By the way, it's relevant—in fact, highly relevant!—to my thesis in this book as a whole to mention that when I first discussed the foregoing question ("What does Query Q1 mean?") with Codd himself and another colleague, Nat Goodman, *we all got it wrong*. I mean, we concluded our discussion—and let me add that the discussion in question was a pretty lengthy one, too—by agreeing that interpretation a. was the correct one. Then we broke up the meeting and went our separate ways. And when I got home, I thought about the query some more, and got more and more confused, and finally decided to just "play computer" and work through the query one step at a time, just as I've done above. That's when I discovered that, lo and behold, interpretation b., not a., was actually the correct one.

To repeat, therefore: We all got it wrong. Even Codd got it wrong!—and he *believed* in 3VL and nulls and thought they were A Good Thing, which Goodman and I most certainly didn't.

*Note:* Despite our poor showing here, I think it's fair to claim that all three of us did at least understand the concepts involved pretty well. And yet, to say it one more time, we all got it wrong. So what are the chances, do you think, that users in general will deal with these matters correctly, 100% of the time?

## QUERY Q2

Of course, if interpretation b. is the right one for Query Q1, the obvious next question is: How can we formulate a query for interpretation a. ("Query Q2")? (We must be able to, of course. If we couldn't, then there'd be something wrong with our query language; I mean, there'd be some sense in which it was incomplete. See Chapter 1, footnote 9.)

Just to remind you, interpretation a. was:

a. Get suppliers who aren't known to supply part P2 (i.e., they might supply part P2, but the system doesn't definitely know they do, nor does it definitely know they don't).

Observe now that, as the remark in parentheses suggests, this natural language interpretation could perhaps be reduced to the arguably simpler form:

a. Get suppliers who might supply part P2.

Note carefully, however, that *might* here must be clearly understood as meaning "possibly but not definitely, and not definitely not either, according to the system's knowledge"—which, you might be forgiven for thinking, is a rather heavy semantic load for one little five-letter word to bear. But let that pass.

So we want to exclude any suppliers who, according to the system's knowledge, either definitely do supply part P2 or definitely don't. Here then is a first attempt at a formulation of the query:

```
S WHERE EXISTS SP
             ( MAYBE ( SP.SNO = S.SNO AND SP.PNO = 'P2' ) )
```

("suppliers for whom there exists a shipment saying they might supply part P2"). However, this formulation is incorrect (though it does happen to produce the right answer, given sample data as previously stated). In order to show why it's incorrect, let me add another row to table SP—viz., a row for supplier S3 and part P2—thus:

SP

| SPNO | SNO | PNO | QTY |
|---|---|---|---|
| SP1 | S1 | P1 | 300 |
| SP2 | S2 | P2 | 200 |
| SP3 | S3 | *null* | 400 |
| SP4 | S3 | P2 | 500 |

Now consider what happens when we examine the sole row for supplier S3 in table S:

- The expression in the WHERE clause becomes

```
EXISTS SP
     ( MAYBE ( SP.SNO = 'S3' AND SP.PNO = 'P2' ) )
```

  which evaluates to TRUE, since there does exist a row in table SP—namely, the row (SP3,S3,NULL,400)—for which the subexpression

```
SP.SNO = 'S3' AND SP.PNO = 'P2'
```

  (representing the MAYBE argument) evaluates to UNKNOWN, and MAYBE UNKNOWN evaluates to TRUE. Thus, supplier S3 does appear in the final result. But we don't want it to! Why not? Because what we want is an expression that represents interpretation a. That is, (a) we're looking for suppliers who might supply part P2, but aren't definitely known either to do so or not to do so, and (b) there's another row in table SP—namely, the row (SP4,S3,P2,500)—that says that in fact supplier S3 definitely does supply part P2.

It follows that the correct interpretation of our first attempt—our attempt, that is, at a formulation for interpretation a.—isn't interpretation a. at all, but is instead something like this: "Get suppliers who, regardless of whether they're definitely known to supply part P2, are definitely known to be *possibly* suppliers of part P2." (I hope that's perfectly clear.)

Here then is a second attempt:[2]

---

[2] The syntactic difference between our two attempts is worth highlighting. To be specific, the first had EXISTS (MAYBE (...)), while the second has MAYBE (EXISTS (...)).

```
S WHERE MAYBE
      ( EXISTS SP ( SP.SNO = S.SNO AND SP.PNO = 'P2' ) )
```

("suppliers for whom there might be a shipment, but isn't definitely known to be a shipment or known not to be a shipment, showing that the supplier supplies part P2"). This formulation is correct. *Exercise:* Convince yourself that this is so.

## NOT IS NOT "NOT"

At this point, I think I want to repeat, or at any rate paraphrase, something I said in Chapter 2 (footnote 13)—namely, if you're not confused by all this, then you haven't been paying attention. And my next observation, I think, serves only to reinforce that message. To be specific:[3]

- Let *X* be a Boolean variable (i.e., a variable of type BOOLEAN).

- In a 3VL system, then, the possible values of *X* are TRUE, UNKNOWN, and FALSE. (A state of affairs, incidentally, that makes the very idea of calling *X* a "Boolean" variable a little questionable in the first place—but, again, I'll let that pass.)

- If we say "*X* is NOT TRUE," we mean the value of *X* is FALSE.

- But if we say "*X* is not TRUE," we mean, of course, that the value of *X* is either UNKNOWN or FALSE (!).

In other words, the "NOT" of 3VL is not the "not" of ordinary English. The possibilities of confusion are endless.

Let me add a few postscripts to the foregoing:

- Recall the question "What does Query Q1 mean?" and the fact that Codd, Goodman, and I all got it wrong, at least initially. For the record, it was precisely a confusion over NOT vs. "not" that caused us to do so.

---

[3] The example that follows elaborates on a point also previously made in Chapter 2, in footnote 5.

- Some years ago I used to write a regular monthly column ("According to Date") for the magazine *Database Programming & Design*, and I usually closed that column with a kind of "puzzle corner" problem for my readers, giving the answer in a later installment. Now, the December 1992 installment was all about nulls and 3VL, and one of the things I stressed in that installment was the danger of confusing *not* and NOT. And what the puzzle corner problem in that installment did was this: It asked the reader to give a natural language interpretation of a certain SQL-like query—much as I've been doing in this chapter, in fact.

  Among the correspondence I received following that installment was a letter from the SQL project leader at the time—I'll call him Albert—at the National Institute of Standards and Technology (NIST), objecting strongly to just about everything I'd said in my original column. I won't bother to repeat all of Albert's arguments here, or my responses to them; I'll just note that his letter finished up by (a) claiming that SQL provides "an understandable and intuitively pleasing answer to the puzzle corner problem," and then (b) giving that answer—which was, of course (surprise, surprise), wrong. What's more, it was wrong *precisely* because Albert himself had fallen into the trap of confusing *not* and NOT, which was a large part of the point of my original column. It was beautiful. I couldn't have made my point any more plainly if I'd rigged Albert's response myself. As I wrote in my commentary at the time, it seems to me that there's probably a moral here.

- Finally, note the title of this section. What I've been arguing is that, in 3VL, NOT doesn't mean "not" (lowercase). Well, now let me add that in SQL (as opposed to 3VL as such), NOT doesn't mean "NOT" (uppercase)!—at least, not always.[4] To be specific, again let *X* be a variable of type BOOLEAN, and let *X* have the value TRUE. In SQL, then, if we say *X* is NOT TRUE, we mean *X* is FALSE; but if we say *X* IS NOT TRUE (note the uppercase IS), we mean *X* is either FALSE or UNKNOWN.[5]

---

[4] If you see what I mean! Perhaps I should have written "NOT always." But I'm not sure (or NOT sure?) that would have been any clearer.

[5] I've characterized this problem as "NOT is not *not*," but I suppose I could equally well have characterized it as "IS is not *is*." In fact, I do seem to recall somebody or other once saying "Well, it depends on what the meaning of *is* is."

## UNKNOWN IS NOT "UNKNOWN"

In the previous section I showed that NOT is not "not"—and perhaps you'll recall from Chapter 3 that UNKNOWN is not "unknown," either. For ease of reference, at least, I'll briefly review this latter point in the present section (after all, it does raise various questions of intuition, and that's what this chapter is supposed to be all about). Briefly:

- Again let *X* be a Boolean variable.
- In 3VL, then, the possible values of *X* are TRUE, UNKNOWN, and FALSE.
- If we say "*X* is UNKNOWN," we mean the value of *X* is the truth value UNKNOWN.
- But if we say "*X* is unknown," we mean, of course, that we don't know the value of *X*.

To put it another way: If *X* is UNKNOWN, then *X* = *X* gives TRUE;[6] if *X* is unknown, then *X* = *X* gives UNKNOWN. Once again, I hope that's perfectly clear.

Incidentally, SQL falls into exactly the foregoing trap, because—despite the fact that it does support the UNKNOWN keyword—it makes the same mistake as Codd did and uses null to represent the UNKNOWN truth value. This mistake is just as significant an error as it would be to represent the value zero by NULL! To spell the point out:

- Like zero, the truth value UNKNOWN is indeed a value.

---

[6] Though not (or NOT?) if we follow Codd and use null to represent UNKNOWN; then it'll give UNKNOWN (or rather NULL). See the remarks almost immediately following, regarding SQL.

- NULL is *not* a value—it's a marker, or flag, that's supposed to represent precisely the fact that there is no value.

- Representing a value of any kind, but most especially a truth value, by something that means there isn't a value is clearly a logical mistake.

  Time, I think, to remind you of that quote from Wittgenstein—

  *All logical differences are big differences.*

—and the corollary:

*All logical mistakes are big mistakes.*

## WHICH 3VL?

I gave the following 3VL truth tables for IF (implication) and IFF (equivalence) in the previous chapter:

| IF | *t* | *u* | *f* |
|---|---|---|---|
| *t* | *t* | *u* | *f* |
| *u* | *t* | *u* | *u* |
| *f* | *t* | *t* | *t* |

| IFF | *t* | *u* | *f* |
|---|---|---|---|
| *t* | *t* | *u* | *f* |
| *u* | *u* | *u* | *u* |
| *f* | *f* | *u* | *t* |

And I went on to show that, given these definitions, certain expressions—specifically, the expressions IF *P* THEN *P* and *P* IFF *P*—that were tautologies in 2VL (in fact, very "obviously" so) were no longer tautologies in 3VL. Here now is another important example of the same phenomenon: Given the foregoing definitions, the statement

```
( P IFF Q ) ≡ ( ( IF P THEN Q ) AND ( IF Q THEN P ) )
```

is, again, a tautology in 2VL but not in 3VL.

Now, I explained in Chapter 3 why the fact that certain 2VL tautologies weren't 3VL tautologies could be a problem, and I don't want to repeat that explanation here. But could we perhaps retrieve the situation by defining IF and IFF a little differently? To be specific, what would happen if, in the case where *P* and *Q* are both UNKNOWN, we were to define IF *P* THEN *Q* and *P* IFF *Q* both to return TRUE instead of (as above) UNKNOWN? Note, incidentally, that this isn't just idle speculation on my part—there's at least one famous logician (Jan Łukasiewicz) whose writings support exactly this position.

Given those changes, the truth tables will look like this (changes highlighted in bold):

| IF | *t* | *u* | *f* |
|---|---|---|---|
| *t* | *t* | *u* | *f* |
| *u* | *t* | **t** | *u* |
| *f* | *t* | *t* | *t* |

| IFF | *t* | *u* | *f* |
|---|---|---|---|
| *t* | *t* | *u* | *f* |
| *u* | *u* | **t** | *u* |
| *f* | *f* | *u* | *t* |

Now IF *P* THEN *P* and *P* IFF *P* are tautologies after all (note that both truth tables now have nothing but TRUE in the diagonal from top left to bottom right). And it follows immediately that

```
( P IFF Q ) ≡ ( ( IF P THEN Q ) AND ( IF Q THEN P ) )
```

is now a tautology as well (in this new, revised 3VL, that is). Unfortunately, however, the following now isn't:

```
( IF P THEN Q ) ≡ ( ( NOT P ) OR Q )
```

(*Exercise:* Check this claim.) So problems of intuition remain—not the same problems as before, of course, but problems nonetheless.

Be all that as it may, the foregoing discussion raises a more fundamental point—an important point, in fact, though it doesn't seem to get much attention in the database literature. Recall that in 2VL there are exactly 20 connectives, or logical operators—four monadics and 16 dyadics. Of course, this state of affairs is a logical consequence of the fact that there are exactly 20 truth tables in 2VL—again, four monadic ones and 16 dyadic ones. So how many connectives are there in 3VL?

Well, it's obvious that a monadic truth table in 3VL has to take the following general form—

| *Op* | |
|---|---|
| *t* | *a* |
| *u* | *b* |
| *f* | *c* |

—where *a*, *b*, and *c* stand for the result of applying the operator *Op* to the truth value shown at the left of the pertinent row. Now, each of *a*, *b*, and *c* can be any one of the three truth values TRUE, UNKNOWN, and FALSE (*t*, *u*, and *f* for short); so there are 3 × 3 × 3 = 27 monadic truth tables, and hence 27 monadic 3VL connectives.

As for the dyadics, the truth table takes this general form:

| *Op* | *t* | *u* | *f* |
|---|---|---|---|
| *t* | $a_1$ | $a_2$ | $a_3$ |
| *u* | $b_1$ | $b_2$ | $b_3$ |
| *f* | $c_1$ | $c_2$ | $c_3$ |

Since each of $a_1$, $a_2$, ..., $c_3$ can be any one of *t*, *u*, and *f*, there are 3 × 3 × 3 × 3 × 3 × 3 × 3 × 3 × 3 = $3^9$ = 19,683 dyadic truth tables, and hence 19,683 dyadic 3VL connectives.

Now, *every* 3VL has to support all of these connectives—all 19, 710 of them—because if it doesn't, it isn't a 3VL.[7] But which connective corresponds to which truth table? Or to put it another way, which operator do we choose to call NOT, and which OR, and which AND, and which IF (and so on)? Different choices lead to different 3VLs.

Perhaps you can see now, if you didn't before, why we should be very skeptical regarding claims that either SQL or the relational model—meaning, here, the model as "extended" in Codd's 1979 paper—"supports three-valued logic." The question is: *Which* three-valued logic? Which logic are we talking about? No one in the database world has ever answered this question satisfactorily, so far as I'm aware. (Indeed, I don't think anyone in that world has answered it at all. Nor do I know of anyone else who has even asked it, except perhaps David McGoveran.)

What's more (and arguably more important, in fact), no 3VL preserves all of the desirable properties of 2VL. For example, in some 3VLs

```
( IF P THEN Q ) ≡ ( ( NOT P ) OR Q )
```

is a tautology, but

```
IF P THEN P
```

[7] In other words (to repeat from Chapter 1, footnote 9), every 3VL, in order to be a "full function" 3VL in the first place, has to be *truth functionally complete*.

isn't, while in other 3VLs it's the other way around.

For a much more extensive discussion of such matters, I refer you to the four-part paper "Nothing from Nothing," by David McGoveran (Chapters 5-8 of the book *Relational Database Writings 1994-1997*, by David McGoveran, Hugh Darwen and myself, Addison-Wesley, 1998).

# Chapter 5

# Three-Valued Logic: Why Stop There?

The relational model was born in 1969, when Codd published his first relational paper ("Derivability, Redundancy, and Consistency of Relations Stored in Large Data Banks," IBM Research Report RJ599, August 19th, 1969). That paper didn't mention nulls at all; instead, it defined the model as being based (very solidly based, I'd say) on classical two-valued logic, 2VL. Ten years later, however, Codd published his 1979 paper ("Extending the Database Relational Model to Capture More Meaning," *ACM Transactions on Database Systems 4*, No. 4, December 1979). That was the paper in which, in an attempt to deal with the problem of missing information, he added nulls and switched from two- to three-valued logic, 3VL. But he didn't stop there! A few years later, he published another paper—"Missing Information (Applicable and Inapplicable) in Relational Databases" (*ACM SIGMOD Record 15*, No. 4, December 1986)—in which he added a second kind of null, and switched from three- to four-valued logic accordingly.[1] Such matters are the concern of the present chapter.

## A MORE CAREFUL TREATMENT OF 3VL

I'll begin with a more careful tutorial treatment of nulls and 3VL—more careful, I mean, than the treatment I've been giving these matters in this book prior to this point. *Note:* The discussion that follows is an edited version of one that first appeared in my own detailed review of Codd's RM/V2 book (viz., *The Relational Model for Database Management Version 2 – A Critical Analysis*, Technics, 2024).

---

[1] Subsequently he incorporated that paper more or less verbatim into his book *The Relational Model for Database Management Version 2* (Addison-Wesley, 1990). As noted in the preface, I'll refer to that book from this point forward as just "the RM/V2 book," or sometimes "Codd's RM/V2 book."

As explained at length in earlier chapters, Codd's approach to the missing information problem was based on what he originally called *nulls*. (That was the term he used in his 1979 paper. In the RM/V2 book, however, he switched to the term *marks*. For reasons of familiarity, however, I'll stay with nulls—for the time being, at any rate.) Now, the basic thinking behind nulls is as follows:

> If some piece of information is missing for some reason (as in, e.g., "present address unknown," or "speaker to be announced"), the location in the database where that information would otherwise have appeared is (a) left empty—conceptually empty, at any rate[2]—and (b) marked with a special flag called a null to show that it is indeed conceptually empty and contains no actual value.

By way of example, consider the suppliers and parts database. Suppose the status value for supplier S6 (name Gomez, city Madrid) is currently missing:

| S6 | Gomez | | Madrid |
|---|---|---|---|

Please observe now—very carefully!—that what this picture represents *isn't a tuple*. Why not? Because a tuple by definition is a set of values, one value (of the pertinent type) for each component of the tuple in question, and nulls by definition aren't values: They're *markers*, or *flags*. So anything that involves such a marker or flag simply isn't a tuple: again, by definition. It follows that (as I put it in Chapter 2, albeit in slightly different words):

- A "tuple" that "contains a null" isn't a tuple.
- A "relation" that contains such a "tuple" isn't a relation.

---

[2] Note, therefore, that I'm now explicitly departing from the conventional, albeit *very* informal, perception—which of course I did tacitly adopt in earlier chapters—that a row might actually "contain a null" in one or more of its column positions (or in other words at one or more "locations," to use the term introduced in the main text above). As I hope that main text makes clear, the logically correct way to think about these matters is *not* to consider such a location as containing anything at all, but rather to consider it "marked" in some way. *Note:* That said, however, let me say too that—at least in his earlier writings, including his 1979 paper in particular—Codd himself often departed from this proper way of thinking and talked instead in terms of nulls being "contained in" positions in rows (and hence, indirectly, in positions in tables too).

- More fundamentally, a "type" that "contains a null" isn't a type (because types too are sets of values).

And hence:

- **Nulls break the relational model.** Or to put it more politely, perhaps: Nulls represent a major departure from, and/or a major extension to, the basic prescriptions of the relational model. As such, they need to be justified very, very carefully before they can be accepted—if indeed they ever can.

As previously noted, therefore, even just to talk about these matters properly requires us to suspend disbelief, as it were, and pretend that the idea of "relations containing nulls" makes some kind of logical sense—despite the fact that it very clearly doesn't. Still, so be it; let's adopt the fiction, at least for the time being, that relations (or tables) can indeed contain tuples (or rows) with marked or flagged components, and let's see where adopting that fiction takes us.

Well, one obvious question that arises immediately is as follows (I deliberately spell it out very carefully, one step at a time):

- Suppose *A* and *B* are locations in the database.

- Suppose *A* is marked, or flagged, as "containing a null."

- What then can we say about the comparison $A = B$?

Let me elaborate. First of all, of course, it's conventional in computing to understand the expression $A = B$ as meaning, not that *A* and *B* are one and the same location, but rather that the values in those two locations are equal. But if *A* is marked, there simply *is* no value in *A*—in which case, what can $A = B$ possibly mean? In particular, what can it mean if *B* happens to be marked as well? (*Pause for thought here.*)

Well, personally, I don't think there's any way such a comparison can be said to have any sensible meaning at all. But Codd disagreed; that is, he thought that nulls could be made to make sense. Here in essence is what he proposed:

> Again consider the comparison $A = B$. If $A$ is marked or $B$ is marked or both, then that comparison should return, not TRUE or FALSE, but rather a "third truth value" called UNKNOWN.

In other words, he proposed that we should replace our conventional two-valued logic (2VL) by a three-valued logic (3VL).

Now I'd like you to consider the following argument (which again I want to spell out very carefully, one step at a time):

- Let *P* be a proposition—for example, let *P* be the proposition "Barack Obama was born in the year 1963."

- Now, I don't know offhand whether *P* is true or false, but it certainly is one or the other. Thus, the fact that I don't know which it is doesn't say anything about *P* as such; rather, what it does say something about is **my knowledge of** *P*. (Actually, what it says is: *The proposition "I know the truth value of P" is false*. Let's call this italicized proposition *Q*.)

- Observe now that the two propositions *P* and *Q* aren't the same!—there's an obvious and important logical difference between them.

- Thus, to pretend that UNKNOWN should be treated on an equal footing with TRUE and FALSE is to mix and muddle some fundamentally different things, and it's bound to lead to error and confusion. Which it very demonstrably does.

### *A Clarification*

To wind up this preliminary section—this "more careful treatment" of what nulls and 3VL are all about, I mean—there's one more point I need to make: one more point, that is, that I want to spell out explicitly. (Actually the point is obvious, but I don't want it to be lost, or overlooked.)

In my exploration above of what I referred to as "one obvious question," I began by saying:

> *Suppose A and B are locations in the database.*

What I carefully didn't say was:

> *Suppose A and B are* distinct *locations in the database.*

The reason I didn't, of course, is because that assumption is unnecessary. That is, everything I said regarding *A* and *B* earlier in the present section still holds true if *A* and *B* are in fact one and the same location. In particular, therefore, I note once again that Codd's 3VL scheme violates *The First Axiom of Equality* (viz., that *X* = *X* for all *X*).

## KINDS OF MISSING INFORMATION

One point I hope the previous section makes clear is this: It would be—in fact, it *is*—very difficult even just to talk about these matters in a way that makes strict logical sense. For example, it would be very cumbersome, to say the least, if we had to make statements like this all the time:

> We didn't know what value to put in the position in the database where we would have recorded Joe's salary if we'd known what it was, so we haven't put any value there—instead, we've left it empty, and we've marked that position with a special flag called a null to show what we've done.

So of course what we do in practice is this: We *simplify*—we say things like "Joe's salary is null," and we hope and trust, and possibly even believe, that this simple statement will be sufficient to convey to users the message that:

a. There's certainly a position (or "slot") in the database for recording Joe's salary, but

b. There's no value recorded at that position, because we don't know what value to put there, and so

c. The position in question is marked or flagged accordingly.[3]

---

[3] As an aside, I note that SQL products do typically represents nulls in precisely this manner (i.e., by, in effect, (a) marking the pertinent storage location on the disk and accordingly (b) treating as irrelevant whatever bit string happens to be stored at that location). Moreover, I tend to agree with what Codd said in later writings( i.e., that some kind of systematic "mark" terminology would be preferable to the more usual "nulls" terminology), but as I've already said I'll stay with the latter for reasons of familiarity. Most of the time, at any rate.

Though I frankly doubt whether abbreviated statements such as "Joe's salary is null" are really understood in such a precise and careful way, either (a) by very many users or (b) very much of the time.

All of that said, however, for obvious reasons I'll make use myself of such abbreviated statements ("Joe's salary is null" and the like) from time to time in what follows. Not without misgivings, though! I must stress that this way of talking, and indeed thinking, is really quite sloppy; and it's unfortunate, therefore, that both the IS_NULL operator introduced in Chapter 2, and (more to the point) SQL's analog of that operator, do tend to encourage it.

To repeat, then: Null is a marker, or flag. Crucially, it's not a value as such. That's why, as noted several times in this book already, the term *null value* is deprecated, strongly. In fact, it's a contradiction in terms.

Now, there are many reasons why a given piece of information might be missing, and hence many possible interpretations of the assertion that "*X* is null" for some *X*. In other words, there are many different kinds of nulls. Here are some of them.

- Value not applicable

  Suppose the database includes an employee table EMP, with columns ENO, DNO, JOB, SALARY, and COMMISSION, and suppose too that the property COMMISSION applies only to employees in the sales department. Also, let Joe be an employee, but let Joe not be in that department. Then the statement "Joe's commission is null" means Joe doesn't have a commission, because the property of having a commission doesn't apply to him.

  *Note:* In the RM/V2 book Codd calls this kind of null an *I-mark* (I for *inapplicable*).

- Value unknown

  In contrast to the previous example, the statement "Joe's salary is null" presumably means Joe does have a salary (because all employees have a salary), but we don't know what it is—the value is unknown.

  *Note:* In the RM/V2 book Codd calls this kind of null an *A-mark* (A for *applicable*—the property of having a salary does apply to Joe, because it applies to all employees, but the actual value is unknown). The term *A-mark* thus refers to what in his 1979 paper Codd called just a null as such.

- Value doesn't exist

  Consider the property "has a social security number." In the U.S., at least, this property applies to employees in general—in fact, it applies to U.S. residents in general—but not everyone actually has a social security number.[4] Thus, the statement "Joe's social security number is null" could simply mean that no social security number exists for Joe. Note the difference between this example and the first example above ("value not applicable"). In this example, the property of having a social security number is certainly applicable to Joe, because it's applicable to every U.S. resident; it's just that Joe doesn't actually happen to have one at this time.

- Value undefined

  Certain items are explicitly undefined: for example, the result of dividing something by zero, or the maximum value in an empty set. Thus, for example, in a table *T* with columns *A*, *B*, *C*, and *D*, where *A* stands for "person," *B* for "number of payments made," *C* for "total payment made," and *D* for "average payment made," *D* will be undefined—another kind of null—for anyone who has made no payments at all.

  *An aside here regarding SQL:* As you probably know, SQL actually defines the AVG (as well as the MAX, MIN, and SUM) of an empty set to be unknown, not undefined. A more appropriate approach, if the system doesn't support "undefined" (which SQL doesn't), would be to allow an optional second argument to be specified on invocations of such operators, representing the value to be returned if the first argument is empty. It would then be an error if that second argument is omitted and the first argument is indeed empty.

  Incidentally, the "empty set" result in the specific case of SUM should be zero anyway, not undefined (SQL is doubly wrong in this particular instance). After all, in the example, if *B* (number of payments) is zero, then *C* (total payment) should clearly be zero as well.

---

[4] I know this for a fact because it happened to me—I was a (legal!) immigrant and U.S. resident for well over two years before I acquired a social security number.

- Value not valid

  During data entry, it might be discovered that some value is invalid—e.g., employee age = 80, whereas employees are required to retire at 65. There might be good reasons for entering the employee into the database anyway, but marking the employee's age as invalid, if for no other reason than to permit subsequent analysis in order to discover, precisely, which values in the original data were in fact not valid.

- Value not supplied

  "Refused to answer" or "no comment" are perfectly legitimate responses to certain questions (e.g., in census operations and the like). Again, there might be good operational reasons for distinguishing such cases appropriately in the database, instead of just marking them as "unknown."

- Value is the empty set

  Let table XDE be the *left outer natural join* of departments and employees over {DNO} (department number).[5] Further, let department *d* have no employees at this time. Then there'll be exactly one row in table XDE for department *d*, with a null in the employee number position. That null means that the set of employees in department *d* is an empty set.

  Note, moreover, that the SQL expression

  ```
  SELECT DNO , COUNT(*)
  FROM   XDE
  GROUP  BY DNO
  ```

  will return a count of one, not zero, for department *d*. This result is at best counterintuitive, at worst just plain wrong.

So that's seven kinds of nulls. And there are certainly other possibilities as well; for example, the nulls generated by outer union seem to be different in kind from *all* of the ones discussed above. (I'll have more to say about outer union in a later section in this chapter.) The overriding point, though, is that each kind of null has its own special properties and its own special behavior; thus,

---

[5] I'll have a lot more to say about outer join later in this chapter.

representing and manipulating them all in the same kind of way is clearly not the right thing to do.

By the way, this latter observation raises another point: namely, that in a system that supports just one kind of null, say "value unknown," it's quite likely that users will use that null for purposes for which it's not appropriate. In other words, the fact that "null support" is provided at all might lull users into a false sense of security ("missing information?—don't worry about it, the system can handle it"). As a concrete example of such misuse, once again let Joe be an employee not in the sales department. In a "one null" system, then, it's possible—even likely—that Joe's commission will be represented by means of a "value unknown" null, whereas it should of course be a "value doesn't apply" null. One consequence of such a mistake is that, in attempting to compute Joe's total compensation (salary plus commission), the system will give "unknown" (see later), whereas of course the result should be just Joe's salary.[6]

What's more, the foregoing argument will always apply, mutatis mutandis, so long as the system supports fewer kinds of nulls than are logically necessary. In other words, simply adding support for a "value doesn't apply" null might solve the specific problem identified in the previous paragraph, but it won't solve the general problem. In fact, a system that does support nulls, but not at the 100% level (whatever that level might be, I suppose I should add), is just as open to abuse—perhaps even more so, perhaps even dangerously more so—than a system that doesn't support nulls at all.

Now, in Codd's approach, the introduction of a single kind of null (i.e., his original null, later renamed the A-mark) required an extension of the traditional two-valued logic (2VL) to a logic of three values (3VL), and the introduction of a second kind (his I-mark) required a further extension to a logic of four values (4VL). Thus, to deal with the seven kinds of nulls identified above will presumably need a logic of at least nine different truth values! In general, in fact, it seems that *n* kinds of nulls will require an (*n*+2)-valued logic. This fact alone, I believe, should at the very least give us pause.[7] But matters are worse than that ... In fact, it's easy to see that—in principle, at any rate—the number of different kinds of nulls required is quite literally infinite. For consider:

---

[6] In the RM/V2 book Codd says the sum of (a) a "value does not apply" null or I-mark and (b) a genuine numeric value should be "value does not apply." But the total compensation for an employee for whom the commission property is inapplicable should clearly be just that employee's salary; in other words, contrary to what Codd says, "*V*+*i*" (where *V* is a genuine value and *i* is an I-mark) should surely give *V*, not *i*.

[7] It's relevant here to remind you of the following point from Chapter 3: If $m > n$, then *m*-valued logic will always be less optimizable than *n*-valued logic, because there'll be fewer tautologies in an *m*-valued logic than there are in an *n*-valued logic.

- Again let table EMP have columns ENO, DNO, JOB, SALARY, and COMMISSION, and let COMMISSION apply only to employees in the sales department.

- Suppose now that employee Joe's DNO slot is "A-marked," meaning that Joe does have a department but we don't know what it is.

- All right; so what do we do about employee Joe's commission? It surely must be null—the information is surely missing—*but we don't know whether that null should be an A-mark or an I-mark*: If Joe is in the sales department it should be an A-mark, otherwise it should be an I-mark. But *we don't know* whether or not Joe is in the sales department! So we don't know what kind of null we need for Joe's commission.

- So it looks as if need a new kind of null (a new kind of mark, if you prefer), meaning "either an A-mark or an I-mark, but we don't know which." Call this new kind of null "null-3" (A- and I-marks being null-1 and null-2, respectively).

- Now we need a new kind of null to represent "either null-1 or null-2 or null-3, but we don't know which." Call this one "null-4."

- Now we need a new kind of null to represent "either null-1 or null-2 or null-3 or null-4, but we don't know which." Call this one "null-5."

And so on, ad infinitum.

## THE OUTER JOIN OPERATOR

You're probably familiar with the basic idea of outer join, but let me review it briefly here anyway. First of all, then, please note that by that term I mean the outer *natural* join specifically, unless the context demands otherwise. Here's a simple example. Suppose the current values of tables S and SP are as follows:

S

| SNO | SNAME | STATUS | CITY |
|---|---|---|---|
| S2 | Jones | 10 | Paris |
| S5 | Adams | 30 | Athens |

SP

| SNO | PNO | QTY |
|---|---|---|
| S2 | P1 | 300 |
| S2 | P2 | 400 |

Note in particular that there are currently no shipments for supplier S5. As a consequence, the join (the regular or "inner" join, that is) of these two tables looks like this:

| SNO | SNAME | STATUS | CITY | PNO | QTY |
|---|---|---|---|---|---|
| S2 | Jones | 10 | Paris | P1 | 300 |
| S2 | Jones | 10 | Paris | P2 | 400 |

So we might say—speaking *very* loosely, please note!—that the inner or regular join in this example "loses information" for supplier S5: Because there's no row in the shipments table for supplier S5, there's nothing for the S5 row in the suppliers table to join to, and so there's no row for S5 in the result.

The outer join is intended to address such problems (if they really are problems). More specifically, the outer join "preserves" information where the inner join "loses" it. Here for example is the outer join of tables S and SP as shown above:

| SNO | SNAME | STATUS | CITY | PNO | QTY |
|---|---|---|---|---|---|
| S2 | Jones | 10 | Paris | P1 | 300 |
| S2 | Jones | 10 | Paris | P2 | 400 |
| S5 | Adams | 30 | Athens | *null* | *null* |

As you can see, this result does have a row for supplier S5—it consists of the row for S5 from the suppliers table, extended with nulls in the PNO and QTY positions—and information regarding that supplier is thus preserved. Despite the picture, though, please remember that those positions don't really "contain a null." Rather, they're marked, or flagged, to show that (conceptually, at any rate) they don't actually contain anything at all.

Let me note as an aside that if we assume for the moment that NULL is a legal scalar expression—by the way, do you think it is?—then outer join can be defined in terms of other operators. For example, the following expression could be used to construct the outer join result just shown:[8]

```
( S JOIN SP )
  UNION
( EXTEND ( S NOT MATCHING SP ) :
                { PNO := NULL , QTY := NULL } )
```

As a further aside, I note that the foregoing expression in itself demonstrates rather clearly one of the things that's wrong with the whole outer join idea. The "S JOIN SP" portion of the expression yields a table whose predicate looks something like this:[9]

> *Supplier SNO is under contract, is named SNAME, has status STATUS, is located in city CITY, and supplies part PNO in quantity QTY.*

And the EXTEND portion of the expression yields a table whose predicate looks something like this:

> *Supplier SNO is under contract, is named SNAME, has status STATUS, is located in city CITY, and doesn't supply any part in any quantity.*[10]

So there are clearly two different predicates here (with, incidentally, different numbers of parameters), *and so there ought to be two different tables.* One looks like this (it's the regular join):

| SNO | SNAME | STATUS | CITY | PNO | QTY |
|---|---|---|---|---|---|
| S2 | Jones | 10 | Paris | P1 | 300 |
| S2 | Jones | 10 | Paris | P2 | 400 |

---

[8] The expression makes use of the relational operators EXTEND and NOT MATCHING, both of which I strongly believe should be supported in practice. Here are the definitions. First, let *T* not have a column called *C*; then EXTEND *T* : {*C* := *exp*} returns a table with (a) heading the heading of *T* extended with column *C* and (b) body the set of all rows *r* such that *r* is a row of *T* extended with a value for *C* that's computed by evaluating *exp* on that row of *T*. Second, let $T_1$ and $T_2$ be joinable, and let $T_1$ have columns $C_1$, $C_2$, ..., $C_n$ (only); then $T_1$ NOT MATCHING $T_2$ is shorthand for $T_1$ MINUS ($T_1$ MATCHING $T_2$), and $T_1$ MATCHING $T_2$ in turn is shorthand for ($T_1$ JOIN $T_2$) {$C_1$,$C_2$, ..., $C_n$}.

[9] This predicate and the next one should both really be prefixed by "We believe that" or some such phrase, but I'm overlooking this point here for simplicity.

[10] I hope you agree, therefore, that the nulls in this example are of the "value doesn't exist" variety.

And the other looks like this (no nulls, observe):

| SNO | SNAME | STATUS | CITY |
|---|---|---|---|
| S5 | Adams | 30 | Athens |

In other words, outer join is a kind of shoehorn operation—it "force fits" rows into a place where they don't really fit at all. In the case at hand, the rows being forced are rows of table SP, and what they're being forced into, or onto, is the regular natural join of tables S and SP.

By the way, here's a thought for you to ponder: If we call the usual join the regular or natural join—as indeed we do—then why don't we call the outer join an irregular or unnatural join?

### *Which Outer Join?*

Actually, there are several different varieties of outer join: to be specific, left, right, and full versions of outer natural join and left, right, and full versions of outer theta join. (I remind you from Chapter 2 that *theta* here stands for any of the usual scalar comparison operators "=", "≠", "<", and so on.) Broadly speaking, the left joins preserve information from the first or left operand table; the right joins preserve information from the second or right operand table; and the full joins do both. Thus, the example discussed in the previous subsection is a left join—a left outer natural join, to be precise.

Unfortunately, however, no matter which particular version of outer join we're talking about, the fact is that the operator suffers from a number of what, in a paper I wrote several years ago,[11] I called "Nasty Properties." I don't propose to discuss those properties in detail here, but at least I'll summarize them for purposes of reference:

1. Outer equijoin[12] isn't a restriction of Cartesian product.

2. Restriction doesn't distribute over outer equijoin.

---

[11] "Watch Out for Outer Join," in the book *Relational Database Writings 1989-1991*, by C. J. Date and Hugh Darwen (Addison-Wesley, 1992).

[12] An "equijoin" is a theta join in which theta is equals ("=").

3. $A \leq B$ isn't equivalent to $A < B$ OR $A = B$.[13]

4. $A < B$ AND $B < C$ doesn't imply $A < C$.

5. Outer natural join isn't a projection of outer equijoin.

I've said I don't plan to discuss these Nasty Properties in detail here; however, I will at least mention that several early SQL products got into considerable trouble over them. Of course, what those products all did do was this: They all supported SQL's original SELECT – FROM – WHERE construct. The trouble is, the Nasty Properties effectively conspire to undermine the assumptions underlying that construct. As a consequence, it turns out that if we want to extend that construct to support some kind of outer join, then:

1. Property No. 1 implies that just extending the WHERE clause won't work.

2. Property No. 2 implies that ANDing an outer join and a restriction doesn't work, implying again that just extending the WHERE clause won't work.

3. Property No. 3 implies that expressing the join condition in the WHERE clause won't work.

4. Property No. 4 implies that outer joins of more than two tables can't be formulated without nested expressions, which at that time SQL didn't support.

5. Property No. 5 implies that just extending the SELECT clause won't work.

*Note:* The underlying problem in all of the above is that SQL at the time didn't properly support the regular or *inner* join; instead, it required the user to formulate such a join by, in effect, spelling out the definition of that operator as an explicit Cartesian product (FROM clause), followed by an explicit restriction (WHERE clause), followed by an explicit projection (SELECT clause). Thus, the obvious solution—indeed, the one that was eventually adopted—was, first, to add explicit inner join support; second, to extend that support to take care of

[13] This particular claim is somewhat simplified as stated. What it means is that the "less than or equals" outer join isn't equivalent to the union of the "less than" and "equals" outer joins.

outer joins as well. But of course that solution introduced a major problem of its own: namely, that large portions of the existing language were now effectively redundant and could be deleted without significant loss of function.[14]

## AN OUTER JOIN EXAMPLE

You might have noticed that I was (deliberately, of course) ducking an issue in the foregoing section. The issue in question is as follows:

- Outer join generates nulls.
- But there are many kinds of nulls, so what kind does outer join generate?

Well, let's consider an example. Suppose we're given tables as follows (shown just in outline for simplicity):

```
EMP  { ENO , DNO , SALARY }
     KEY { ENO }
     FOREIGN KEY { DNO } REFERENCES DEPT

DEPT { DNO , BUDGET }
     KEY { DNO }

PGMR { ENO , LANG }
     KEY { ENO }
     FOREIGN KEY { ENO } REFERENCES EMP
```

What these tables are supposed to mean is, I hope, intuitively obvious—except perhaps for table PGMR, where the intended meaning is that the specified employee is a programmer and is skilled in the specified programming language. Also, let's agree for simplicity that (a) each programmer is skilled in just one language; (b) column DNO in table EMP has "nulls allowed"; (c) all other columns have "nulls not allowed." Now consider the following outer joins:

- *Left outer natural join of EMP with PGMR:* Rows in the result for employees who aren't programmers will "contain a null" in the LANG

---

[14] In practice, of course, they can't be deleted, owing to what Hugh Darwen calls *The Shackle of Compatibility*. So the language must forever remain highly redundant, with all the problems such redundancy brings in its wake. See Chapter 4 ("Redundancy in SQL") of my book *Stating the Obvious, and Other Database Writings* (Technics, 2020).

column. Those nulls will presumably be of the "value not applicable" variety.

- *Left outer natural join of DEPT with EMP:* Rows in the result for departments with no employees will "contain a null" in the ENO and SALARY columns. The ENO nulls will presumably be of the "value doesn't exist" variety. As for the SALARY nulls, the same might be said of them too—but the reason why some particular SALARY value doesn't exist is because no corresponding employee exists, a state of affairs that might suggest the need for some different kind of null.

- *Left outer natural join of EMP with DEPT:* Rows in the result for employees whose DNO is null in table EMP will "contain a null" in the DNO and BUDGET columns. The DNO nulls will presumably be of the "value unknown" variety. As for the BUDGET nulls, the same might be said of them too—but the reason why some particular BUDGET value is unknown is because the corresponding department is unknown, a state of affairs that (again) might suggest the need for some different kind of null.

- *Full outer natural join of EMP and DEPT and PGMR:* Rows in the result will, in general, "contain nulls" in any or all of several different columns, meaning ... Well, meaning what, exactly? It looks as if what's needed is a mechanism that will allow us to specify, for any particular outer join invocation, which kinds of nulls are to be generated in which columns of the result. In fact, we might even need to be able to specify different kinds of nulls for the *same* column (in different rows, of course). For example, suppose some of the nulls in column DNO of table EMP mean "department unknown," others mean "department not listed in table DEPT," and others mean "department doesn't exist." What kind of nulls should be generated in the BUDGET column?

## RELATION VALUED ATTRIBUTES

Actually, as you might know, there's an alternative approach to the problem that outer join is supposed to address, an approach that

a. Doesn't involve nulls at all;

b. Doesn't involve outer join either;

c. Doesn't do violence to the relational model (in fact, we're talking about a truly relational approach to the problem); and

d. Is, to my mind, an altogether more elegant solution.

The approach in question makes use of *relation valued attributes* (RVAs). An RVA is simply an attribute—a column, if you prefer—whose type is some relation type. Here's an example. Consider once again tables S and SP as shown a few pages back:

S

| SNO | SNAME | STATUS | CITY |
|---|---|---|---|
| S2 | Jones | 10 | Paris |
| S5 | Adams | 30 | Athens |

SP

| SNO | PNO | QTY |
|---|---|---|
| S2 | P1 | 300 |
| S2 | P2 | 400 |

Given these sample values, the relational expression

```
EXTEND S : { PQ_REL := ( SP MATCHING S ) { PNO , QTY } }
```

produces the following result:

<table>
<tr><th>SNO</th><th>SNAME</th><th>STATUS</th><th>CITY</th><th>PQ_REL</th></tr>
<tr><td>S2</td><td>Jones</td><td>10</td><td>Paris</td><td><table><tr><th>PNO</th><th>QTY</th></tr><tr><td>P1</td><td>300</td></tr><tr><td>P2</td><td>400</td></tr></table></td></tr>
<tr><td>S5</td><td>Adams</td><td>30</td><td>Athens</td><td><table><tr><th>PNO</th><th>QTY</th></tr><tr><td></td><td></td></tr></table></td></tr>
</table>

And column PQ_REL in this result is, precisely, an RVA.

Let me immediately address one obvious objection to this example, and others like it. To be specific, you might be thinking that RVAs violate the prescriptions of the relational model; in particular, you might be thinking the result just shown violates first normal form, 1NF. Well, they don't, and it doesn't. The truth is, many people—beginning, I'm sorry to say, with Codd himself—were confused over these issues for many years, and in some cases probably still are. (Indeed, I was confused myself for a long time, as can be seen from some of my own earlier writings on such matters.) For a detailed account of the true state of affairs, I refer you to Chapter 8 ("What First Normal Form Really Means") of my book *Date on Database: Writings 2000-2006* (Apress, 2006).

Back to the example. Of course, the important point about that example is that, in that EXTEND result, *the empty set of parts supplied by supplier S5 is represented by an empty set*, and not by some mysterious "null." What a good idea—to represent an empty set by an empty set! In fact, let me elaborate on this point:

- Let tables $T_1$ and $T_2$ both have a column *C*, but let there be a value *c* of column *C* in table $T_1$ that doesn't appear in $T_2$. Then, logically speaking, the *only* legitimate interpretation we can put on that state of affairs is that *the set of rows in* $T_2$ *matching that value c in* $T_1$ *is empty*. And that's *all* we can say!—again, logically speaking. Whether that empty set denotes unknown, or not applicable, or not supplied, or undefined, or any of the myriad other meanings that can be or have been attached to nulls at one time or another, is something that in my opinion is not only beyond the purview of the model, but must forever remain so.

- It follows that there'd be no need for outer join at all, as that operator is usually understood, if only RVAs were supported.

## OTHER OUTER OPERATORS

For completeness, let me just say a quick word about the other so called "outer" operators, viz., outer union, outer intersection, and outer difference. In fact, let me focus on outer union in particular.

Let $T_1$ and $T_2$ be tables. If we're to be able to form the regular (i.e., inner) union of these two tables, they must be of the same type; equivalently, their headings must be the same. For outer union, by contrast, columns with the same name must still be of the same type, but $T_1$ might have columns that $T_2$ doesn't, or vice versa, or both. For example, let $T_1$ and $T_2$ be the projections of the suppliers table on columns {SNO,STATUS} and {SNO,CITY}, respectively. Here are some sample values:

$T_1$

| SNO | STATUS |
|---|---|
| S1 | 20 |
| S5 | 30 |

$T_2$

| SNO | CITY |
|---|---|
| S1 | London |
| S3 | Paris |

These tables clearly have different headings and are thus of different types,[15] and so we can't form their regular relational union. However, we *can* form their outer union. If we do, the result will look like this (and I'm very tempted to add "believe it or not," but that would be inappropriate in a book of this kind, so I won't):

| SNO | STATUS | CITY |
|---|---|---|
| S1 | 20 | London |
| S5 | 30 | *null* |
| S3 | *null* | Paris |

As an exercise, you might like to try writing out a formal definition of this operator (a definition of outer union in general, I mean, not just one tailored to this specific example).

Well, perhaps it's not very fair of me to ask such a thing. Let me elaborate briefly. Consider the operators of the relational algebra we're already familiar with. Each such operator is carefully defined in such a way that if (a) we know the table predicate(s) for the input table(s), then (b) we know the table predicate for the output table too. For example, consider the suppliers and parts database and the join of suppliers and shipments, S JOIN SP:

- The predicate for the suppliers table S is:

[15] Codd would say they're not "union compatible." See Chapter 2, footnote 14.

*Supplier SNO is under contract, is named SNAME, has status STATUS, and is located in city CITY.*

- The predicate for the shipments table SP is:

  *Supplier SNO supplies part PNO in quantity QTY.*

And it follows immediately that the predicate for the result of the expression S JOIN SP is:

*Supplier SNO is under contract, is named SNAME, has status STATUS, is located in city CITY,* **and** *supplies part PNO in quantity QTY.*

(I.e., it's just the logical AND of the predicates for the input tables.)

Returning to tables $T_1$ and $T_2$ as defined above, then (i.e., as the projections of table S on columns {SNO,STATUS} and {SNO,CITY}, respectively), here are two questions:

1. (*Easy*) What are the predicates for $T_1$ and $T_2$?

2. (*Hard*) What's the predicate for the outer union of $T_1$ and $T_2$?

Here for the record is the answer to the first question:

- $T_1$: *There exists some name SNAME and there exists some city CITY such that supplier SNO is under contract, is named SNAME, has status STATUS, and is located in city CITY.* Or, less precisely and formally, just: *Supplier SNO has status STATUS.*

- $T_2$: *There exists some name SNAME and there exists some status STATUS such that supplier SNO is under contract, is named SNAME, has status STATUS, and is located in city CITY.* Or, less precisely and less formally, just: *Supplier SNO has status STATUS.*

I'll leave the second question to you!—except to note that, as I'm sure you've realized, it's effectively just different wording for the exercise I suggested earlier—viz., write out the formal definition of the outer union operator—but now tailored to this specific example.

And I think I'll leave it at that. If you want to know more about the outer versions of union, intersection, and difference, then I'll have to refer you to (a) Codd's RM/V2 book, and/or (b) my own review of that book, viz., *The Relational Model for Database Management Version 2 – A Critical Analysis* (Technics, 2024).

## FOUR-VALUED LOGIC

As its title suggests, the overall premise, or rather question, for this chapter is this: Once the decision has been made to go beyond conventional two-valued logic, why stop at three? After all, as you certainly know by now even if you didn't before, there are many reasons for information to be missing. So if we accept the premise that our approach to the missing information problem is to be based on nulls and many-valued logic, it follows that we do have to go beyond 3VL, possibly a long way beyond. And in fact that was exactly what Codd did: He did go one step beyond (though only one step). To be specific, he proposed that database systems should support two kinds of nulls, and therefore be based on four-valued logic, 4VL, instead of just 3VL.

Well, I have no intention of going into great detail on 4VL; I believe I've already shown, more than sufficiently, that 3VL suffers from very serious problems, and 4VL is much worse. So I'll limit myself in the present section to just a few pertinent observations.

First of all, we need a name for the new (fourth) true value. Following Codd, let's call it INAPPLICABLE (*i* for short). Now, recall that (a) 2VL has a total of 20 connectives, four monadics and 16 dyadics, and (b) 3VL has a total of 19,710 connectives, 27 monadics and 19,683 dyadics. So what about 4VL?

Well, a monadic truth table in 4VL has to take the following general form:[16]

| *Op* | |
|---|---|
| *t* | *a* |
| *u* | *b* |
| *i* | *c* |
| *f* | *d* |

[16] I'll retain the 3VL *u* for unknown. Be aware, however, that Codd—in my opinion, confusingly, and unnecessarily so—uses *a* ("applicable but unknown"), not *u*, with the immediate consequence that it looks as if his 4VL is incompatible with his 3VL. Which as a matter of fact it is (though not for that reason), as I'll show.

Since each of *a*, *b*, *c*, and *d* can be any one of the four truth values *t*, *u*, *i*, and *f*, it follows that there are $4^4 = 4 \times 4 \times 4 \times 4 = 256$ monadic truth tables, and hence 256 monadic 4VL connectives.

As for the dyadics, the truth table takes the general form

| *Op* | *t* | *u* | *i* | *f* |
|---|---|---|---|---|
| *t* | $a_1$ | $a_2$ | $a_3$ | $a_4$ |
| *u* | $b_1$ | $b_2$ | $b_3$ | $b_4$ |
| *i* | $c_1$ | $c_2$ | $c_3$ | $c_4$ |
| *f* | $d_1$ | $d_2$ | $d_3$ | $d_4$ |

Each of $a_1$, $a_2$, ..., $d_4$ can be any one of *t*, *u*, *i*, and *f*, and so there are $4^{16}$ = 4,294,967,296 (!) dyadic truth tables, and hence 4,294,967,296 dyadic 4VL connectives.

Now, every 4VL supports all of these connectives—both the monadics and the dyadics, all 4,294,967,552 (which is to say, over *four billion*) of them in total—because if it doesn't, it isn't a 4VL. But which connective corresponds to which truth table? Or to put it another way, which of those four billion plus operators do we choose to call NOT, and which OR, and which AND, and which IF (and so on)? Different choices lead to different 4VLs.

Just for the record, I summarize below the situation in general with respect to the number of connectives in different logics (the symbol "^" means "raised to the power of"):

| | *monadics* | *dyadics* |
|---|---|---|
| 2VL | 2 | 16 |
| 3VL | 27 | 19,683 |
| 4VL | 256 | 4,294,967,296 |
| ... | | |
| *n*VL | *n*^*n* | *n*^(n²) |

To repeat, different operator choices lead to different logics—and in the case of 4VL in particular, Codd actually changed his choices, not once but twice (changing first his definition of OR, and subsequently his definition of NOT).[17] So which particular 4VL was he talking about? Note that different 4VLs differ

[17] See Chapter 18 ("Why Three- and Four-Valued Logic Don't Work")) of my book *Date on Database: Writings 2000-2006* (Apress, 2006) for more specifics regarding those changes.

in particular with respect to which statements are tautologies in that logic. For example:

- In Codd's first 4VL, none of the following is a tautology (though they *are* all tautologies in 2VL):

```
IF P THEN P

P IFF P

IF P THEN Q ≡ ( NOT P ) OR Q

P IFF Q ≡ ( ( NOT P ) OR Q ) AND ( ( NOT Q ) OR P )

NOT ( P AND Q ) ≡ ( NOT P ) OR ( NOT Q )

NOT ( P OR Q ) ≡ ( NOT P ) AND ( NOT Q )

FORALL X ( P ) ≡ NOT EXISTS X ( NOT P )
```

  Observe that the foregoing list includes De Morgan's Laws in particular (Refer to Chapter 1 if you need to refresh your memory regarding De Morgan's Laws.)

- In Codd's second 4VL, the same is true.

- In Codd's third 4VL, De Morgan's Laws do now work—but De Morgan's Laws aren't everything, of course. And in any case there's another, more serious criticism that applies to Codd's third 4VL. Returning for a moment to three-valued logic, it's easy to see that Codd's 3VL truth tables for NOT, OR, and AND reduce to those for 2VL if we simply delete the rows and columns corresponding to "the third truth value" *u*. But no analogous property holds for Codd's third 4VL! That is, if we delete the rows and columns for "the fourth truth value" *i* from the 4VL truth tables for NOT, OR, and AND, we do *not* obtain the corresponding 3VL truth tables; to be more specific still, we're left with the fact that NOT *u* is defined to return *i*, a truth value that doesn't exist at all in Codd's 3VL.

The title of this chapter asks, rhetorically, "Why Stop at 3VL?" Personally, of course, I think we should stop at *2VL*—but at least I hope I've shown by now that, bad though 3VL certainly is, 4VL is much worse.

## A DEEPER QUESTION

*Note: I'm afraid this section is little more than a placeholder. The issue is important, in fact very important, and I'll be relying on it heavily in later chapters (in Chapter 7 in particular). However, to give it the full background explanation here that it requires, and indeed deserves, would take up more space than would be appropriate, given the general objectives for this book as a whole. But more details can be found in several other writings of mine; see, for example, Chapter 3, "TABLE_DUM and TABLE_DEE," of my book Database Dreaming Volume II (Technics, 2022).*

I'll begin by reciting a few simple and well known facts:

- Relations have headings.

- Headings are sets (sets of attributes, or columns).

- Sets can contain any number of elements, including zero.

- Let *R* be a relation with heading *H*; then the number of attributes, or columns, in *H* is the degree of both *H* and *R*.

From the foregoing facts taken together, it follows in particular that *a relation can have an empty heading*—i.e., a heading consisting of zero attributes—and thus be of degree zero.

Next question: Can a relation of degree zero contain any tuples, or rows? *Answer:* Perhaps a little surprisingly, yes, it can—it can contain a tuple, or row, with zero components. (After all, recall from the preface that a tuple too is a set, and so a tuple too can be empty.) I'll refer to such a tuple for brevity as a 0-tuple.

So a relation of degree zero can contain a 0-tuple. But it can't contain two!—because, by definition, all 0-tuples are duplicates of one another (in fact, there's only one 0-tuple in the universe, as it were). Hence, there are precisely two relations of degree zero; one has just one tuple (the 0-tuple), and the other has no tuples at all. And—again, perhaps a little surprisingly—these two special relations are extremely important: so important, in fact, that we have special pet names for them: We call them TABLE_DEE and TABLE_DUM, or DEE and DUM for short.[18] To spell out the details:

- TABLE_DEE is the unique relation with no attributes but one tuple (or no columns but one row, if you prefer).

- TABLE_DUM is the unique relation with no attributes and no tuples either (or no columns and no rows, if you prefer).

It's rather hard to draw pictures of these relations!—in fact, this is the place where thinking of relations as tables breaks down somewhat (which makes those pet names a little unfortunate, perhaps). But you should pay careful attention to these two relations nevertheless, because as I've said they're really important.

So why are they so important? Actually there are several answers to this question, but the most fundamental one has to do with their *meanings*, which are true and false (or yes and no, if you prefer), respectively: TABLE_DEE means true, or yes, and TABLE_DUM means false, or no.[19] They have the most fundamental meanings of all.

Let me illustrate this point before going any further. Consider the query "Is any supplier in Athens?"—a true/false or yes/no query, you'll observe. In a proper relational language, then, we could formulate this query as follows:

```
( S WHERE CITY = 'Athens' ) { }
```

In other words, restrict suppliers to just the ones in Athens, and project the result over no columns. If the result of the restriction contains at least one row, that projection will produce TABLE_DEE (true, or yes); otherwise it'll produce TABLE_DUM (false, or no).[20]

So what about SQL? Well, SQL does at least support the idea that the result of any query in a relational system should be a relation (or a table at any rate; I choose to overlook, for the moment, the fact that SQL tables are at best

---

[18] For the benefit of readers who might not be native English speakers, I should explain that these names are basically just wordplay—due to Hugh Darwen, I should add—on Tweedledee and Tweedledum, who were originally characters in a children's nursery rhyme and were subsequently incorporated into Lewis Carroll's *Through the Looking-Glass and What Alice Found There* (1871).

[19] Here's a mnemonic device for remembering which is which: DEE and "yes" both contain an *e*.

[20] In case the point isn't obvious, let me elaborate briefly. Let *R* be a relation (or table), Then—fully in accordance with the definition of projection in general, of course—the projection *R*{ } of *R* on no columns returns TABLE_DUM if *R* is empty, TABLE_DEE otherwise.

only approximations to relations as such). So we ought to be able to formulate the foregoing query in SQL like this:

```
SELECT /* no columns at all */
FROM   S
WHERE  CITY = 'Athens'
```

Unfortunately, however, SQL doesn't support the special tables that represent true and false, and so it can't actually do true/false queries in the manner suggested. (In particular, it doesn't allow the SELECT clause to specify an empty list of operands.) Instead, therefore, we have to do something like this:

```
SELECT *
FROM   S
WHERE  CITY = 'Athens'

IF result is empty
THEN return 'no'
ELSE return 'yes'
```

To repeat, therefore, TABLE_DEE can be interpreted as yes, or true, and TABLE_DUM can be interpreted as no, or false. So now we come to the real point of this section:

- There are exactly two relations of degree zero, DEE and DUM. Moreover, in 2VL, there are exactly two truth values as well, TRUE and FALSE; and DEE and DUM correspond directly and respectively to those two truth values.

- In 3VL, by contrast, there are three truth values, TRUE, UNKNOWN, and FALSE—*but there are still only two degree zero relations*, DEE and DUM, and they still correspond directly and respectively to the truth values TRUE and FALSE.

- So what corresponds to UNKNOWN?

Or more colloquially: Who is DEE and DUM's other brother?

I've posed this question to numerous people (professional logicans included), and I've been seriously impressed—not positively, let me add—by the total inability of anyone I've ever asked to come up with a sensible answer.[21]

### *An Old Riddle*

That question—"Who's DEE and DUM's other brother?"—reminds me irresistibly of the following, which I believe is a very old riddle indeed:

> *How many legs does a dog have, if we call a tail a leg?*

I'd like you to take a few moments to think about how you'd answer this question before reading any further.

The answer, of course, is four. Calling a tail a leg doesn't *make* it a leg! And, coming back to the matter at hand, calling UNKNOWN a truth value doesn't make it a truth value. After all, I could say that &%$*@#!? is another integer!—but that wouldn't make it another integer. No: The set of integers is what it is; it's fixed; and there's no way we can add another one to the set (or take one away, for that matter). And the same goes for truth values as well; that is, the set of truth values is fixed (at least, it is in classical logic), and there's no way we can add another one to the set, or take one away. Or to put the matter another way, let me come back to, and paraphrase, that argument from the beginning of the chapter:

- Let *P* be the proposition "Barack Obama was born in the year 1963."

- *P* is certainly either true or false.

- Of course, I might not know which it is, but my not knowing is a very different matter from it actually being one or the other. That is, the truth value of *P* might be unknown as far as I'm concerned—but "unknown as far as I'm concerned" isn't a truth value! It's just a statement about my own knowledge (or lack of same, rather). As I put it earlier, to say *P* is

---

[21] With one possible exception, my friend David McGoveran, who came up with: "Well. surely it's obvious—the answer's TABLE_*DUH*."

"unknown as far as I'm concerned" is to say, more precisely, that the proposition "I don't know the truth value of *P*" is true. No third truth value is involved, or indeed needed, and no 3VL is involved or needed either.

- Thus, pretending that

  a. My not knowing whether *P* is true or false

  should be treated on an equal footing with

  b. The fact that *P* certainly is one or the other

  is to mix and muddle some very different things, and it's bound to lead to problems. Which, as I said before, it very demonstrably does.

## CLOSING REMARKS

Nulls and 3VL are supposed to be a solution to the "missing information" problem—but I believe I've shown by now that, to the extent they can be considered a "solution" at all, they're a disastrously bad one. But there are still a few more points I'd like to make, points that I think can be taken as further evidence (at least anecdotal evidence) in support of my position with respect to these matters.

- *System R:* Relational ideas first began to take off, in the research world at any rate (universities and the like), soon after the publication of Codd's original papers in the early 1970s. At the same time, however, there was a lot of skepticism too, at least in the commercial arena. To be specific, many people felt that, no matter what other advantages they might enjoy, relational systems would and could never achieve the kind of performance needed for database systems in "the real world." Well, System R proved them wrong. System R was a research prototype, built in the mid 1970s in the IBM Research Lab in San Jose, California, whose main goal was to demonstrate that a relational system could be built that displayed at least acceptable performance—and in that goal it succeeded admirably. Indeed, there can be little doubt that the subsequent almost universal acceptance of relational technology owes a great deal to the fact that System R was so successful. And one consequence of that success was that IBM began to build, and of course later to market, what became the DB2 product range; and I think it's fair to say that having the weight of IBM behind it was a huge factor in "making relational respectable," as it were. In particular, of course, those IBM products used SQL as their access language; other vendors thus soon began to do the same, and SQL quickly became the de facto standard. Subsequently, of course, it became a formal standard as well—not just in the U.S., but worldwide.

So the reason why SQL occupies the dominant position it does today, and the reason why nulls in particular are supported now in so many products, can be traced all the way back to System R. And yet ... Soon after the System R project was completed, back in the 1970s, one of the original project leaders—I'll call him George—told me that if they could do it all again, they wouldn't do nulls. In his opinion nulls were nothing but a horrible mistake: not least in the way they had "repercussions *everywhere*," as he put it. I find these admissions interesting! After all, today's products support nulls precisely because they support SQL. So the entire "nulls industry," if I might call it that, is founded on what George, who was in the best of all positions to know, thought was a mistake.

- *DB2:* Talking of DB2, there's another point I'd like to make. Like all SQL DBMSs, DB2 supports a system catalog. Of course, that catalog is effectively a small SQL database in its own right—and like other databases, it's subject to the missing information problem (for example, some SQL tables, I'm sorry to say, have no key). So does DB2 use nulls to represent that missing information? No.[22] In other words, DB2 doesn't use its own "missing information" mechanism to deal with missing information! I think that should tell you something.

- *X3H2:* X3H2 is the American National Standards Institute (ANSI) committee responsible (in the U.S.) for the SQL standard. I was on the X3H2 mailing list for a while—this was several years ago—and received occasional communications from them accordingly. Those communications were always headed with a list of addressees, giving, for each addressee, his or her name and affiliation (e.g., IBM, Oracle,

---

[22] Well, the answer was certainly *no* back in the days when I was forced to pay attention to DB2 specifics—but that was a long time ago, and I frankly don't know whether the answers is still *no* today. But even if it isn't, my point, I think, is valid nonetheless.

Department of Defense, etc.). But I was working for myself and thus didn't have an affiliation. So was my affiliation given as null? Of course not!—it was simply left blank.

- *Einstein:* One of the many wonderful things Albert Einstein said was the following:

  > Everything should be made as simple as possible—*but no simpler*.

  And that, in a nutshell, is what I think is wrong with nulls: They represent an oversimplified solution to a very complicated problem (viz., the problem of missing information). Oversimplifying can be harmful to your health.

Finally, I'd like to describe, and respond to, an argument that I've often heard in connection with my position on these matters. That argument goes something like this:

> All those examples you give of where nulls lead to wrong answers [*in this connection, see Chapter 3 in particular*] are very artificial. Real world queries aren't like that! More generally, most of your criticisms seem very academic and theoretical—I bet you can't show any real practical situations where nulls have given rise to the kinds of problems you worry about, and I bet you can't prove such practical situations do occur.

Needless to say, I have several responses to these criticisms. The first is: How do we know that nulls haven't caused real practical problems, anyway? It seems to me that if some serious real world situation—an oil spill, a collapsed bridge, a wrong medical diagnosis—were found to be due to nulls, there might be valid reasons (nontechnical ones, I mean) why the information would never get out. We've all heard stories of embarrassing failures caused by software glitches of other kinds, even in the absence of nulls; in my opinion, nulls can only serve to make such failures more likely.

Second, suppose someone—me, for example—were to go around claiming that some particular software product or application contained a serious logical error due to nulls. Can you imagine the lawsuits?

Third and most important, I think those of us who criticize nulls don't need to be defensive, anyway; I think we should stand those counterarguments on their head, as it were. After all, it's undeniable that nulls can lead to errors in certain cases. So it's not up to us to prove that those "certain cases" might include practical, real world situations; rather, it's up to those who want to defend nulls to prove that they don't. And I venture to suggest that, in practice, it would be quite difficult, and very likely impossible, to prove any such thing.

Of course, if nulls are prohibited, then missing information will have to be handled by some other means. But of course those other means are a big topic in their own right, and they deserve chapters of their own (see Chapters 7 and 8). Here I'll just note that the SQL mechanism of (nonnull) default values can be used in simple cases, and I'll have more to say regarding that possibility in Appendix A; but for a more comprehensive approach to the problem—including in particular an explanation of how you can still get "don't know" answers when you want them, even from a database without nulls—I refer you again to Chapters 7 and 8.

# Chapter 6

# Three-Valued Logic: Some SQL Flaws

As everyone knows, relational DBMSs in the commercial world—or would-be relational DBMSs, at any rate—all support the language SQL. The name "SQL" was originally an abbreviation for "Structured Query Language," and it was usually pronounced *sequel*; now that the language is an official international standard, however, the name isn't officially an abbreviation for anything at all, and it's officially pronounced just *ess cue ell*. Nevertheless, many people still pronounce it *sequel* anyway, and that's the pronunciation I've been assuming, and will continue to assume, throughout the present book.

Of course, I've mentioned SQL in this book quite a few times already, at least in passing. But now it's time to get a little more specific and say more about SQL as such. That's the purpose of the present chapter.

As I really hope you appreciate by now, it's my position that three-valued logic, 3VL, is a disastrously bad "solution" to the missing information problem. It's so bad, in fact, that personally I don't regard it as a solution at all. But of course SQL supports it, and so we're more or less stuck with it. Well ... perhaps I should say rather that SQL *tries* to support it; because the truth is, SQL's "support" for 3VL is deeply flawed and, I would argue, not really a proper implementation of 3VL at all. To elaborate briefly:

a. First of all, as previous chapters have shown in detail, 3VL as such suffers from all kinds of problems—problems that are so serious in themselves that, to repeat, I don't believe 3VL is a solution at all.

b. Second, SQL tries to implement 3VL *but gets it wrong*. I mean, not only does SQL suffer from all of the intrinsic problems of 3VL as described in previous chapters, but it manages to introduce additional problems of its own—problems over and above those intrinsic ones.

Personally, I believe the intrinsic problems mentioned under point a. are bad enough to serve as complete showstoppers. But even if they weren't, I would argue that the additional problems mentioned under point b. are bad enough to serve as showstoppers too! In other words, even if I were a fan of 3VL as such (which I'm obviously not), I'd still do everything in my power to avoid using SQL's version of it, in any shape or form.

The rest of this chapter goes into more detail on such matters.

## NULL vs. UNKNOWN

My first point is just a reminder. Recall from Chapter 4 that SQL (following Codd, I'm sorry to have to say) makes the mistake of using null to represent the UNKNOWN truth value. As noted in that chapter, this mistake is just as bad as it would be to use null to represent, say, the numeric value zero. (After all, UNKNOWN is certainly a *value*—it's "the third truth value"—and a value is the one thing that a null, whatever it else it might be, is most definitely not.) So right away we see that SQL's 3VL support is based on some pretty shaky foundations.

Let me remind you also that, although SQL is always described as "being based on 3VL" or "supporting 3VL," no one has ever defined exactly which 3VL that might be. See Chapter 4 for further elaboration of this point.

## IS NOT NULL vs. NOT IS NULL

I described SQL's IS NULL and IS NOT NULL operators in Chapter 2. Here once again are the definitions (*V* here denotes an arbitrary scalar value, nonnull by definition):

| | IS NULL | IS NOT NULL |
|---|---|---|
| NULL | *t* | *f* |
| *V* | *f* | *t* |

But now let me stress the point that *V* here is, specifically, a *scalar* value. As noted in passing in Chapter 2, SQL does pay at least some kind of lip service to the idea that values might be not scalars but rows (or possibly even tables, but I don't want to discuss this latter possibility any further). Here's an example of a row value in SQL:

```
ROW ( 'S1' , 'Smith' , 20 , 'London' )
```

Now, SQL does explicitly allow the IS NULL and IS NOT NULL operators to be applied to rows as well as scalars—implying, therefore, that (as far as SQL is concerned, at any rate) *rows as such* can be either null or nonnull. By way of illustration, let $X_1$ and $X_2$ each be what SQL calls a "value expression" (which is to say, either a scalar expression or a row expression,[1] though definitely not a table expression), and let *V* be the following row:

```
ROW ( X1 , X2 )
```

Then the expression

```
V IS NULL
```

is defined to be shorthand for the following:

```
X1 IS NULL AND X2 IS NULL
```

As an aside, therefore, let me now point out that (a) if *V* is indeed a row, and (b) if *V* IS NULL is true, then (a) and (b) together don't actually mean that (c) *V* is null![2]—rather, it means that every component of *V* is null, which is a logically different state of affairs. But that's not the main point I want make here. Let me continue with that main point. Next, then, the expression

```
V IS NOT NULL
```

is defined to be shorthand for the following:

```
X1 IS NOT NULL AND X2 IS NOT NULL
```

So suppose *V* is, say,

```
ROW ( NULL , 42 )
```

---

[1] Note, therefore, that rows can contain rows as components, with all that that fact implies.

[2] Understand, then, that "*V* IS NULL" and "*V* is NULL" (or "*V* is null") mean different things.

(so $X_1$ is null and $X_2$ is 42). Then *V* IS NULL and *V* IS NOT NULL both return FALSE! In other words, SQL regards *V* as being neither null nor nonnull, and thus apparently doesn't believe in *The Law of the Excluded Middle*.[3] I'll pause here to let you think about that one for a moment or two.

There's more. As I've said,

```
V IS NULL
```

is shorthand for:

```
X1 IS NULL AND X2 IS NULL
```

It follows that

```
NOT V IS NULL
```

is shorthand for:

```
NOT ( X1 IS NULL AND X2 IS NULL )
```

or in other words

```
X1 IS NOT NULL OR X2 IS NOT NULL
```

—which isn't the same as the expansion given above for *V* IS NOT NULL! As you'll recall, this latter was as follows:

```
X1 IS NOT NULL AND X2 IS NOT NULL
```

In SQL, therefore, we have that:

```
V IS NOT NULL ≢ NOT V IS NULL
```

Who designed this language?

Let me add a brief postscript to the foregoing. It's based on text from Chapter 1, "Equality," of my book *Stating the Obvious, and Other Database Writings* (Technics, 2020). The SQL standard in its discussion of what it calls "null predicates"—a terrible name if there ever was one, incidentally, for more

---

[3] Let *P* be a proposition, Then *The Law of the Excluded Middle* states that exactly one of *P* and its negation NOT *P* must be true and the other one must be false.

reasons than I care to count—says the following (I'm paraphrasing fairly liberally here, but only for clarity, not in such a way as to misrepresent the intended sense):

> Let *X* be the expression *r* IS NULL, where *r* is a row value. If *r* is the null value, then *X* evaluates to TRUE; otherwise, if the value of every field in *r* is the null value, then *X* evaluates to TRUE; otherwise *X* evaluates to FALSE.

This text indicates rather clearly that SQL considers a null row and a row containing nothing but nulls as two different things—despite the fact that they both give TRUE if they're compared with NULL.[4] It also indicates very clearly that as I've "explained" above, a row such as ROW (NULL,42) is definitely *not* considered to be null.[5] (Of course, to repeat, it's definitely not considered to be not null, either.)

## IN vs. EXISTS

Recall now from Chapter 4 that, at least in 2VL, each of IN and EXISTS can be defined in terms of the other. To be specific, if *V* is a value, *X* is a set, and *Y* is a range variable that ranges over *X*, then the expressions

```
V IN X
```

and

```
EXISTS Y ( Y = V )
```

are equivalent. Thus, the following SQL expressions ought logically to be equivalent too:

```
V IN ( SELECT Y                EXISTS ( SELECT Y
       FROM   X                         FROM   X
       WHERE  bx )                      WHERE  bx
                                        AND    V = Y )
```

---

[4] Provided the comparison takes the form *r* IS NULL, that is. If by contrast it takes the form *r* = *r*′, where *r*′ IS NULL gives TRUE, it gives UNKNOWN. I hope that's clear.

[5] At the same time, however, ROW (NULL,42) doesn't "compare equal" to itself. Since we've just learned that the row ROW (NULL,42) isn't considered to be null, we see now that null isn't the only thing in SQL that's considered not to be equal to itself. Where does this madness end?

(I show the expressions side by side for ease of comparison, and I deliberately omit a few syntactic niceties, such as parentheses, that might be needed in practice.)

Well, I say these expressions "ought to be" equivalent, and indeed they are equivalent in 2VL. But what about 3VL? Well, here's a concrete example. Consider the query "Get parts whose weight is different from that of every Paris part." Here's a would-be formulation using IN:

```
SELECT P.*
FROM   P
WHERE  NOT P.WEIGHT IN
     ( SELECT Q.WEIGHT
       FROM   P AS Q
       WHERE  Q.CITY = 'Paris' )
```

And here's another, using EXISTS:

```
SELECT P.*
FROM   P
WHERE  NOT EXISTS
     ( SELECT Q.WEIGHT
       FROM   P AS Q
       WHERE  Q.CITY = 'Paris'
       AND    Q.WEIGHT = P.WEIGHT )
```

Now suppose there's just one part in Paris, and—with apologies for the sloppy phrasing, both here and in the explanation to follow—the weight of that part is null. Then:

- In the first formulation (the one using IN), the parenthesized subexpression evaluates to a set containing nothing but a null, and the Boolean expression in the WHERE clause thus becomes

  ```
  NOT P.WEIGHT IN ( NULL )
  ```

  The IN returns UNKNOWN; NOT UNKNOWN also returns UNKNOWN; that UNKNOWN then gets coerced to FALSE; and the net result is that no parts are retrieved at all.

- In the second formulation (the one using EXISTS), the parenthesized subexpression evaluates to an empty set (why, exactly?), and the Boolean expression in the WHERE clause thus becomes

  ```
  NOT EXISTS ( empty )
  ```

  The EXISTS returns FALSE; NOT FALSE returns TRUE; and the net result is that every part is retrieved.

So, first of all, the two formulations are certainly not equivalent, and neither should be transformed into the other. But in a sense, of course, *both* of the answers are wrong!—the only logically correct answer is something like "*The system doesn't know* which parts, if any, have a weight that's different from that of every Paris part." Here, therefore, I think a case might be made that the system really is lying to us. But that's not the point I want to make (serious though I think it is); rather, the point is that the answers are different, and hence that a certain expression transformation (or "query rewrite") that looks as if it should be valid, and indeed is valid in 2VL, *isn't* valid in 3VL. I think we should all take this point to heart as a warning of some kind.

I want to say a little more about EXISTS, though. Consider the following quantified expression (but please note carefully that it's a *logical* expression, not a SQL expression—I'm not using SQL syntax here):

```
EXISTS X ( P ( X ) )
```

Suppose now that (a) at least one possible value for *X* does exist—i.e., *X* ranges over a nonempty set—but that (b) *P*(*X*) evaluates to UNKNOWN for all such values. In 3VL, then, the foregoing quantified expression should evaluate to UNKNOWN also. But the analogous expression in SQL never will! Here's a simple illustration of the point. Let table *T* have just one column, *C*, and just one row, and let the sole row and column intersection within *T* contain a null.[6] Then the SQL expression

```
EXISTS ( SELECT C FROM T )
```

---

[6] By the way, here's a question for you to ponder: Are the SQL expressions SELECT *C* FROM *T* and SELECT *C* FROM *T* WHERE TRUE—both of which are syntactically legitimate, let me note—logically equivalent?

should return UNKNOWN but will in fact return TRUE (because the EXISTS argument is considered to be nonempty). In other words, EXISTS in SQL isn't a faithful implementation of the existential quantifier of 3VL.[7] Now, we've seen in previous chapters that, in both 3VL and SQL,

*NOT is not "not"*

and

*UNKNOWN is not "unknown"*

And in SQL specifically:

*NOT is not "NOT"*

Well, now we can add

*EXISTS is not "exists"*

to the SQL list.

## AGGREGATE OPERATORS

As noted in Chapter 5, SQL's aggregate operators SUM, AVG, MAX, and MIN all return null if their argument is empty. One consequence of this state of affairs is that, once again, certain expression transformations that ought to be valid in fact aren't so, in SQL. The following example illustrates this point. The query is "Get parts whose weight is greater than that of every Paris part." The first attempt at a formulation uses ">ALL" (which is an example of what SQL calls a *quantified comparison*):

```
SELECT P.*
FROM   P
WHERE  P.WEIGHT >ALL
     ( SELECT Q.WEIGHT
       FROM   P AS Q
       WHERE  Q.CITY = 'Paris' )
```

---

[7] A more intuitively appropriate name for it might be IS NOT EMPTY.

But if some given weight is greater than that of all Paris parts, then it must surely be greater than that of the heaviest Paris part. This consideration thus leads to a second putative formulation:

```
SELECT P.*
FROM   P
WHERE  P.WEIGHT >
     ( SELECT MAX ( Q.WEIGHT )
       FROM   P AS Q
       WHERE  Q.CITY = 'Paris' )
```

Now suppose there are no parts in Paris. Then:

- In the first formulation, the parenthesized subexpression evaluates to an empty set. The ">ALL" comparison thus returns TRUE, and the net result is that every part is retrieved.

- In the second formulation, the parenthesized subexpression requires MAX to be applied to an empty set and thus returns a null. The comparison in the outer WHERE clause thus returns UNKNOWN; that UNKNOWN then gets coerced to FALSE, and the net result is that nothing is retrieved.

Do you think either of these answers is correct? If so, which one? And what does the example tell us about expression transformations in general?

## INTEGRITY CONSTRAINTS

Let *tx* be a SQL table expression, and let *tx* involve one or more WHERE clauses; let such a WHERE clause be called "outermost" if it's not nested within some other clause; and let *bx* be the boolean expression immediately following the keyword WHERE in an outermost WHERE clause within *tx*. Then I've said several times already (though I might not have been quite so careful about pinning down the precise context on those previous occasions)[8] that if *bx* evaluates to UNKNOWN, then that UNKNOWN gets coerced to FALSE. But sometimes it gets coerced to TRUE instead! To be specific, this latter behavior

---

[8] That said, the definition of that "precise context" as I give it here still isn't fully watertight. For SQL's own definition of the true state of affairs, I refer you to Appendix B.

occurs in the context of integrity constraints. For example, suppose we want to define a constraint to the effect that the average supplier status value must be at least ten. Here's one way such a constraint can be formulated in SQL:[9]

```
CREATE ASSERTION CX37 CHECK
   ( ( SELECT AVG ( STATUS ) FROM S ) ≥ 10 ) ;
```

However, suppose table S is currently empty. Then the foregoing AVG invocation will return null; the parenthesized subexpression SELECT ... FROM S will thus return null also; and the comparison will thus become "null ≥ 10" accordingly, which will return UNKNOWN. So if that UNKNOWN were to be coerced to FALSE, the integrity check would fail! In such a context, therefore, UNKNOWN is coerced to TRUE instead.

I'll leave it to you to judge whether such behavior is reasonable, or whether it's the best solution to the problem. *Hint:* It isn't.

Here's another example involving integrity constraints in SQL that might not unreasonably strike you as a little odd. Suppose the following sequence of events occurs:

1. An integrity constraint (or "assertion") is defined to the effect that shipment quantities must be greater than zero:

   ```
   CREATE ASSERTION CX52 CHECK
        ( NOT EXISTS ( SELECT * FROM SP WHERE QTY ≤ 0 ) ) ;
   ```

2. A row is inserted into the shipments table as follows:

   ```
   INSERT INTO SP ( SNO , PNO , QTY )
               ROW ( 'S5' , 'P6' , NULL ) ;
   ```

   *Note:* You should check for yourself to see exactly how and why this INSERT satisfies (or perhaps I should rather say, fails to violate) Constraint CX52.

3. The following query, or table expression, is then evaluated:

   ```
   SELECT * FROM SP WHERE QTY > 0
   ```

---

[9] Constraints are called assertions in SQL—sometimes, but not always. It is not known why this is.

Given this sequence of events, what happens is that

a. As already noted, the INSERT in Step 2 will succeed, but

b. The inserted row won't appear in the result of the SELECT in Step 3.

And yet, knowing that shipment quantities are supposed to be greater than zero, the user would surely be within his or her rights to expect that SELECT to be logically equivalent to just SELECT * FROM SP—which will, of course, produce a different result (to be specific, it will return that inserted row). I regard this state of affairs as yet another of the vast—infinite?—number of absurdities that nulls inevitably seem to give rise to.

## THE UNIQUE OPERATOR

SQL's UNIQUE operator is used—to quote the standard—to "test for the absence of duplicate rows." (Of course, no such test would ever be needed in the relational world, but we're not in the relational world here, we're in the SQL world.) The syntax is UNIQUE (*tx*), where *tx* is a table expression. Let *T* be the table denoted by *tx*. Then as the standard puts it:

> If there are no two rows in *T* such that the value of each column in one row is nonnull and is not distinct from the value of the corresponding column in the other row, then the result [is TRUE; otherwise it's FALSE].

*Note:* The meaning of the foregoing sentence doesn't exactly leap off the page, does it. If you're having trouble construing it, therefore, here's an example that might help. Suppose table *T* looks like this:

| T | ... | C | | ... | | ... |
|---|---|---|---|---|---|---|
| | ... | 1 | | | | ... |
| | ... | 2 | | | | ... |
| | ... | 3 | | | | ... |
| | ... | *null* | | | | ... |
| | ... | *null* | | | | ... |

Then the expression UNIQUE (SELECT *C* FROM *T*) will give TRUE. Note, therefore, that UNIQUE can give TRUE when it might have been expected—since null isn't supposed to be equal to anything, not even itself—to give UNKNOWN. (Compare EXISTS in SQL, which also sometimes gives TRUE when it might have been expected to give UNKNOWN.)

However, the principal purpose of UNIQUE is, I strongly suspect, to "simplify" (?) the standard's definition of what it means for some column or column combination *C* to be a key for some table *T*, taking into account the possibility that *C* might have "nulls allowed." For example, the CREATE TABLE statement shown in the preface to this book for the suppliers table S contains this specification:

```
UNIQUE ( SNO )
```

The semantics of such a specification are explained by the standard as follows (of course, I've adapted the standard's own generic phrasing to apply to the specific case at hand, but note the reference to the UNIQUE operator in particular):[10]

> The constraint UNIQUE (SNO) is not satisfied if and only if EXISTS (SELECT * FROM S WHERE NOT (UNIQUE (SELECT SNO FROM S))) is true.

Well, I hope that's perfectly clear.

Here now are some questions for you. Let *k1* and *k2* be values (possibly "null values," if you'll allow me to use such a term), both of the same type. In SQL, then, what exactly do a., b., and c. below mean?

a. *k1* and *k2* are distinct for the purposes of a comparison (e.g., in a WHERE clause).

b. *k1* and *k2* are distinct for the purposes of key uniqueness.

c. *k1* and *k2* are distinct for the purposes of duplicate elimination.

I suggest you take a moment or two to think about these questions before continuing.

---

[10] Of course, column SNO in table S should probably have "nulls not allowed" anyway (despite the fact that it wasn't actually defined that way in the preface to this book), but this state of affairs doesn't materially affect the discussion.

——— ♦♦♦♦♦ ———

*Answer:* No two of a., b., c. are equivalent! Statement a. follows the rules of SQL's 3VL; statement b. follows the definition of SQL's UNIQUE operator; and statement c. follows SQL's definition of duplicates. In particular, if *k1* and *k2* are both null, then (believe it or not) a. gives UNKNOWN, b. gives FALSE, and c. gives TRUE. To elaborate:

a. With SQL's 3VL, the comparison *k1* = *k2* (in, e.g., a WHERE clause), gives TRUE if *k1* and *k2* are both nonnull and are equal; FALSE if *k1* and *k2* are both nonnull and are unequal; and UNKNOWN otherwise.

b. With SQL's UNIQUE operator, the comparison *k1* = *k2* gives TRUE if *k1* and *k2* are both nonnull and are equal, FALSE otherwise.

c. With SQL's definition of duplicates (e.g., as in DISTINCT), the comparison *k1* = *k2* gives TRUE if *k1* and *k2* are either both nonnull and equal or both null, FALSE otherwise.

I should mention too that throughout the foregoing, "equal" and "unequal" are to be interpreted in accordance with SQL's own somewhat idiosyncratic definition of the "=" operator. See, e.g., my book *SQL and Relational Theory*, 3rd ed. (O'Reilly, 2015) for further explanation of this point.

As an aside, I remark that SQL does get itself into extraordinary difficulties over the apparently simple concept of "distinctness." Here's another quote from the standard to illustrate the point:

> Two multisets *A* and *B* are distinct if [and only if] there exists a value *V* in the element type of *A* or *B*, including the null value, such that the number of elements in *A* that are not distinct from *V* does not equal the number of elements in *B* that are not distinct from *V*.

*Note:* A *multiset*, also known as a *bag*, is like a set except that it permits duplicates. It might help to observe that, e.g., the multisets {*x*,*y*} and {*x*,*y*,*y*} aren't considered to be equal.

## RECOMMENDATIONS

So suppose you decide you'd like to avoid nulls entirely in your use of SQL. As far as I'm concerned, that would be an eminently sensible decision; in fact, I think it's the *only* sensible decision. The first thing to do, then, is specify NOT NULL, either explicitly or implicitly, for every column of every base table; then nulls will never occur in the database as such. Unfortunately, however, certain SQL expressions can still yield results, dynamically, that contain nulls; that is, even if the database as such is 100% "null free," nulls can still be generated at run time.[11] Here in outline are a few of the situations in which this phenomenon can occur (but note that the list that follows is definitely not exhaustive):

- Aggregate operators such as SUM, MAX, and MIN return null if their argument is empty.

- If a scalar subquery evaluates to an empty table, that empty table is coerced to a null. *Note:* Loosely speaking, a scalar subquery is a SELECT – FROM – WHERE expression that's nested inside another such expression and is such that it necessarily yields a table of exactly one column and at most one row.

- If a row subquery evaluates to an empty table, that empty table is coerced to a row of all nulls. *Note:* Loosely speaking, a row subquery is a SELECT – FROM – WHERE expression that's nested inside another such expression and is such that it necessarily yields a table of exactly one row.

- Outer operations (outer joins in particular) are expressly designed to produce nulls in their result.

- If the ELSE option is omitted from a CASE expression, an ELSE option of the form ELSE NULL is assumed.

- The expression NULLIF $(X,Y)$ returns null if $X = Y$ evaluates to TRUE.

- Let table $T_2$ have a foreign key referencing table $T_1$. Then if the "referential triggered action" ON DELETE SET NULL is specified for that foreign key,

---

[11] In views in particular, of course.

deleting a row from $T_1$ can generate nulls in $T_2$ (obviously enough). A similar remark applies to ON UPDATE SET NULL, of course.

### *Dos and Don'ts*

Here then are some explicit suggestions for avoiding nulls as much as possible:[12]

- Do specify NOT NULL, at least implicitly, for every column in every base table.

- Don't use the keyword NULL in any other context whatsoever (i.e., anywhere other than a NOT NULL constraint or logical equivalent).

- Don't use the keyword UNKNOWN in any context whatsoever.

- Don't omit the ELSE option from a CASE expression, unless you're certain it would never have been reached anyway.

- Don't use NULLIF.

- Don't use outer join, and don't use the keywords OUTER, FULL, LEFT, and RIGHT (except possibly as suggested in the second COALESCE example below).

- Don't use IS TRUE, IS NOT TRUE, IS FALSE, or IS NOT FALSE. The reason is that, if *bx* is a boolean expression, then the following equivalences fail to hold only if nulls are present:

  ```
  bx IS TRUE       ≡  bx
  bx IS NOT TRUE   ≡  NOT bx
  bx IS FALSE      ≡  NOT bx
  bx IS NOT FALSE  ≡  bx
  ```

  In other words, IS TRUE and the rest are distractions at best, in the absence of nulls.

---

[12] The list is deliberately incomplete. For further details, please refer to the book from which it's taken—namely, my book *SQL and Relational Theory*, 3rd ed. (O'Reilly, 2015).

- Finally, do use COALESCE on every scalar expression that might "evaluate to null" without it.

In case you're not familiar with COALESCE, let me elaborate briefly on it here. Essentially, COALESCE is an operator that lets you replace a null by some nonnull value "as soon as it appears" (i.e., before it has a chance to do any further damage). Here's the definition:

> **Definition (COALESCE):** Let *a*, *b*, ..., *c* be scalar expressions. Then the SQL expression COALESCE (*a*,*b*,...,*c*) returns null if its arguments are all null, or the value of its first nonnull argument otherwise.

Of course, to use this operator sensibly, you do need to ensure that at least one of *a*, *b*, ..., *c* is indeed nonnull! Here's a fairly realistic example:

```
SELECT S.SNO , ( SELECT COALESCE ( SUM ( SP.QTY ) , 0 )
                 FROM   SP
                 WHERE  SP.SNO = S.SNO ) AS TOTQ
FROM   S
```

In this example, if the SUM invocation "evaluates to null"—which will happen in particular for any supplier such as supplier S5, given our usual sample data, with no matching shipments—then the COALESCE invocation will replace that null by a zero. Given that usual sample data, then, the expression overall will produce the following result:

| SNO | TOTQ |
|---|---|
| S1 | 1300 |
| S2 | 700 |
| S3 | 200 |
| S4 | 900 |
| S5 | 0 |

Here's a second example of the use of COALESCE to get rid of nulls (as you can see, it involves explicit use of SQL's outer join operator):

```
SELECT SNO , COALESCE ( PNO , 'nil' ) AS PNO
FROM   S NATURAL LEFT OUTER JOIN SP
```

Here's the result (note the row for supplier S5 in particular):

| SNO | PNO |
|---|---|
| S1 | P1 |
| S1 | P2 |
| S1 | P3 |
| S1 | P4 |
| S1 | P5 |
| S1 | P6 |
| S2 | P1 |
| S2 | P2 |
| S3 | P2 |
| S4 | P2 |
| S4 | P4 |
| S4 | P5 |
| S5 | *nil* |

Note, however, that the row for supplier S5 is still "telling a lie," in a sense. After all, is *nil* a real part number? I don't think so. So the result overall, even though it does avoid nulls, still misrepresents the semantics of the situation.[13] The truth is, padding rows in an outer join with real values instead of nulls just tends to hide the fact that outer join is simply not a respectable operation. Much better to avoid it altogether.

## CLOSING REMARKS

The overall message of this chapter, to repeat, is as follows: Even if the 3VL "solution" to the missing information problem were clean and elegant—which it isn't—SQL's implementation of that "solution" would still be deeply flawed. In fact, it manages to introduce numerous additional problems of its own, and in a nutshell makes an already bad situation much worse. I've given several examples of those additional problems in this chapter, but I don't want you to think the treatment has been in any way exhaustive, because it hasn't.

So what can be done? As I've said before (e.g., in the preface), the missing information is a real problem. How then are we supposed to handle it, if we can't use 3VL or SQL? Well, that's the topic for the next two chapters.

---

[13] Here's a question for you to ponder: What's the predicate for that result?

# Chapter 7

# Two–Valued Logic: "Don't Know" Answers

In this chapter I show how, even in a database system that's built strictly in accordance with the principles of two-valued logic—no nulls, in other words, and no 3VL—it's still possible to get "don't know" answers to queries (when "don't know" is the right answer, of course!). The key to achieving this desirable goal is something called *The Closed World Assumption.* *Note:* I did discuss the CWA briefly in Chapter 1 and again in Chapter 4, but now it's time to get a little more specific.

## *THE CLOSED WORLD ASSUMPTION*

Anyone who uses a relational database—or, more realistically, a SQL database—is crucially dependent on *The Closed World Assumption* (CWA for short). But what does this statement mean?

Well, note first that the CWA is indeed an *assumption.* As this fact might suggest, the dependence I just referred to tends to be implicit; I mean, the assumption as such is rarely spelled out in so many words. So one thing I want to do in this chapter is this: I want to make that implicit assumption explicit—I want to explain exactly what *The Closed World Assumption* is, and in particular I want to show why it's to be preferred over the alternative, *The Open World Assumption* or OWA.

I'll begin with a little background: In October 2006 I participated in a workshop in Edinburgh, Scotland, with the title "The Closed World of Databases Meets the Open World of the Semantic Web." Here's a quote from the announcement for that workshop:

> [The] database community traditionally operates under the closed world assumption ... while the semantic web community [operates under] an open world assumption ... .

I didn't believe this claim when I first read it, and I don't believe it now. To be more specific, I don't believe people in the "semantic web community" do actually operate under *The Open World Assumption*; they might think they do, but if so, then I don't think they can mean the same thing by that term as I do. By contrast, we in the database community most certainly do operate under *The Closed World Assumption*; however, I should immediately add that we're often sloppy in specifying just what the specific "world" is that's "closed." Part of my aim in this chapter is to shed some light on this latter issue also.

With regard to that workshop announcement, incidentally, I have to say too that I do detect a certain bias in the wording! As we all know, the terms *closed* and *open* carry a certain amount of semantic baggage with them, along the lines of "closed bad, open good" (think of closed vs. open minds, for example). Thus, if you want to claim that closed is better, you tend to find yourself at a bit of a disadvantage right from the outset, inasmuch as you typically have to adopt a somewhat defensive position. So another aim of this chapter is to show that, in this context at least, closed is good, not bad.

*Note:* Given the truth of the foregoing, it might be nice to come up with some better terminology—in particular, with a more positive sounding term than "closed world." But I won't attempt such a thing here.

## DEFINITIONS

The CWA has its origins in some papers by Raymond Reiter.[1] Basically what it says is this: *Everything stated or implied by the database is true, and everything else is false*. For example, consider the usual suppliers table S:

---

[1] Raymond Reiter: "On Closed World Data Bases," in Gallaire and Minker (eds.), *Logic and Data Bases* (Plenum Press, 1978), and "Towards a Logical Reconstruction of Relational Database Theory," in Brodie, Mylopoulos, and Schmidt (eds.), *On Conceptual Modelling: Perspectives from Artificial Intelligence, Databases, and Programming Languages* (Springer-Verlag, 1984). *Note:* The CWA is very closely related to the idea of *negation as failure*, which was described, albeit in a different context, in another paper in that same Plenum Press collection, viz., "Negation as Failure," by K. L. Clark.

| SNO | SNAME | STATUS | CITY |
|---|---|---|---|
| S1 | Smith | 20 | London |
| S2 | Jones | 10 | Paris |
| S3 | Blake | 30 | Paris |
| S4 | Clark | 20 | London |
| S5 | Adams | 30 | Athens |

Just to remind you, the corresponding table predicate is:

- *Supplier SNO is under contract, is named SNAME, has status STATUS, and is located in city CITY.*

So we can see that (e.g.) the following is a true proposition at this time:

- *Supplier S1 is under contract, is named Smith, has status 20, and is located in city London.*

We can also see that (e.g.) the following is a false proposition at this time:

- *Supplier S6 is under contract, is named Gomez, has status 30, and is located in city Madrid.*

By the way, note that the CWA says that everything stated *or implied* by the database is true. Thus, for example, we can see from the foregoing sample value that *Supplier S1 is under contract and has some name and some status and is located somewhere* is a true proposition, one that's implied by what the database says about supplier S1 but isn't stated, as such, explicitly. Here are some more examples of propositions that are implied (and that we can therefore assume to be true) but aren't stated explicitly by the sample value shown above for table S:

- *Supplier S1 is under contract.*

- *Supplier S1 is located somewhere.*

- *Supplier S1 has some status.*

And here are some propositions that we can assume to be false, because they're neither stated explicitly nor implied by that same sample value:

- *Supplier S6 is under contract.*
- *Supplier S6 is located somewhere.*
- *Supplier S1 is located in Paris.*

With respect to these latter examples, by the way, another way to say the same thing is that we can assume the following propositions are true, because their *negation* is neither stated explicitly nor implied:

- *Supplier S6 isn't under contract*—or (perhaps better) *It's not the case that supplier S6 is under contract.*
- *It's not the case that supplier S6 is located somewhere.*
- *It's not the case that supplier S1 is located in Paris.*

Here now is a slightly more precise definition of the CWA (more precise, that is, than the one given in Chapter 1):

> **Definition (*Closed World Assumption*):** Let table *T* have predicate *P*. Then (a) if row *R* appears in *T* at a given time, then the instantiation of *P* corresponding to *R* is assumed to be true at that time; conversely, (b) if row *R* could appear in *T* at a given time but doesn't, then the instantiation of *P* corresponding to *R* is assumed to be false at that time. Loosely speaking, in other words, row *R* appears in table *T* at a given time if and only if it satisfies the predicate for table *T* at that time. What's more, it follows that if proposition *Q* is represented by a row that appears in some table that can be derived from the tables in the database at a given time, then proposition *Q* can be (and is) assumed to be true at that time.

As an aside, I note that it follows from the foregoing definition that if tables $T_1$ and $T_2$ have predicates $P_1$ and $P_2$, respectively, and if $P_1$ and $P_2$ are both currently satisfied by the same row *R*, then *R* must currently appear in both $T_1$ and $T_2$. As a rule of thumb (but it's *only* a rule of thumb, of course), it's a good idea to design the database in such a way as to ensure that $P_1$ and $P_2$ are specific enough to preclude such a situation (so long as $T_1$ and $T_2$ are both base tables, at any rate).

Other, more formal definitions and discussions of the CWA can be found elsewhere—for example, in the book *Principles of Database and Knowledge-Base System Volume I*, by Jeffrey D. Ullman (Computer Science Press, 1988). Though perhaps I should caution you that *more formal* doesn't necessarily mean *more accurate* ... For example, here's a quote from that book:

> The CWA lets us "deduce" facts of the form $\neg p(a1,...,ak)$ whenever the usual form of deduction does not yield $p(a1,...,ak)$.[2]

This sentence can't really mean what it says—which is, to paraphrase, that whenever a query fails to yield a result that includes a row representing some proposition *P*, then we're allowed to deduce that *P* is false. For example, the expression

```
S WHERE CITY = 'Oslo'
```

certainly fails to yield a result that includes a row representing the fact that supplier S1 is under contract; so apparently we're allowed to deduce the fact that supplier S1 is *not* under contract (!).[3]

I'll close this section with a definition of *The Open World Assumption* or OWA:

> **Definition (*Open World Assumption*):** Let table *T* have predicate *P*. Then (a) if row *R* appears in *T* at a given time, then the instantiation of *P* corresponding to *R* is assumed to be true at that time; conversely, (b) if row *R* could appear in *T* at a given time but doesn't, then the instantiation of *P* corresponding to *R* is not assumed either to be true or to be false at that time (i.e., it's unknown whether it's true—it might be, and it might not). Loosely speaking, in other words, row *R* appears in table *T* at a given time only if—not if and only if—it satisfies the predicate for table *T* at that time. However, it does at least follow that if proposition *Q* is represented by a

---

[2] The symbol "$\neg$" here denotes the logical operator NOT.

[3] I think the sentence should rather have read as follows: "The CWA lets us deduce facts of the form $\neg p(a1,...,ak)$ whenever $p(a1,...,ak)$ can't be obtained via the usual form of deduction." I'll say it again: Negation can be tricky.

row that appears in some table that can be derived from the tables in the database at a given time, then proposition *Q* can be (and is) assumed to be true at that time.

As you'll recall, I characterized the CWA thus: *Everything stated or implied by the database is true, and everything else is false*. Analogously, the OWA can be characterized thus: *Everything stated or implied by the database is true, and everything else is unknown.*

## WHY THE CWA IS PREFERRED

Now I want to explain why, from a practical point of view as well as a theoretical one, the CWA is to be preferred over the OWA. As a basis for examples, I'll use a reduced version of the suppliers table, one that has just two column, viz., SNO and CITY (but I'll continue to refer to that reduced table as "table S," for simplicity). Here then is an appropriate SQL definition:

```
CREATE TABLE S
  ( SNO   CHAR(5)       ,
    CITY VARCHAR(25)  ,
    UNIQUE ( SNO ) )  ;
```

And here's the table predicate:

*Supplier SNO is under contract and is located in city CITY.*

A sample value for this simplified suppliers table is shown below (and I'll assume this particular value throughout the remainder of this chapter, barring explicit statements to the contrary):

S

| SNO | CITY |
|---|---|
| S1 | London |
| S2 | Paris |
| S3 | Paris |
| S4 | London |
| S5 | Athens |

I now propose to consider the query *Is supplier S1 in London?* Three points arise immediately. The first is that this is an extremely simple query—indeed, it's close to being the simplest possible query we might consider asking of a table like table S. Nonetheless, it's perfectly adequate to illustrate the points I want to make, and I'll stay with it until further notice.

The second point is that the query is expressed in natural language, of course, and (as is so often the case with natural language statements) it's somewhat imprecise and/or incomplete, if not downright ambiguous. In fact, there are at least two possible interpretations that whoever stated the query in the first place might have had in mind:

1. *Is it the case that supplier S1 is under contract and in London?*

2. *Is it the case that, if supplier S1 is under contract, then that supplier is in London?*

Observe that there's certainly a logical difference between these two interpretations. To be specific, if there were no row for supplier S1 in table S, then we would expect the answer *no* under the first interpretation but the answer *yes* under the second. (I'm appealing here to the conventional definition of logical implication, according to which (as we saw in Chapter 1) the expression IF *P* THEN *Q* is defined to be equivalent to (NOT *P*) OR *Q* and thus returns FALSE if *P* is true and *Q* is false, TRUE otherwise.)

From this point forward, I'll abbreviate the two candidate interpretations slightly, as follows:

1. *Is supplier S1 under contract and in London?*

2. *If supplier S1 is under contract, is that supplier in London?*

Also, I'll assume until further notice that the first of these two interpretations is the one intended.

The third point arising is that (as in effect I've already pointed out) the query is a yes/no query—it expects the answer *yes* or *no*. Of course, it was a deliberate decision on my part to use such a query as a basis for my discussions, because yes/no queries illustrate some of the issues I want to examine in a very direct way. One problem caused by that decision, however, is that (as we saw in Chapter 5) SQL doesn't properly support such queries, and so I can't show my examples in SQL even if I wanted to. However, relational algebra does properly support such queries, of course; so here then is an algebraic formulation of the sample query, first interpretation (viz., "Is supplier S1 under contract and in London?"):

```
( S WHERE SNO = 'S1' AND CITY = 'London' ) { }
```

*Explanation:* The expression in parentheses (S WHERE ... 'London') yields either (a) a nonempty table (actually containing just one row) if supplier S1 is represented in table S as being under contract and in London, or (b) an empty table otherwise (i.e., if either there's no row for S1, or there is such a row but the CITY value isn't London). Call this intermediate result *R*. Then the expression *R*{ } denotes the projection of *r* on no columns at all. Since it's on no columns, the result of that projection is necessarily either TABLE_DEE or TABLE_DUM—TABLE_DEE if *R* is nonempty, TABLE_DUM otherwise. And as we saw in Chapter 5, these two possible results effectively denote *yes* and *no*, respectively, and the overall expression thus does indeed represent the query we want it to.

However, let's examine the foregoing conclusions a little more carefully. Those conclusions, paraphrased, are that

a. The overall expression gives either TABLE_DEE (if supplier S1 is represented in table S as being under contract and in London) or TABLE_DUM (otherwise), and hence that

b. The expression in question does indeed represent the query *Is supplier S1 under contract and in London?*

To spell the point out:

- If the result is TABLE_DEE (*yes*), it means supplier S1 is under contract and in London.

- If the result is TABLE_DUM (*no*), it means *it's not the case that* supplier S1 is under contract and in London—which means in turn that supplier S1 either isn't under contract or isn't in London. (Given the semantics of the situation, however, we can be a little more precise here: It means either that supplier S1 isn't under contract at all or that supplier S1 is under contract but isn't in London. Being in London but not under contract doesn't make any sense, gven the context.)

Note very carefully, however, that the foregoing interpretation *relies implicitly on the CWA*—and to be completely accurate in spelling out that interpretation, I ought really to have said as much. What would happen if we were operating under the OWA instead?

Well, under the OWA, if the result is TABLE_DEE, it would still mean that supplier S1 is under contract and in London. But what if it's TABLE_DUM? Apparently, we'd have to understand a result of TABLE_DUM as meaning *it's unknown whether* supplier S1 is under contract and in London. What are the implications of this state of affairs? One important one is as follows:

- First of all, we do need to be clear that the proposition *Supplier S1 is under contract and in London* actually does evaluate to either true or false (for otherwise it wouldn't be a proposition, by definition).

- Let me refer to that proposition as *P*. Then a result of TABLE_DUM doesn't mean that *P* evaluates to some "third truth value" that we might call UNKNOWN; it simply means we don't know which of TRUE and FALSE it does evaluate to. In other words, a result of TABLE_DUM means *we don't have enough information* to determine whether *P* is true or false.

- And as I explained at length in Chapter 5, there's a huge logical difference between (a) *our not knowing* whether some proposition *P* is true or false and (b) that proposition *P* actually *being* either true or false. Indeed, an attempt to pretend otherwise—i.e., an attempt to pretend that our not knowing whether *P* is true or false is the same kind of thing, logically speaking, as *P* actually being either true or false—is a huge logical mistake! And it's precisely that mistake that leads us into the quagmire of three-valued logic, and nulls, and the whole mess of "missing information" as currently "supported" by SQL.

As a matter of fact, I really hope a warning flag was raised in your brain the moment I first mentioned the term "unknown"—especially when I raised the possibility of our not knowing whether some proposition is true or false being regarded as the same kind of thing as that proposition actually being either true or false. That way madness lies! The fact is, as I've argued many, many times and in many, many places (in this book and elsewhere), the whole notion of three-valued logic (3VL) is simply incompatible with the relational model.

To recap, then: We've seen that, under the OWA, if the result of some yes/no query is TABLE_DUM, then that result has to be interpreted as meaning *we don't know* something; in other words—very loosely, and modulo the foregoing discussion—TABLE_DUM has to mean *unknown.* But in that case we longer have a table that means good old plain *no*![4] And yet we're surely entitled, even under the OWA, to expect to get plain *no* as the right answer to certain queries. For example, consider the alternative interpretation of our original natural language query: *If supplier S1 is under contract, is that supplier in London?* Surely we'd be within our rights to expect to get the answer *no* to this query if table S shows supplier S1 as under contract but in some city other than London.

Let's consider this example more closely. First of all, observe that table S satisfies the functional dependency (FD) {SNO} → {CITY}.[5] As a consequence of this FD, the answer to the query should definitely be *no* if table S shows supplier S1 as under contract but in some city other than London (note that the table can't possibly show supplier S1 as being in London and in some other city simultaneously, thanks to the FD).[6] Here then is an expression—deliberately spelled out a step at a time—that's guaranteed to evaluate to (a) TABLE_DUM if table S shows supplier S1 as under contract but in some city other than London, (b) TABLE_DEE otherwise::

```
WITH ( TA := S WHERE SNO = 'S1' AND CITY ≠ 'London' ,
       TB := TA { } ) :
TABLE_DEE MINUS TB
```

*Explanation:*

---

[4] Just to spell the point out (apologies if you think this is just repetition, but I really want to be crystal clear here): Under the CWA, TABLE_DEE means *yes* and TABLE_DUM means *no*; but under the OWA, TABLE_DEE means *yes* and TABLE_DUM means *unknown*, and there's no "other brother" that can be used to represent *no*.

[5] In fact, {SNO} is the sole key for that table, and there are always FDs "out of keys" to everything else in the pertinent table. See, e.g., my book *Database Design and Relational Theory*, 2nd ed. (Apress, 2019) for further discussion of such matters.

[6] Actually, to say the FD is the reason why the table can't show some supplier as being in two cities at once is to put the cart before the horse. In fact, of course, the FD holds *because* no supplier can be in two cities at once.

- Intermediate result *TA* is nonempty (containing just the supplier row for supplier S1) if and only if table S shows supplier S1 as under contract and in some city other than London.

- Thus, intermediate result *TB* is TABLE_DEE if table S shows supplier S1 as under contract and not in London, TABLE_DUM otherwise.[7]

- The expression TABLE_DEE MINUS *TB* then returns either TABLE_DEE or TABLE_DUM according as *TB* is TABLE_DUM or TABLE_DEE (in other words, it returns the *complement* of *TB*, in effect replacing TABLE_DUM by TABLE_DEE and TABLE_DEE by TABLE_DUM).

If the final result is TABLE_DUM, therefore, it means that table S shows supplier S1 as under contract and not in London—precisely the situation in which, I previously claimed, the right answer should be *no*. To repeat, therefore, there are situations, even under the OWA, in which we must be allowed to obtain *no* as the right answer to certain queries; hence, there are situations, even under the OWA, in which TABLE_DUM must mean *no*.

From examples like the foregoing, I conclude that we must reject the suggestion that if we accept the OWA, then TABLE_DUM no longer means *no*. I conclude further that there's no relation that means *unknown*: TABLE_DEE means *yes* and TABLE_DUM means *no*, and there's no "third relation with no attributes"—no "brother" to TABLE_DEE and TABLE_DUM, as I put it earlier—that might be considered to represent "the third truth value" (if I might be permitted to speak as if there were such a thing, just for the moment). And I conclude still further that the OWA and the relational model are fundamentally at odds with one another.

As a matter of fact, I don't need to appeal to the alternative interpretation of the original query—*If supplier S1 is under contract, is that supplier in London?*—in order to show that, even under the OWA, a result of TABLE_DUM sometimes has to mean *no*. Let's go back to the first interpretation: *Is supplier S1 under contract and in London?* Here again is the formulation I gave previously:

---

[7] See Chapter 5, footnote 20.

```
( S WHERE SNO = 'S1' AND CITY = 'London' ) { }
```

Suppose once again that we're operating under the OWA. As I said previously, then, we apparently have that:

- If the result is TABLE_DEE (*yes*), it means supplier S1 is under contract and in London.

- If the result is TABLE_DUM (*unknown*), it means we don't know whether supplier S1 is under contract and in London.

Abstracting a little, this latter possibility means that a certain 3VL expression of the form *P* AND *Q*, where *P* and *Q* are propositions, evaluates to UNKNOWN. (In our example, *P* is SNO = 'S1' and *Q* is CITY = 'London'.) Now, according to both Codd and SQL, if the 3VL expression *P* AND *Q* evaluates to UNKNOWN, it means either that (a) *P* and *Q* both evaluate to UNKNOWN or that (b) one evaluates to UNKNOWN and the other to TRUE. In the case at hand, however, there's no way that one of the propositions *P* and *Q* can possibly be unknown and the other true, because:

- If there's a row for supplier S1 in table S at all, then *Supplier S1 is under contract* is true and *Supplier S1 is in London* is either true or false, depending on whether the CITY value in that row is London or something else. It follows that there can't be a row for supplier S1 in table S at all.

- Hence, both propositions—SNO = 'S1' and *Q* is CITY = 'London'—are unknown (remember that we're operating under the OWA here). In particular, therefore, the proposition *Supplier S1 is under contract* is unknown.

The net of this argument is: If the query result is TABLE_DUM, there can't be a row in table S for supplier S1 at all—meaning, to repeat, that *we don't know whether* supplier S1 is under contract.

But now suppose supplier S1 is under contract but is in some city other than London. In this case, table S will contain a row saying supplier S1 is under contract. Yet the expression shown previously—

```
( S WHERE SNO = 'S1' AND CITY = 'London' ) { }
```

—will yield the result TABLE_DUM, which (according to the analysis of the previous paragraph) the OWA tells us has to mean *we don't know* whether supplier S1 is under contract. But we *do* know! So the OWA has given us the wrong answer.

## TABLE PREDICATES REVISITED

As we've seen, yes/no queries do always deliver yes/no answers, under the CWA. However, this state of affairs does *not* mean that such an answer can never be understood as meaning "don't know"! It's simply a matter of being careful about what question that yes/no answer is an answer to. In order to explain this point, I first need to step back a bit; to be specific, I need to review, and expand on, that whole business of table predicates as previously discussed in Chapters 1 and 2.

When I introduced the reduced version of the suppliers table S near the beginning of the previous section, I said the predicate was *Supplier SNO is under contract and is located in city CITY.* But it isn't—not really. To see why not, consider what happens if the user tries to insert a new row into the table, perhaps like this (using SQL syntax):

```
INSERT INTO S ( SNO , CITY ) ROW ( 'S6' , 'Madrid' ) ;
```

In effect, the user is asserting with this INSERT that there's a new supplier, S6, with city Madrid. Now, the system obviously has no way of telling whether that assertion is true—all it can do, and all it does do, is check that if the requested insertion is performed, it won't cause any integrity constraints to be violated. If that check succeeds, then the system accepts the new row, *and interprets it as representing a "true fact" from this point forward.*

We see, therefore, that rows in table S don't necessarily represent actual "true facts" about the real world; rather, they represent *what the user tells the system* about the real world, or in other words the user's *knowledge* of the real world. Thus, the predicate for table S isn't really just *Supplier SNO is under contract and is located in city CITY;* rather, it's ***We know that*** *supplier SNO is under contract and is located in city CITY.* And the effect of a successful INSERT is to make the system aware of something the user already knows. Thus, the database doesn't contain "the real world" (of course not); what it contains is, rather, *the system's knowledge of* the real world. And the system's knowledge in turn is derived from the user's knowledge (of course!—there's no magic here).

By the way, even the terms *know* and *knowledge* might be a little strong in contexts such as the ones at hand—the terms *believe* and *beliefs* might be better—but I'll stay with *know* and *knowledge* for the purposes of the present discussion.

So when we pose a query, by definition that query can't be a query about the real world; instead, it is—it has to be—a query about the system's knowledge of the real world. For example, the query I discussed in the previous section (*Is supplier S1 under contract and in London?*) really means ***According to the system's knowledge,*** *is supplier S1 under contract and in London?* Or equivalently: ***Do we know that*** *supplier S1 is under contract and in London?* Or equivalently again: ***Does the database say that*** *supplier S1 is under contract and in London?* In practice, of course, we almost never talk in such precise terms; we usually elide all those qualifiers ("according to the system's knowledge," "do we know that," "does the database say that," and so on). But even if we do elide them, we certainly need to understand that, conceptually, they're there—for otherwise we'll be really confused. (Though perhaps I should note for the record that such confusions aren't exactly unknown in practice.)

It follows from the foregoing discussion that the algebraic expression

```
( S WHERE SNO = 'S1' AND CITY = 'London' ) { }
```

doesn't really represent the query *Is supplier S1 under contract and in London?*—despite the fact that earlier in this chapter I said it did. Rather, it represents the query ***Do we know that*** *supplier S1 is under contract and in London?* And it follows further that:

- If the result is TABLE_DEE (*yes*), it means we do know that supplier S1 is under contract and in London.

- If the result is TABLE_DUM (*no*), it means *we don't know whether* supplier S1 is under contract and in London. And that's a "don't know" answer if ever you saw one.

## PUTTING IT ALL TOGETHER

Consider once again the question of whether supplier S1 is in London (for simplicity, let's ignore the part about the supplier being under contract). From the discussion so far, then, it should be clear that:

a. If a row for supplier S1 appears in table S and the CITY value in that row is London, it means yes, we know supplier S1 is in London.

b. If a row for supplier S1 appears in table S but the CITY value in that row is something other than London, it means no, we know supplier S1 isn't in London.

c. And if no row for supplier S1 appears in table S at all, it means we don't know whether supplier S1 is in London.[8]

Even under the CWA, therefore—and, praise be, without having to delve into three-valued logic!—we can formulate queries that return a true /false /don't know answer. Here's a possible formulation in relational algebra for the particular case in hand:

```
( EXTEND ( S WHERE SNO = 'S1' AND CITY = 'London' ) { } :
         { ANSWER := 'true        ' } ) { ANSWER }
  UNION
( EXTEND ( S WHERE SNO = 'S1' AND CITY ≠ 'London' ) { } :
         { ANSWER := 'false       ' } ) { ANSWER }
  UNION
( EXTEND ( RELATION { TUPLE { SNO 'S1' } }
                              MINUS S { SNO } ) { } :
         { ANSWER := 'don''t know' } ) { ANSWER }
```

As you can see, this expression takes the form *a* UNION *b* UNION *c* (where each of *a*, *b*, and *c* denotes a table of one column), and it should be clear

---

[8] More precisely, it means there's no city *C* such that we know that "S1 is in *C*" is true. Note carefully that it *doesn't* mean we know that "S1 is under contract" is false. S1 might indeed be under contract—but since we don't know the city, there's no row we can insert into the table.

PS: Of course, if "S1 is under contract" *is* false, then it's certainly the case that there's no city *C* such that "S1 is in *C*" is true. So if no row for supplier S1 appears in table S at all, a strict interpretation of that state of affairs is *either* that (a) there's no supplier S1 at all *or* that (b) there *is* a supplier S1, but the city is unknown. Now, whether you think "don't know" is a reasonable response to the query, in the case where there's actually no supplier S1 at all, is a matter I leave to your judgment. But I stress the point that, in that case, *the system doesn't know* that there's no supplier S1; all it knows is that it doesn't know the city for supplier S1, regardless of whether such a supplier actually exists.

that exactly one of *a*, *b*, and *c* evaluates to a table containing just one row and the other two evaluate to a table containing no eows at all. (In fact, of course, *a*, *b*, and *c* correspond respectively to the three cases a., b., and c. identified above.) The overall result thus consists of a table of one column and one row; the single column, ANSWER, is of type CHAR, and the single row contains the appropriate ANSWER value. And the trick—though it isn't really a trick at all—is that the ANSWER value in question is a character string, not a truth value. Thus, there's no need to get into the 3VL quagmire in order to formulate queries that can yield "true," "false," or "don't know" answers, if that's what the user wants.

By the way, we can even formulate such queries in SQL, despite the fact that (as noted earlier) SQL doesn't really support yes/no queries properly. To illustrate, here's a SQL analog of the foregoing relational algebra expression:

```
SELECT 'true       ' AS ANSWER
FROM ( SELECT SNO
       FROM   S
       WHERE  SNO = 'S1'
       AND    CITY = 'London' ) AS POINTLESS
UNION
SELECT 'false      ' AS ANSWER
FROM ( SELECT SNO
       FROM   S
       WHERE  SNO = 'S1'
       AND    CITY ≠ 'London' ) AS POINTLESS
UNION
SELECT 'don''t know' AS ANSWER
FROM ( VALUES ( 'S1' )
       EXCEPT
       SELECT SNO
       FROM   S ) AS POINTLESS
```

(As for those *AS POINTLESS* specifications, they're pointless, but they're required by the SQL standard.)

Chapter 8

# Two-Valued Logic: Missing Information and Database Design

In the previous chapter I showed how we can get "don't know" answers out of a completely null-free database—i.e., without having to use any such suspect notion as nulls or three-valued logic at all. However, the database I used for my examples in that chapter didn't actually involve any "missing information," in the usual sense of that term, at all. As a consequence, those examples didn't address the more general question of how we might handle missing information as such—how we might represent the fact that some piece of information is missing, I mean, and how we might perform queries on such a representation, whatever it turns out to be. Now I turn my attention to these matters.

## THE DECOMPOSITION APPROACH

The book *Database Explorations*, by Hugh Darwen and myself (Trafford, 2010), discusses several possible approaches to the missing information problem, all of which avoid the use of nulls and 3VL. In what follows I describe one of those approaches—the one that, in practice, is probably the easiest to implement—in some detail. The approach in question is known as the *decomposition* approach, because it involves decomposing, in a variety of ways, tables that might appear to require nulls into ones that don't. In other words, the emphasis is on designing the database in such a way as to avoid a perceived need for nulls. As a consequence, the approach:

- Has no notion of null or any other construct that's allowed to appear where a value is expected and yet isn't itself a value;
- Relies exclusively on classical two-valued logic (2VL), instead of three-valued logic (3VL) or, more generally, *n*-valued logic (*n*VL) for some $n > 2$;
- Abides by *The Information Principle* (see below); and
- Is capable of dealing with missing information of any number of different kinds.

### *The Information Principle*

I'd like to elaborate briefly on *The Information Principle*, because it's important. The principle is due to Codd, and "The Information Principle" was his original name for it. But the first time he mentioned it in writing was, I believe, in his articles "Is Your DBMS Really Relational?" and "Does Your DBMS Run by the Rules?" (*Computerworld*, October 14th and 21st, 1985), and there he referred to as "The Information Rule." And then in the RM/V2 book he renamed it again, calling it "The Information Feature." Personally, I think the original name is best, and that's the one I'll use by preference. Anyway, here now is how Codd stated the principle in 1985, in the first part of that two-part article:

> **Definition (*Information Principle*):** All information in a relational database is represented explicitly at the logical level and in exactly one way—by values in tables.[1]

I heard Codd refer to this principle on more than one occasion as *the* fundamental principle underlying the relational model. Why is it so important? There are two main reasons:

1. Relations ("tables") are both necessary and sufficient to represent absolutely any data whatsoever at the user (or "logical") level; thus, the

---

[1] Here for interest is part of Codd's own elaboration of this principle in that 1985 article: "Even table names, column names, and domain names are represented as character strings in some tables. Tables containing such names are normally part of the built-in system catalog. The catalog is accordingly a relational database itself—one that is dynamic and active and represents the metadata (data describing the rest of the data in the system)." PS: That "normally" is a little puzzling, though (?).

relational model gives us everything we need in this respect, and it doesn't give us anything we don't need.

2. It's axiomatic that if there are *n* different ways of representing data, we need *n* different sets of operators. For example, if we had arrays as well as relations, we'd need a full complement of array operators as well as a full complement of relational ones.[2] If *n* is greater than one, therefore, we have more operators to implement, document, teach, learn, remember, and use (and choose among). But those extra operators add complexity, not power! There's nothing that can be done—nothing useful, at any rate—if *n* is greater than one that can't be done if *n* equals one (and in the relational model, of course, *n* does equal one).

Given all of the above, then, I find it supremely ironic that Codd's nulls violate his own *Information Principle*. How do they do so? Actually, the answer is immediately and transparently obvious:

a. The principle says the database contains nothing but values.

b. Nulls aren't values.

One last point: I have to say I don't think the principle is very well named. It might more accurately be called *The Principle of Uniform Representation*, or even *The Principle of Uniformity of Representation*, since the crucial point about it is that it implies that all information in a relational database is represented in the same way: namely, as relations, and nothing but relations. But these names are a bit of a mouthful, and I suppose "The Information Principle" is at least pithier.

### *An Introductory Example*

Be all that as it may, here's a simple example to show what the decomposition approach might look like in practice. Suppose we don't know whether there's a supplier S7 under contract and located in Athens. Obviously, then, the row

---

[2] We'd also need operators for converting arrays into relations and vice versa, and guidance as to when it was better to use arrays and when relations. *Note:* None of this is to say that relational databases are the best solution for all possible kinds of data and all possible applications. However, what certainly is the case is that the range of kinds of data and applications for which relational databases are suitable is extraordinarily large.

```
ROW ( 'S7' , 'Athens' )
```

doesn't satisfy the predicate for table S—which is, to repeat from Chapter 7, *We know that supplier SNO is under contract and is located in city CITY.* (I assume for the time being, as I did in the previous chapter, that table S has just two columns, SNO and CITY.) It follows that we can't, and mustn't, insert that row into that table. As Wittgenstein famously said:[3]

> *Was sich überhaupt sagen lässt, lässt sich klar sagen; und wovon man nicht reden kann, darüber muss man schweigen.*

In English:

> What can be said at all can be said clearly; and whereof one cannot speak, thereon one must remain silent.

In the example, we can't "speak of" supplier S7 being in Athens (because we don't know whether that's a "true fact" or not), and so indeed we mustn't "speak of it." In other words, we mustn't insert the row (S7,Athens) into the suppliers table S.[4]

But suppose now that we do at least know that supplier S7 exists, even if we don't know the corresponding city. Of course, it's still the case that there's no city *C* such that the row (S7,*C*) satisfies the predicate for table S; so there's still no row for supplier S7 that we can legitimately insert into table S. Nevertheless, we might still want to record the fact that we do at least know that supplier S7 exists, even though we don't know the city. In that case, then there are two things we can do—two approaches we can adopt, that is—which I'll refer to as Darwen's approach and McGoveran's approach, respectively, since Hugh Darwen and David McGoveran were the first to describe them (as far as I know, at any rate):

---

[3] In *Tractatus Logico-Philosophicus* (1921, translated by Frank Ramsey).

[4] That (S7,Athens) should of course really be, slightly more correctly, ('S7', 'Athens'). From this point forwards I'll drop the quote marks in regular text, for simplicity.

- In Darwen's approach,[5] we retain table S unchanged, with its predicate *We know that supplier SNO is under contract and is located in city CITY*, but we introduce a second table, which I'll call CITY_UNKNOWN, with just one column, SNO, and predicate *We know that supplier SNO is under contract but we don't know the corresponding city.* In the example at hand, the result looks like this:

S

| SNO | CITY |
|---|---|
| S1 | London |
| S2 | Paris |
| S3 | Paris |
| S4 | London |
| S5 | Athens |

CITY_UNKNOWN

| SNO |
|---|
| S7 |

Of course, no supplier number can appear in both tables (that's an integrity constraint on this design).

- McGoveran's approach[6] also involves two tables: one (which I'll continue to call S) with a single column, SNO, and predicate *We know that supplier SNO is under contract*, and the other (which I'll call SC) with columns SNO and CITY and predicate *We know that supplier SNO is located in city CITY.* In the example at hand, the result looks like this:

S

| SNO |
|---|
| S1 |
| S2 |
| S3 |
| S4 |
| S5 |
| S7 |

SC

| SNO | CITY |
|---|---|
| S1 | London |
| S2 | Paris |
| S3 | Paris |
| S4 | London |
| S5 | Athens |

---

[5] Described in "How to Handle Missing Information Without Using Nulls" (presentation slides), by Hugh Darwen, *www.thethirdmanifesto.com* (May 9th, 2003).

[6] Described in Chapter 8 ("Nothing from Nothing, Part 4 of 4: It's in the Way that You Use It") of *Relational Database Writings 1994-1997*, by David McGoveran, Hugh Darwen and myself (Addison-Wesley, 1998). *Note:* Ironically enough, McGoveran's approach is almost identical to a scheme proposed by Codd himself in his 1979 paper, albeit in connection with his "extended" model RM/T.

Every supplier number appearing in table SC must also appear in table S (that's an integrity constraint—in fact, a foreign key constraint—on this design).

As you can see, both of the foregoing approaches involve some kind of decomposition: to be specific, decomposition of the original suppliers table into two separate tables (hence the title of this section). The approaches are conceptually very similar, of course. For definiteness, I'll focus from this point forward on Darwen's approach specifically.

## A DETAILED EXAMPLE

I revert now to our usual suppliers table S, with its four columns SNO, SNAME, STATUS, and CITY. The following picture shows a version of that table in which certain information is missing—but now I choose to represent the fact that the information in question is missing by means of shading, to stress the point that we're definitely not talking about data values here. Note that we can't say—at least, we can't say legitimately—that the picture shows a *relation*, precisely because of those shaded entries. In fact, we can't legitimately say the picture shows a *value*, as such, at all—not of any kind.

| SNO | SNAME | STATUS | CITY |
|---|---|---|---|
| S1 | Smith | 20 | London |
| S2 | Jones | 10 | |
| S3 | Blake | | Paris |
| S4 | Clark | | |

*Note:* I omit the usual row for supplier S5 merely by way of simplification. There's no ulterior motive.

Now, the corresponding predicate is supposed to be as follows:

*We know that supplier SNO is under contract, is named SNAME, has status STATUS, and is located in city CITY.*

For present purposes, however, let's simplify this predicate by dropping both the qualifying "We know that" and the bit about the supplier being under contract, thus:

> *Supplier SNO is named SNAME, has status STATUS, and is located in city CITY.*

Observe now that this predicate is at best approximate. It would be appropriate if it weren't for those shaded entries. After all, the following—obtained from the foregoing predicate by substituting values from the row shown for supplier S1, which has no shaded entries—is certainly a meaningful instantiation of this predicate (i.e., it's a meaningful proposition):

> *Supplier S1 is named Smith, has status 20, and is located in city London.*

But if we try to do the same thing for the row for supplier S2, we obtain:

> *Supplier S2 is named Jones, has status 10, and is located in city* .

And this certainly isn't a meaningful instantiation, or proposition; in fact, it doesn't make any sense at all.

Another interesting question is: What are the data types for columns STATUS and CITY? (I'm assuming here for the sake of the example, and I'll continue to assume throughout the rest of this chapter, that shaded entries don't appear, and won't ever appear, in the other two columns, SNO and SNAME.) In SQL in particular, the shaded entries in columns STATUS and CITY can be interpreted as meaning the pertinent entries "are null"; in the preface to this book, however, I said the (SQL) data types of those columns are INTEGER and VARCHAR(25), respectively, and null certainly isn't a value of either of those types. In fact, of course, null isn't a value at all, and so it can't sensibly be said to be of any type at all.[7]

---

[7] In SQL, by contrast, it's considered to be of *every* type! To quote the standard: "Every data type includes a special value, called the *null value* [*sic*] … [that] is neither equal to any other value nor not equal to any other value." (And the standard could have gone on to say, and I think should have done so, that "the null value" is neither equal to itself nor not equal to itself. However, what it actually does say is that "in some contexts, multiple null values are treated together." Well, I guess that certainly clears up any possible confusion over such matters, doesn't it.)

From this preliminary discussion, it should be clear that what we need to do is get rid of those shaded entries—and decomposition (in fact, two kinds of decomposition, vertical and horizontal) can be used to achieve this goal.

## VERTICAL DECOMPOSITION

The first step in that process of getting rid of those shaded entries is to apply *vertical* decomposition to produce a set of tables with the property that no table ever has more than one column with any such entries. (Note that vertical decomposition in this sense—vertical because the dividing lines in the decomposition are between columns, so to speak—is very reminiscent of what we already do when we do classical normalization.) For the table from the previous section, the result of this step is the following collection of tables SN, ST, and SC:

SN

| SNO | SNAME |
|---|---|
| S1 | Smith |
| S2 | Jones |
| S3 | Blake |
| S4 | Clark |

ST

| SNO | STATUS |
|---|---|
| S1 | 20 |
| S2 | 10 |
| S3 | |
| S4 | |

SC

| SNO | CITY |
|---|---|
| S1 | London |
| S2 | |
| S3 | Paris |
| S4 | |

Now, the "obvious" predicates for these tables are as follows:

- SN: *Supplier SNO is named SNAME.*
- ST: *Supplier SNO has status STATUS.*
- SC: *Supplier SNO is located in city CITY.*

In fact the "obvious" predicate is indeed the correct one in the case of table SN. But those "obvious" predicates for tables ST and SC are still only approximate, because of those shaded entries—and that's why we need horizontal decomposition, which we'll get to in the next section. First, however, note that each of tables SN, ST, and SC has just two columns. But this state of affairs is a fluke, in a way; it's a direct result of my choice of example. If the example were different—e.g., if we knew that column STATUS, as well as columns SNO and SNAME, will never contain any shaded entries—then the appropriate vertical decomposition would be as follows:

SNT

| SNO | SNAME | STATUS |
|---|---|---|
| S1 | Smith | 20 |
| S2 | Jones | 10 |
| S3 | Blake | 30 |
| S4 | Clark | 20 |

SC

| SNO | CITY |
|---|---|
| S1 | London |
| S2 | |
| S3 | Paris |
| S4 | |

*Note:* I'm assuming here, just for the sake of the example (but in accordance with our usual sample values), that suppliers S3 and S4 have status 30 and 20, respectively, instead of those STATUS values being missing as they're supposed to be in our current running example.

## HORIZONTAL DECOMPOSITION

In horizontal decomposition, the dividing lines are between rows, so to speak, instead of between columns. The basic motivation for such decomposition is this: We shouldn't try to use the same table to represent two or more different predicates. For example, consider table SC again as shown in the previous section. In that table, the row for supplier S1 means: *Supplier S1 is located in London*. By contrast, the row for supplier S2 means: *We don't know where supplier S2 is located* (at least, let's agree for the time being that that's what it means). So different rows correspond to different predicates, and the "obvious" predicate I gave for table SC in the previous section—*Supplier SNO is located in city CITY*—doesn't in fact apply to every row.

Now, we might think about trying a different predicate, perhaps as follows (note the OR, which I've shown in uppercase bold for emphasis):

> *Supplier SNO is located in city CITY* ***OR*** *we don't know where supplier SNO is located.*

But this predicate doesn't work either. If we try to instantiate it with values (or "values," rather, since  certainly isn't a value) from the row for supplier S2, we get:

> *Supplier S2 is located in city* **OR** *we don't know where supplier S2 is located.*

And the first half of this sentence—Supplier S2 is located in city —still doesn't make sense, because isn't a legitimate city name and can't legitimately be substituted as an argument for the CITY parameter in the putative predicate. Clearly, what we need to do is break that would-be predicate into two separate pieces, as it were (more precisely, we need to break the two disjuncts apart, *disjunct* being the correct term for a sentence that's OR'ed with another); in other words, we need to apply *horizontal* decomposition to table SC, to obtain one table for each disjunct. Here's the result:

SC

| SNO | CITY |
|---|---|
| S1 | London |
| S3 | Paris |

SUC

| SNO |
|---|
| S2 |
| S4 |

As you can see, we now have two tables, viz.:

a. An abbreviated version of table SC (for which I've retained that same name SC, for convenience), containing just the original SC rows that had no shaded entries in column CITY, and

b. Another table SUC ("suppliers with an unknown city"), containing just the original SC rows that did have shaded entries in column CITY—except that the CITY column in that table, if we'd kept it, would have contained nothing but shaded entries, and so we can discard it without losing any information.

The predicates for these two tables are as follows:

- SC: *Supplier SNO is located in city CITY.*
- SUC: *We don't know where supplier SNO is located.*

Observe in particular that the predicate for this new version of table SC has two parameters, SNO and CITY, and that table has two columns accordingly; by contrast, the predicate for table SUC has just one parameter, SNO, and that table has just one column accordingly.

Of course, we can and should perform an analogous horizontal decomposition on table ST. Heres the result:

ST

| SNO | STATUS |
|---|---|
| S1 | 20 |
| S2 | 10 |

SUT

| SNO |
|---|
| S3 |
| S4 |

The predicates for these tables as follows:

- ST: *Supplier SNO has status STATUS.*
- SUT: *We don't know supplier SNO's status.*

*Note:* The five tables we've wound up with—viz., SN, SC, SUC, ST, and SUT—are all "truly relational," and so we could if we wanted switch now to the more formal terminology of relations, tuples, and attributes. For consistency, however, I'll continue to talk in terms of tables, rows, and columns throughout the remainder of this chapter.

## WHAT DO THE SHADED ENTRIES MEAN?

Let's ignore status values for the moment and concentrate on cities. Here again is the "supplier cities" table SC as it was before we performed horizontal decomposition on it:

SC

| SNO | CITY |
|---|---|
| S1 | London |
| S2 | |
| S3 | Paris |
| S4 | |

Previously, I assumed those shaded entries in the CITY column meant *we don't know* the applicable supplier city—i.e., the supplier does have a city, but we don't know what it is. But of course our not knowing is only one of many possible reasons why we might not be able to use a genuine city name as some entry in that column. For example, it might be that the notion of having a city doesn't apply to some suppliers (perhaps they conduct their business entirely online). If so, we might say, *very* loosely, that table SC, with those shaded entries in the CITY column, has a predicate looking something like this:

> *Supplier SNO is located in city CITY* ***OR*** *we don't know where supplier SNO is located* ***OR*** *supplier SNO isn't located anywhere.*

Note, therefore, that those shaded entries now potentially have two distinct interpretations: Some of them mean we don't know the applicable city; others mean the property of having a city doesn't apply. So, again, we apply horizontal decomposition, this time to obtain three tables: SC (suppliers with a known city), SUC (suppliers with an unknown city), and SNC (suppliers with no city at all). If we assume for the sake of the example that supplier S2 has an unknown city and supplier S4 doesn't have a city at all, then the result of this decomposition will look like this:

SC

| SNO | CITY |
|---|---|
| S1 | London |
| S3 | Paris |

SUC

| SNO |
|---|
| S2 |

SNC

| SNO |
|---|
| S4 |

The predicates are:

- SC: *Supplier SNO is located in city CITY.*
- SUC: *We don't know where supplier SNO is located.*
- SNC: *Supplier SNO doesn't have a location.*

As the foregoing example suggests, therefore, the decomposition approach allows us to represent as many different kinds of missing information as we like. To be specific, if there are *n* distinct reasons for supplier cities to be missing, there'll be $n + 1$ tables having to do with suppliers and cities. Two possible objections thus immediately spring to mind:

1. Aren't we going to wind up with an awful lot of tables?

2. As a consequence, aren't some queries going to get awfully complex? For example, suppose we just want to retrieve everything in the database having to do with suppliers (the analog of "SELECT * FROM S" in SQL); aren't we going to have to do a lot of joins, or (worse) outer joins?

I'll come back to the second of these issues in the section "Queries," later. As for the first, well, there are several points I want to make. Suppose for the moment that we're in the SQL environment, and let *C* be a column in that environment that permits nulls. Then:

- If the nulls in column *C* all represent the same kind of missing information—and if the same is true for all such columns *C*—then the number of tables resulting from the decomposition approach is exactly the same as the number resulting from a good relational design. (To repeat something I said in Chapters 2 and 5, nulls "break the relational model." The fact is, the presence of such a column *C* in some table *T* means that the table *T* in question is certainly not a *relational* table. Proper relational design requires elimination of such columns.)

- The situation is worse if the nulls in column *C* represent two or more distinct kinds of missing information and proper decomposition hasn't been done. In such a case, there'll certainly be fewer tables—but the apparent simplicity of such a design is spurious: Those tables aren't relational, they don't faithfully reflect the real world, they no longer have clear predicates, and queries are more susceptible to errors of formulation or errors of interpretation or both.

Now, there's a tactic we might consider if we want "to be truly relational" and yet still reduce the number of tables, which I'll illustrate with reference to the example in which the CITY property is unknown for some supplies and inapplicable for others. In terms of that example, the tactic would involve combining tables SUC and SNC into a single table with two columns, SNO and

REASON, where REASON indicates the reason why the applicable supplier has no recorded city:

| SNO | REASON |
|---|---|
| S2 | *d/k* |
| S4 | *n/a* |

But now we have to define appropriate values, and spell out their interpretations, for column REASON (in the example, I've used *d/k* for "don't know" and *n/a* for "not applicable"). In fact, if the decomposition approach requires *n* missing information tables, the "combination" approach as sketched here requires *n* missing information reasons. So the combination approach is, in effect, no less complex than the decomposition approach.

Finally, you might be thinking that such an "awful lot of tables" is going to lead to a very inefficient use of storage. Well, if you're thinking that, then I'm afraid you might be right, given the implementations typically found in today's SQL systems. But there are better implementations! In particular, an implementation based on *The TransRelational Model™* wouldn't be subject to any such criticism. For further details, I refer you to my book *Go Faster! The TransRelational™ Approach to DBMS Implementation* (2002, 2011), available as a free download from Ventus Publishing (*http://bookboon.com/en/go-faster-ebook*).

## INTEGRITY CONSTRAINTS

Throughout the remainder of this chapter, then, let's agree that:

- There's just one reason why STATUS values might be missing: namely, we don't know the value.
- There are just two reasons why CITY values might be missing: namely, either we don't know the value or no such value exists.

So far, then, our suggested overall design for the running example looks like this:

SN

| SNO | SNAME |
|---|---|
| S1 | Smith |
| S2 | Jones |
| S3 | Blake |
| S4 | Clark |

ST

| SNO | STATUS |
|---|---|
| S1 | 20 |
| S2 | 10 |

SUT

| SNO |
|---|
| S3 |
| S4 |

SC

| SNO | CITY |
|---|---|
| S1 | London |
| S3 | Paris |

SUC

| SNO |
|---|
| S2 |

SNC

| SNO |
|---|
| S4 |

Note, however, that the foregoing design needs certain integrity constraints to be enforced in order to hold it together, so to speak. The constraints in question are as follows:

1. Each table has {SNO} as a key.

2. Each row in SN has a matching row in exactly one of ST and SUT, and conversely.

3. Each row in SN has a matching row in exactly one of SC, SUC, and SNC, and conversely.

The first of these is just a conventional key constraint on each of the six tables, and it can be dealt with by means of conventional KEY specifications. As for the second, one possible formulation is as follows:

```
CONSTRAINT ...
      SN { SNO } = ( ST { SNO } UNION SUT { SNO } )
      AND
      IS_EMPTY ( ST { SNO } INTERSECT SUT { SNO } ) ;
```

*Explanation:* This constraint consists as you can see of two Boolean expressions ANDed together:

- The first states, in effect, that every supplier number in SN also appears in at least one of ST and SC. Note in particular that the "=" in that Boolean expression denotes *relational* equality—it represents an equality comparison between two relations. That Boolean expression overall is thus an example of what's called, for obvious reasons, an *equality dependency* or EQD.[8]

- The second states, in effect, that no supplier number appears in both ST and SC (IS_EMPTY is an operator that returns TRUE if its sole operand, a relation, has cardinality zero, FALSE otherwise). In fact, that second Boolean expression also represents a certain EQD, albeit one in slightly concealed form. To elaborate briefly: Any expression of the form

```
IS_EMPTY ( rx )
```

(where *rx* is a relational expression) is logically equivalent to an equality comparison of the form

```
rx { } = TABLE_DUM
```

(where, to remind you, the expression *rx*{ } denotes the projection of the relation denoted by *rx* over no columns at all).

By the way, it's worth pointing out in this example that the expression denoting the IS_EMPTY argument—

```
ST { SNO } INTERSECT SUT { SNO }
```

—could equally well have been formulated thus (why, exactly?):

```
ST { SNO } JOIN SUT { SNO }
```

Turning now to the third constraint, it's very similar to the second, of course, but slightly lengthier:

---

[8] Note that if an EQD is in effect that spans two or more tables, then certain updates on any individual one of those tables will necessarily cause that EQD to be violated—implying, therefore, that the tables in question had better be updated "simultaneously," as it were. But then a similar remark applies in the case of foreign key constraints also, as I'm sure you realize. In fact, EQDs and foreign key constraints have a lot in common. See my book *Database Design and Relatonal Theory*, 2nd ed. (Apress, 2019) for an extended discussion of such matters.

```
CONSTRAINT ...
      SN { SNO } = ( SC { SNO } UNION SUC { SNO }
                                UNION SNC { SNO } )
      AND
      IS_EMPTY ( SC { SNO } INTERSECT SUC { SNO }
                            INTERSECT SNC { SNO } ) ;
```

*Note:* As an exercise, try formulating the foregoing constraints in SQL.

## QUERIES

Now I return to the second of the possible objections I raised in the section before last: viz., given a "fully decomposed" design like the one discussed in the previous section, aren't some queries going to get awfully complex? In particular, what's involved with that specific design in doing a query analogous to the "simple" SQL query SELECT * FROM S?

Before I address that issue, let me first point out that some queries—queries, I venture to suggest, that are more likely to be needed in practice than ones like SELECT * FROM S—are actually easier to formulate with the fully decomposed design. As a trivial example, the query "For suppliers for whom CITY is both applicable and known, get supplier numbers and cities" becomes just

```
SELECT SNO , CITY
FROM   SC
```

instead of:

```
SELECT SNO , CITY
FROM   S
WHERE  CITY IS NOT NULL
```

Be that as it may, let's consider the "SELECT * FROM S" question. More precisely, let's see how the original suppliers table (or a respectable version of that table, rather) can be recovered from the fully decomposed design—where by *respectable* I mean the result will contain proper data values everywhere (no shaded entries! no nulls!) and might thus look like this:

| SNO | SNAME | XSTATUS | XCITY |
|---|---|---|---|
| S1 | Smith | 20 | London |
| S2 | Jones | 10 | *d/k* |
| S3 | Blake | *d/k* | Paris |
| S4 | Clark | *d/k* | *n/a* |

First I'll show the solution a step at a time, using the foregoing sample values as a basis for illustrating the result of each step in turn; then I'll bring all the steps together at the end. (Of course, I'll show that solution in relational algebra. As an exercise, you might like to try giving a solution using SQL instead.)

a.
```
WITH ( TA := EXTEND ST :
                 { XSTATUS := CAST_AS_CHAR ( STATUS ) } ) :
```

*TA*

| SNO | STATUS | XSTATUS |
|---|---|---|
| S1 | 20 | 20 |
| S2 | 10 | 10 |

```
/* STATUS values are integers, */
/* but XSTATUS values are CHAR */
/* strings, thanks to the CAST */
/* invocation                  */
```

b.
```
WITH ( TB := TA { SNO , XSTATUS } ) :
```

*TB*

| SNO | XSTATUS |
|---|---|
| S1 | 20 |
| S2 | 10 |

c.
```
WITH ( TC := EXTEND SUT : { XSTATUS := 'd/k' } ) :
```

*TC*

| SNO | XSTATUS |
|---|---|
| S3 | *d/k* |
| S4 | *d/k* |

d.[9] `WITH ( TD := UNION { TB , TC } ) :`

*TD*

| SNO | XSTATUS |
|---|---|
| S1 | 20 |
| S2 | 10 |
| S3 | *d/k* |
| S4 | *d/k* |

e. `WITH ( TE := SC RENAME { CITY AS XCITY } ) :`

*TE*

| SNO | XCITY |
|---|---|
| S1 | London |
| S3 | Paris |

```
/* attribute renaming preparatory */
/* to UNION in Step h.            */
```

f. `WITH ( TF := EXTEND SUC : { XCITY := 'd/k' } ) :`

*TF*

| SNO | XCITY |
|---|---|
| S2 | *d/k* |

g. `WITH ( TG := EXTEND SNC : { XCITY := 'n/a' } ) :`

*TG*

| SNO | XCITY |
|---|---|
| S4 | *n/a* |

---

[9] This step uses the alternative prefix syntax for UNION. Step h. does likewise, and Step i. uses the prefix syntax for JOIN similarly.

h. `WITH ( TH := UNION { TE , TF , TG } ) :`

*TH*

| SNO | XCITY |
|---|---|
| S1 | London |
| S2 | *d/k* |
| S3 | Paris |
| S4 | *n/a* |

i. `S := JOIN { SN , TD , TH }`

S

| SNO | SNAME | XSTATUS | XCITY |
|---|---|---|---|
| S1 | Smith | 20 | London |
| S2 | Jones | 10 | *d/k* |
| S3 | Blake | *d/k* | Paris |
| S4 | Clark | *d/k* | *n/a* |

Putting all of these steps together, then (and simplifying slightly), we have:

```
WITH ( TA := EXTEND ST :
                 { XSTATUS := CAST_AS_CHAR ( STATUS ) } ,
       TB := TA { SNO , XSTATUS } ,
       TC := EXTEND SUT : { XSTATUS := 'd/k' } ,
       TD := UNION { TB , TC } ,
       TE := SC RENAME { CITY AS XCITY } ,
       TF := EXTEND SUC : { XCITY := 'd/k' } ,
       TG := EXTEND SNC : { XCITY := 'n/a' } ,
       TH := UNION { TE , TF , TG } ) :
S := JOIN { SN , TD , TH }
```

Now, it's certainly true that this expression looks a little complicated (or tedious, at any rate), and it might look even more so if I hadn't formulated it a step at a time, using WITH. However:

- Various syntactic shorthands could be defined, if desired, that could be used to simplify it.

- In practice, certain sequences of steps as shown above would probably be combined into single steps.

- I frankly doubt whether results like the foregoing will ever be wanted much in practice anyway, except perhaps as the basis for some kind of periodic report.

- In any case, the complexity, such as it is, can always be concealed by defining that result as a view.

Finally, let me remind you of the claim I made a few pages back, to the effect that an implementation based on *The TransRelational Model*™ would be able to represent the complete set of tables (i.e., SN, ST, SUT, SC, SUC, and SNT) efficiently. Well, I now claim further—as a bonus, if you like—that "complicated" queries like the one discussed above will perform efficiently, too, given such an implementation. Again I refer you to my book *Go Faster! The TransRelational*™ *Approach to DBMS Implementation* for further details.

## PARTIAL INFORMATION

So far in this chapter I've been assuming that if information is missing at all, then it's missing completely; for example, I've assumed that the city for supplier S7 is completely unknown and might in fact be anything at all (any value of the pertinent type, that is). But sometimes information is only partly unknown. For example, we might know with "50 percent certainty"—i.e., we might be "50 percent sure"—that supplier S7 is in Athens. More generally, we might be "*X* percent sure" that supplier SNO is in city CITY. Well, that's a predicate: a predicate with three parameters, in fact, And here's a corresponding table, with three columns:

```
CREATE TABLE SCX
  ( SNO  CHAR(5)              ,
    CITY VARCHAR(25)          ,
    X    INTEGER              ,
    UNIQUE ( SNO , CITY ) ) ;
```

Incidentally, it's interesting to see that this design—note the key constraint UNIQUE {SNO,CITY}—would allow us to say, for example, that we're 50 percent sure that supplier S7 is in Athens *and* 50 percent sure that supplier S7 is in Madrid, thereby providing a mechanism for representing certain kinds of disjunctive information. It would also allow us to say, for example, that we're zero percent sure that supplier S2 is in Athens, thereby providing a mechanism for representing certain kinds of negative information as well ("We're completely unsure that supplier S2 is in Athens").[10] See the section immediately following for further discussion of such possibilities.

## NEGATION AND DISJUNCTION

In the previous chapter I emphasized the crucial role played by *The Closed World Assumption* in connection with missing information. However, I don't want to leave you with the impression that the CWA is a perfect cure for "missing information" ills; au contraire, it's well known that it can lead to difficulties over negative information and disjunctive information. Let's take a closer look.

### *Negation*

Consider the predicate *Supplier SNO isn't located in city CITY.* (For simplicity I'll ignore the part about the supplier being under contract; I'll also ignore the fact that the predicate ought more properly to begin with the qualifier *We know that.* What's more, I'll make similar simplifications throughout the remainder of this chapter, barring explicit statements to the contrary.) Let there be a table, NS, corresponding to this predicate, and let that table contain just one row for supplier S2, with city Athens. Then we can certainly conclude that supplier S2 isn't in Athens. But since there isn't a row in table NS for supplier S2 with city (let's say) Madrid, the CWA allows us—in fact, forces us—to conclude that *it's not the case that supplier S2 isn't in Madrid*, or in other words that supplier S2 *is* in Madrid. At the same time, the CWA also forces us to conclude that supplier S2 is in (say) London, and Berlin, and Rome, and ... (and so on).

Well, that can't be right, of course; so the obvious and highly unsatisfactory implication is that if there are *n* cities in total, table NS will have to contain $n - 1$ rows for each and every known supplier!—one for each and every city the supplier in question is *not* located in. (I'm assuming here, of course, as I've done throughout this chapter so far, that each supplier is supposed to be located in just

---

[10] Note carefully, however, that this proposition isn't equivalent to the proposition *We're completely sure that supplier S2 isn't in Athens.* Or is it? As I've had occasion to remark elsewhere, negation can be tricky ... Here are alternative formulations of the propositions in question that might (or might not!) help. The first is: *We definitely don't know that supplier S2 is in Athens.* The second is: *We don't definitely know that supplier S2 is in Athens.* And if this all reminds you of something we've seen before, then s it should; it's like the difference, discussed in Chapter 4, between the statements *I don't know if you have measles* and *I know you don't have measles.*

one city.) The sad, albeit well known, conclusion is that the relational model and the CWA in combination are simply not well suited to representing this particular kind of negative information. Though I do have to ask: How often in practice do we really want to represent such negative information, anyway?[11]

*Note:* An attendee at one of my live presentations suggested that the answer to the foregoing question is: Very frequently. For example, it might be very important to represent customers who haven't yet been contacted (in connection with the release of a new product, perhaps). But that's easy: We simply define a one-column table with predicate *Customer CUSTNO hasn't yet been contacted*, thereby (in a sense) replacing a negative by a positive.

### *Disjunction*

Consider the predicate

> *Supplier SNO is located in either city CITYA or city CITYB*

—which I'll take to mean, more precisely, that *We know supplier SNO is located in exactly one city, and we know that city is either CITYA or CITYB, but in general we don't know which.* Let there be a table, DS (with columns SNO, CITYA, and CITYB), corresponding to this predicate. Moreover, suppose for the sake of the example that we do know that supplier S3 is in either London or Paris, but we don't know which; suppose, therefore, that table DS contains a row for supplier S3 with CITYA and CITYB equal to London and Paris, respectively ("Supplier S3 is in either London or Paris").

So far, so good. However, now consider this question: Does table DS additionally need to contain a row for supplier S3 with CITYA and CITYB equal to Paris and London, respectively ("Supplier S3 is in either Paris or London")?

- If the answer is *no*, the CWA forces us to conclude that supplier S3 is *not* in either Paris or London, and so we have an obvious contradiction on our hands.

  *Note:* I'm deliberately ignoring here the fact that if table DS is supposed to satisfy the constraint that {SNO} is a key, then the answer to the question must be *no* (the table wouldn't be allowed to contain two distinct rows for the same supplier); I'm concerned with the predicate (i.e.,

---

[11] Represent it explicitly, I mean. The fact that a given supplier isn't located in a given city *is* represented (courtesy of the CWA), implicitly, by the usual suppliers table with its usual key and usual table predicate.

with what the table *means*), not with integrity constraints as such. Predicates take precedence over constraints.[12]

- So the answer must be *yes*. But now we have an obviously bad design, inasmuch as it permits—in fact, requires—some redundancy, just so long as there's at least one supplier with different values for CITYA and CITYB.

Now, we can fix the foregoing problem by tightening up the predicate as follows: *Supplier SNO is located in either city CITYA or city CITYB, and CITYA ≤ CITYB*, where "≤" refers (let's agree for the sake of the example) to alphabetic ordering. With this revised predicate, (a) table DS can't contain the additional row (the one with CITYA and CITYB equal to Paris and London, respectively), and (b) that omission can't be interpreted to mean that supplier S3 is in neither Paris nor London. But I'd be the first to admit that this fix is little more than a trick. What's more, it doesn't even solve all of the problems, anyway! E.g., consider the question: Can table DS additionally contain a row for supplier S3 with CITYA and CITYB equal to London and Madrid, respectively ("Supplier S3 is in either London or Madrid")?

- If the answer is *yes*, it means that supplier S3 must be in London (because that supplier is in exactly one of London and Paris and exactly one of London and Madrid), thereby contradicting our original assumption that we don't know which of London and Paris supplier S3 is located in.

- But if the answer is *no*, the CWA forces us to conclude that supplier S3 is *not* in exactly one of London and Madrid, and again we have a contradiction on our hands.

  *Note:* Again I'm ignoring the fact that if table DS is supposed to satisfy the constraint that {SNO} is a key, then the answer to the question must be *no*; again I'm concerned with the predicate, not with integrity constraints.

Here's another question: Can table DS additionally contain a row for supplier S3 with CITYA and CITYB both equal to London ("Supplier S3 is in either London or London")?

---

[12] What I mean by this remark is that, in principle, we can't even define the constraints for a given table—at least, not legitimately—until we know the predicate for that table.

- The answer can't be *yes*, because such a row would assert definitively that supplier S3 is in London, thereby contradicting our original assumption that supplier S3 is in either London or Paris, but we don't know which.

- But if the answer is *no*, the CWA forces us to conclude that supplier S3 is *not* in London, and again we have a contradiction on our hands.

  *Note:* Yet again I'm ignoring the fact that if table DS is supposed to satisfy the constraint that {SNO} is a key, then the answer to the question must be *no*.

I don't think there's an obvious simple fix to the original predicate that can overcome such problems. I suppose we might try something like:

> *Supplier SNO is located in either city CITYA or city CITYB, and either CITYA < CITYB or CITYA = CITYB (and in the latter case supplier SNO is definitely located in CITYA, or equivalently in CITYB).*

Well, I suppose that might work; but now I want to show that we can fix the various problems I've raised (and fix them more elegantly, in my opinion) by performing more drastic surgery, as it were, on our design.

Before I try to explain what I mean by this remark, let me extend the example to make it a little more general. The discussion so far is sufficient to illustrate the problem but is, of course, very unrealistic; it's not likely that we would know of every supplier that the supplier in question is in exactly one of just two possible cities. Instead, it's more likely—at least, let's agree as much for the sake of the example—that we would know of a given supplier that the supplier in question is in exactly one out of a set of *n* possible cities, where the value of *n* varies from one supplier to another. (In particular, $n = 1$ would correspond to a supplier whose city is definitely known.) For such a situation, a design with a relation valued attribute (RVA) is more appropriate.[13] Here's a sample value, showing that supplier S1 is in either London, Paris, or Athens and supplier S3 is in either London or Paris:

---

[13] Recall from Chapter 5 that RVAs are indeed legal.

```
SCM
┌─────┬──────────────┐
│ SNO │ CITIES       │
├═════┼──────────────┤
│ S1  │ ┌────────┐   │
│     │ │ CITY   │   │
│     │ ├════════┤   │
│     │ │ London │   │
│     │ │ Paris  │   │
│     │ │ Athens │   │
│     │ └────────┘   │
│ S3  │ ┌────────┐   │
│     │ │ CITY   │   │
│     │ ├════════┤   │
│     │ │ London │   │
│     │ │ Paris  │   │
│     │ └────────┘   │
└─────┴──────────────┘
```

Here for the record is a SQL definition (i.e., a CREATE TABLE statement) for such a table:

```
CREATE TABLE SCM
  ( SNO    CHAR(5)                                ,
    CITIES ROW ( CITY VARCHAR(25) ) MULTISET ,
    UNIQUE ( SNO ) )                              ;
```

Recall from Chapter 6 that a *multiset*, also known as a *bag*, is like a set except that it permits duplicates. The foregoing CREATE TABLE defines CITIES values as multisets whose elements are, specifically, rows, each such row containing in turn just a CITY value. *Note:* A separate constraint will be needed in order to ensure that no individual CITIES value contains any duplicate CITY values (exercise for the reader).

Now, we do need to be a little careful over the table predicate when relation valued attributes are involved. We can't just say in the example that the predicate is:

*Supplier SNO is located in exactly one of the cities in CITIES.*

(*Question*: Why not? *Answer*: Because of the CWA, of course, as a moment's reflection should be sufficient to show.) Rather, we have to say something like this:

*Supplier SNO is located in exactly one of the cities in CITIES and not in any city not in CITIES.*

Thus, for example, a relation identical to the one shown above except that the supplier number in the "S3" row is S1 instead of S3 couldn't be a possible value for table SCM as a whole, because it would lead to a contradiction—one row would say, in effect, that supplier S1 might be in Athens but the other would say that's not possible.[14]

Observe that the foregoing design does indeed get over the CWA problem with disjunction. What's more, suppose we change the example as follows: Suppose it's possible for a given supplier to be in *any number of* cities out of a specified set (for example, supplier S1 might in both London and Paris). Table SCM can handle this situation, too, so long as we change the predicate appropriately:

*Supplier SNO is located in at least one (possibly more than one) of the cities in CITIES and not in any city not in CITIES.*

In fact, this design could even handle suppliers who are in no cities at all, if we allow the CITIES value for such suppliers to be an empty table: negative information again, of a kind. (*Exercise:* Would the table predicate need any revision to cater for this possibility?)

I'll close this discussion with another question for you to ponder. Consider the following expression:

```
SCM UNGROUP CITIES
```

Given the sample value shown above for table SCM, this expression will produce the following "ungrouped" result:[15]

---

[14] You might object that the supplier number in the "S3" row couldn't possibly be S1 instead of S3, because {SNO} is a key—but such an argument would be to put the cart before the horse again (compare footnote 12).

[15] I omit a detailed definition of UNGROUP here, but the example should be sufficient to give a general idea of what such a definition might look like. For further details, see, e.g., my book *The **New** Relational Database Dictionary* (O'Reilly, 2016).

| SNO | CITY |
|---|---|
| S1 | London |
| S1 | Paris |
| S1 | Athens |
| S3 | London |
| S3 | Paris |

The question for you is this: Could we use this ungrouped table (instead of the previous version, with its relation valued attribute CITIES) to get around the CWA problems with disjunction? If not, why not? (*Hint:* What would the predicate for that table look like?)

## CLOSING REMARKS

Arguments like the ones I've been presenting, both in this chapter and in its predecessor, make me extremely skeptical of claims (mentioned in that previous chapter) to the effect that "the semantic web community operates under an open world assumption." In fact, I think such claims can make sense only if the "semantic web community" attaches some interpretation to the term "open world assumption" that's very different from the one I do. However, I'll have to leave an explanation of any such different interpretation to someone more knowledgeable than I am with respect to the semantic web (my own perhaps rather superficial search of the literature wasn't much help in this connection).

I also indicated in that previous chapter that, while we in the database community most certainly do rely on *The Closed World Assumption* (at least implicitly), we can be rather sloppy in specifying just what world it is that's closed. As I've tried to show, that world is typically not "the real world" as such but, rather, our knowledge of that real world. Thus, the nonappearance of a given row will typically mean we don't know the truth value of the corresponding proposition—that sounds more like the OWA!—*except* in the important special case when the proposition corresponding to the missing row actually contradicts the proposition corresponding to some row that does appear, in which case we do know the pertinent truth value: namely, FALSE.[16]

---

[16] I'm being sloppy again. What I mean here by "the proposition corresponding to a given row" isn't actually the proposition corresponding to that row, which is of the form "We know that *P* is true" for some proposition *P*. Rather, it's that proposition *P* as such; i.e., it's what's left when the "We know that" portion is removed.

There's one more point I want to make. The fact is, I've been making yet another tacit assumption (!) throughout both the present chapter and its predecessor: I've been assuming that either every table in the database is subject to the CWA or every table in the database is subject to the OWA. But is this assumption reasonable, or necessary? Apparently Codd didn't think so. In his 1979 paper—where he talks about closed and open world *interpretations*, however, rather than assumptions as such—he says this:

> Although the closed world interpretation is usually the one adopted for commercial databases, there is a case for permitting some [tables] ... to have the open world interpretation, while others ... have the closed world interpretation.

It seems to me, however, that allowing a mixture of interpretations in this way (i.e., in the same database) is likely to lead to serious difficulties in making sense of query results—especially if the query in question references both kinds of tables. Perhaps more study is required.

## Appendix A

# Default Values

Many years ago I proposed an approach to missing information based on the *systematic*—I stress that word—use of default values.[1] The present appendix contains a brief summary of that proposal. I make no great claims for it (which is why I relegate it to an appendix instead of including it in the body of this book), but at least I'd like to make the following points:

- First, although the scheme is certainly no panacea, at least it works in simple cases.

- Second, default values are what we use in the real world! For example, suppose we have a form to fill out (a census form, for example) and we can't answer some question on that form for some reason; then we typically respond with a blank—or a dash, or "N/A," or a question mark, or a variety of other possible entries. And each of these possible entries is, precisely, a special value that's agreed by convention to bear some special interpretation.[2] What we most certainly don't do is respond with a (3VL-style) null. *There's no such thing as a null in the real world.*

*Note:* My original "defaults" proposal dealt with just one kind of missing information ("value unknown"), but it could obviously be extended to deal with other kinds as well. If so, however, it would be desirable to replace keywords such as DEFAULT (see below) by some more explicit term such as UNKNOWN. Additional keywords such as INAPPLICABLE, UNDEFINED,

---

[1]In Chapter 21 ("The Default Values Approach to Missing Information") of the book *Relational Database Writings 1989-1991*, by Hugh Darwen and myself (Addison-Wesley, 1992).

[2] An exactly analogous remark applies to reports. In a system that supports nulls, there has to be a means of displaying those nulls in reports. And, of course, what the system does in such cases is precisely this: It displays the null in question as some "special value that's agreed by convention to bear a special interpretation."

PS: I note here that Codd's own RM/V2 book contains several pictures of "tables containing nulls." Do we see any nulls, as such, in those pictures? No, we don't. What we see are *special values*—typically dashes, but sometimes a double question mark, and the book mentions other possibilities in passing as well.

etc., could then be introduced to deal with other kinds of missing information. In this appendix, however, I stay for simplicity with the single DEFAULT of the original proposal.

- Associated with the declaration of each column of each base table is either a DEFAULT clause (specifying the default value—which must be of the appropriate type, of course—for that column), or else the specification NO DEFAULT (meaning the column in question doesn't have a default value). Here's an example (in outline), using an SQL-based syntax:

```
CREATE TABLE S /* suppliers */
     ( SNO    ... NO DEFAULT          ,
       SNAME  ... DEFAULT ( '' )      ,
       STATUS ... DEFAULT ( -1 )      ,
       CITY   ... DEFAULT ( '???' )  ,
       UNIQUE ( SNO ) )               ;
```

  If no default is specified explicitly for a given column (and NO DEFAULT isn't specified), then it might be possible for the system to assume a "default default" (e.g., blanks for a character string column).

- When a new row is inserted into a base table:

  a. A value must be provided for every column that has no default value.

  b. For other columns, the system will supply the applicable default value if the user doesn't provide a value.

- When a column is added to a base table:

  a. The new column must have a DEFAULT specification (i.e., NO DEFAULT can't be specified).

  b. The value of the new column is automatically set to the applicable default value in all existing rows in the table.

- The operator DEFAULT (*R.C*), where *R* is a range variable ranging over some table and *C* is a column of that table, returns the default value applicable to that column. It's an error if no such default value exists.

- When applying an aggregate operator such as AVG to a particular column, the user must explicitly exclude default values, if that's what's desired. For example:

```
SELECT AVG ( SP.QTY )
FROM   SP
WHERE  SP.QTY ≠ DEFAULT ( SP.QTY )
```

- The operator IS_DEFAULT (*R.C*) returns TRUE if its argument *R.C* evaluates to the applicable default value, FALSE otherwise. Thus, the foregoing SELECT could alternatively have been formulated as follows:

```
SELECT AVG ( SP.QTY )
FROM   SP
WHERE  NOT ( IS_DEFAULT ( SP.QTY ) )
```

- Aggregate operators such as AVG are extended to include an optional second argument, defining the value to be returned if the first argument is empty. It's an error if the first argument is empty and the second argument is omitted.

- For some columns it might be the case that every value of the pertinent type (domain) is a legitimate nondefault value. Such cases must be handled by explicit, separate, user controlled indicator columns (as with the host side of the interface in embedded SQL today)—though it would be desirable to be able to tell the system that those separate columns are indeed meant to be indicator columns, and to specify the indicator values declaratively so that the system understands them.

### *Discussion*

Advantages of the foregoing scheme, compared to the 3VL approach described in the body of this book, include the following:

- It's intuitively easier to explain and understand.

- It's also easier to implement.

- It directly reflects the way we handle missing information in the real world.

- There are fewer traps for the unwary.

- As already mentioned, it's extendable to other kinds of missing information without the need to resort to *n*-valued logic for any $n > 2$.

In the RM/V2 book, however, Codd argues strongly against such a scheme on the grounds that (a) it's unsystematic, (b) it misrepresents the semantics, and (c) it's a significant burden on DBAs and users, inasmuch as they have to choose and understand and manipulate the default values (possibly many different default values). My response to these arguments is as follows:

a. "*Unsystematic*": It seems to me that DBAs and users (and DBMSs, I might add) are always going to be able to use system facilities in an unsystematic manner, no matter how carefully defined those facilities might be. The default values approach isn't totally unsystematic. At least the default values are explicitly made known to the system, and appropriate operators are provided to avoid the need for hardcoding those values into programs; in fact, users shouldn't normally even have to know what the specific default values are. A systematic treatment of empty sets is also part of the proposal.

b. "*Misrepresenting semantics*": If default values "misrepresent the semantics," then the 3VL scheme does so too! At the very least, it certainly does so as soon as it becomes necessary to deal with two or more kinds of missing information (and I think it could be argued that it does so even when there's only one kind). To repeat a point from the body of the book: It's at least as dangerous, to my way of thinking, to represent, say, "not applicable" as "value unknown" as it is to represent, say, "value unknown" as "−1"—possibly more dangerous, in fact, because in the first case the user might be lulled into a false sense of security. Indeed, we can see exactly this kind of mistake in the design of the SQL language itself (in other words, system designers and implementers can make just the same kinds of mistakes as users). For example, the fact that SQL defines the MAX of an empty set to be null (meaning "value unknown") is just plain wrong, in my opinion.

c. "*Burden*": I agree that default values represent a significant burden on DBAs and users—but so too does three-valued logic, in my opinion (not to mention four- and five- ... and *n*-valued logic), as I think the discussions in the body of the book have clearly demonstrated. So which burden do you think is the greater?

To conclude, then: I freely admit that the default values scheme isn't a particularly elegant approach to the problem, but I certainly don't think 3VL is any better, and indeed I believe I've shown it's much worse.

## Appendix B

# Syntactic Containment in SQL

In Chapter 6, in the section "Integrity Constraints," I gave the following as a kind of rough and ready definition of what it meant for a WHERE clause to be "outermost" (because it's in the context of such an "outermost" WHERE clause that UNKNOWN gets coerced to FALSE, in SQL):

> Let *tx* be a SQL table expression, and let *tx* involve one or more WHERE clauses; let such a WHERE clause be called "outermost" if it's not nested within some other clause; and let *bx* be the boolean expression immediately following the keyword WHERE in an outermost WHERE clause within *tx*.

However, I did say too that the foregoing definition wasn't fully watertight. Here now for the record is SQL's own definition of the true state of affairs. The text that follows is taken verbatim from Section 6.3.3.1 ("Syntactic containment") of the document *Information technology – Database languages – SQL – Part 1: Framework (SQL/Framework)*, ISO/IEC JTC 1/SC 32 (July 26th, 2003). The division into paragraphs and line spacing in particular are exactly as in that reference.

——— ♦♦♦♦♦ ———

Let <A>, <B>, and <C> be syntactic elements; let *A1*, *B1*, and *C1* respectively be instances of <A>, <B>, and <C>.

In a Format, <A> is said to *immediately contain* <B> if <B> appears on the right-hand side of the BNF production rule for <A>. An <A> is said to *contain* or *specify* <C> if <A> immediately contains <C> or if <A> immediately contains a <B> that contains <C>.

In SQL language, *A1* is said to *immediately contain B1* if <A> immediately contains <B> and *B1* is part of the text of *A1*.

*A1* is said to *contain* or *specify C1* if *A1* immediately contains *C1* or if *A1* immediately contains *B1* and *B1* contains *C1*. If *A1* contains *C1*, then *C1* is *contained in A1* and *C1* is *specified by A1*. *A1* is said to contain *B1 with an intervening* <C> if *A1* contains *B1* and *A1* contains an instance of <C> that contains *B1*. *A1* is said to contain *B1 without an intervening* <C> if *A1* contains *B1* and *A1* does not contain an instance of <C> that contains *B1*.

*A1 simply contains B1* if *A1* contains *B1* without an intervening instance of <A> or an intervening instance of <B>.

*A1 directly contains B1* if *A1* contains *B1* without an intervening <subquery>, <multiset value constructor by query>, <table value constructor by query>, <array value constructor by query>, <within group specification>, or <set function specification> that is not an <ordered set function>.

If <A> contains <B>, then <B> is said to be *contained in* <A> and <A> is said to be a *containing* production symbol for <B>. If <A> simply contains <B>, then <B> is said to be *simply contained in* <A> and <A> is said to be a *simply containing* production symbol for <B>.

*A1* is the *innermost* <A> satisfying a condition *C* if *A1* satisfies *C* and *A1* does not contain an instance of <A> that satisfies *C*. *A1* is the *outermost* <A> satisfying a condition *C* if *A1* satisfies *C* and *A1* is not contained in an instance of <A> that satisfies *C*.

If <A> contains a <table name> that identifies a view that is defined by a <view definition> *V*, then <A> is said to *generally contain* the <query expression> contained in *V*. If <A> contains a <query name> that identifies a <query expression> *QE*, then <A> is said to *generally contain QE*. If <A> contains a <routine invocation> *RI*, then <A> is said to *generally contain* the routine bodies of all <SQL-invoked routine>s in the set of subject routines of *RI*. If <A> contains <B>, then <A> generally contains <B>. If <A> generally contains <B> and <B> generally contains <C>, then <A> generally contains <C>.

NOTE 5 — The "set of subject routines of a <routine invocation> " is defined in Subclause 10.4, "<routine invocation>", in ISO/IEC 9075-2.

In a Format, the verb "to be" (including all its grammatical variants, such as "is") is defined as follows: <A> is said to *be* <B> if there exists a BNF production rule of the form `<A> ::= <B>` . If <A> is <B> and <B> is <C>, then <A> is <C>. If <A> is <C>, then <C> is said to *constitute* <A>. In SQL language, *A1* is said to *be B1* if <A> is <B> and the text of *A1* is the text of *B1*. Conversely, *B1* is said to *constitute A1* if *A1* is *B1*.

## Appendix C

# Much Ado about Nothing

Throughout this book I've been very critical of Codd's ideas for handling missing information, and so it's only fair to give him the right to reply—some chance to defend his ideas, I mean. That's why I wanted to include this appendix. It consists essentially of the text of a debate on the subject between the two of us, a debate in which Codd's primary concern wasn't so much to explain what his approach was—other publications of his do that—as it was to defend that approach from my criticisms.

First let me explain the historical background. In December 1992 and January 1993 I published a pair of articles with the titles "Why Three-Valued Logic Is a Mistake" and "Nothing in Excess," respectively. The articles in question were consecutive installments in the regular series I was doing at the time for the magazine *Database Programming & Design* ("*DBP&D*" for short), and what they did was briefly review a few of the things that I felt at the time were wrong with the idea of using nulls and three-valued logic (3VL) as a basis for handling missing information. Among the letters I received after the articles appeared was one from Codd, who unsurprisingly didn't agree with my criticisms at all. His letter, together with my response to it, grew into a somewhat lengthy debate that subsequently appeared as an article in its own right in a later issue of *DBP&D*. Of course, it goes without saying that the debate didn't lead to any kind of resolution or agreement between us; however, I still think it's useful, inasmuch as it does at least air many of the arguments on both sides of the issue. So what follows is an updated version of that original debate.

*Publishing history:* This is an edited version of, and supersedes, the debate as it first appeared in *Database Programming & Design 6*, No. 10 (October 1993). That original version was later republished as Chapter 9 of my book *Relational Database Writings 1991-1994* (Addison-Wesley, 1995), and then again, with revisions, as Chapter 1 of my book *Database Dreaming Volume II* (Technics, 2022). The present version has been revised again in various minor ways.

## THE *DBP&D* INTRODUCTION

*This section sets the scene. It consists of a lightly edited version of the introduction by DBP&D's own editor, David Stodder, to the debate as originally published.*

A point / counterpoint on the tough issue of missing values ... E. F. Codd and C. J. Date are two of the best known figures in the history, development, and exposition of what was a breakthrough concept in database technology: the relational model. Ever since the model was first defined by Codd in 1970, in his famous paper "A Relational Model of Data for Large Shared Data Banks,"[1] we've been reading, listening to, and interpreting their commentaries on it. While Codd and Date have agreed upon much during the course of the relational model's evolution and implementation, on some issues they definitely don't agree. One important disagreement—and the topic of this special article—centers on the issue of nulls and missing values, and the underlying theoretical problems of three- and four-valued logic.

Both have written extensively on these topics, as is clear from the "References" section in what follows.[2] The [criticisms] presented here were sparked by Date's columns in *DBP&D* last December and January, when he discussed the three-valued logic approach to missing information. Codd then sent us his criticisms of Date's columns; [those criticisms] are presented here. Date then provided a series of rebuttals to specific points of Codd's, which follow Codd's remarks. Finally, we gave Codd a chance to rebut Date's rebuttal.

For the reader's convenience, we've kept Codd's [criticisms] together, so they can be read as a whole. We've noted throughout, however, where Date's specific rebuttals apply, and should be read. This way, the reader can follow Codd's [criticisms] all the way through, and then return to his essay, reading Date's rebuttals as appropriate.

---

[1] Actually Codd first described his model in 1969, not 1970, in an IBM Research Report with the title "Derivability, Redundancy, and Consistency of Relations Stored in Large Data Banks" (IBM Research Report RJ599, August 19th, 1969). The much better known 1970 paper consisted essentially of a somewhat revised version of that 1969 paper. *Note:* That original 1969 version was quite hard to find until it was eventually republished in *ACM SIGMOD Record 38*, No. 1 (May 2009).

[2] I've dropped that section from the present appendix. Instead, I've expanded the relevant references inline, as it were, as part of the main text.

At first, the issues might seem arcane and theoretical, but most developers and DBAs know they're clearly not, and merit serious debate. Missing values remain one of the toughest—and potentially most dangerous—problems in database technology.

## CODD'S COMMENTS

Although Date has been a strong supporter of the relational approach to database management for over 20 years,[3] from time to time I have found that his criticisms of the relational model have been incorrect. I do agree with many of his criticisms of SQL; however, he often fails to make a clear distinction between SQL and the relational model. SQL came after the relational model was described; it was invented by a small IBM group in the Yorktown Heights (N.Y.) Research Laboratory. In my book, *The Relational Model for Database Management Version 2*, I make it clear what semantic properties a relational language should have if it is to conform to the model, and label such a language *RL*. I also describe three major shortcomings of SQL (there are, of course, numerous others):

- As a user option, SQL permits rows to occur within a single relation that are complete duplicates of each other. I call this a *tabular error* because it is based on two misconceptions:

    1. That relations and tables are in one to one correspondence, and

    2. That duplicate rows are essential to some applications.

- Full support of first order predicate logic is sacrificed in the name of user friendliness. I call this a *pyschological mixup*: A logically sound language is absolutely necessary as a foundation. Any useful "user friendly" features should be grafted as a layer on top, along with rigorously defined translation between layers.

- The treatment of missing information is wrong for two reasons:

---

[3] That was in 1993. Now (2024) it's well over 50 years.

1. Support in the language for multivalued logic is grossly inadequate, and

2. A user is permitted to designate a value that is acceptable to a column specifically to indicate the fact that some value is missing from that column. I call this latter error one of *missing value misrepresentation.*

Date has criticized the multivalued logic approach to missing values in the relational model, claiming it can lead to catastrophic errors. He has advocated the missing value misrepresentation approach, which he calls the *default value* approach. In 1986, when Date had his original paper reprinted in the U.S., I prepared a technical response.[4]

The ideas behind Date's default value approach came completely from prerelational products that used single record at a time processing. The default value approach appealed to RDBMS vendors because it placed all of the responsibility for the representation and handling of missing values in a relational database completely on the users. However, I think it is best described as a nonsolution to the problem, and a complete evasion of the issue. The approach contains no clear description of how missing values in a column are to be treated. That means that the treatment will often be invented by application programmers and buried in their programs. It also means that there are likely to be many different treatments buried in numerous programs.

Now that we are dealing with RDBMSs that employ multiple record at a time processing, this default value approach is unacceptable for the following reasons:

1. The *meaning* of the fact that a value is missing from some part or column of a relational database is quite different from the meaning of a value that is legitimate within that part or column.

---

[4] The chronology isn't quite as Codd describes it here. It's true that I published a paper called "Null Values [*sic*] in Database Management"—an invited paper, incidentally—in the proceedings of a U.K. conference in 1982; it's also true that in that paper I criticized nulls and sketched what I called a "less ambitious" alternative approach, based on default values; and finally it's also true that I republished that paper in my book *Relational Database: Selected Writings* (Addison-Wesley) in 1986. But the paper in question was just an expanded version of an IBM Technical Report on the subject ("The Problem of Null Values [*again sic*]," Technical Report TR 03.168) that I originally published in October 1981, something that I'd shown to Codd *and discussed with him, at length, in his office at IBM, prior to publication.* So he shouldn't be claiming as he seems to be doing here that he didn't became aware of that paper until 1986.

2. A single relational request can touch many different columns in a relational database, and therefore it is intolerable that in conceiving such a request the user should have to understand and cope with as many different representations and treatments of missing values as the columns that are touched. In a relational database, both the representation and treatment of missing values *must* be uniform across the entire database.

**See Date's Rebuttal I**

Date and other critics of multivalued logic claim that serious errors are inevitable if a multivalued logic is made available to users. However, such critics have failed to provide a single example of a *severely wrong* answer being delivered as a result of a multivalued logic. A result is severely incorrect if the logical expression is evaluated by the DBMS to be

- *True* when it is actually *false* or *unknown*, or
- *False* when it is actually *true* or *unknown*.

A result is *mildly incorrect* if the DBMS evaluates an expression as *unknown* when it is actually either *true* or *false*. In [my 1979 paper] ... I cited an example of a request *mildly mishandled* by 3VL: For some requests the condition would be evaluated as *unknown* when the correct answer was *true* or *false*, if the DBMS were unable to recognize tautologies. This example shows that simple 3VL should be augmented by some inferential capability. An example would be the following: Suppose that the birth year is recorded for most employees, but is missing from the database for a few. Now, consider the request: Retrieve the serial numbers and names of employees for each of whom

1. The birth year is 1960, or
2. The birth year is earlier than 1960, or
3. The birth year is later than 1960.

Suppose the DBMS does NOT have the capability of recognizing that the whole condition must be *true* for every employee, whether the birth year happens to be missing or not. That is, it is unable to detect tautologies or contradictions.[5] Then for those employees whose birth year is unknown, the DBMS comes up with *unknown* for each of the three subconditions. And, using the rule that for truth values *unknown* OR *unknown* is *unknown*, it evaluates the whole condition to be *unknown*. This is an example of a mild error. This kind of error is just as likely to occur (and other kinds much more likely) if the responsibility for handling missing information is placed totally on the users.

*See Date's Rebuttal II*

Now, an obvious cure for [this kind of mild error] is to equip the DBMS not only with 3VL, but also with the capability of recognizing for any whole condition whether it is a tautology. This would be easy if only propositional logic were being supported. However, the relational model requires the more powerful predicate logic to be supported in specifying the condition part of a request. It is well known that it is a logically undecidable problem to determine whether an arbitrary formula in predicate logic is a tautology or a contradiction.

Therefore, it is pointless to search for an allegedly universal algorithm for detecting all possible tautologies and all possible contradictions. A reasonably good algorithm can be developed that will take care of at least all of the simple cases that will be encountered in commercial activities, and this algorithm should be incorporated into every RDBMS product. The RDBMS will then make mild errors only when a most unusual request is made. An RDBMS must admit its inability to deduce a sound response to a user request whenever this is impossible because of missing values. Also, present treatment by SQL of missing values is, in my opinion, totally unsatisfactory. For a more complete treatment of missing values and a refutation of Date's criticisms, refer to my RM/V2 book.

*See Date's Rebuttal III*

Date's argument that *true* and *false* are the only truth values, and that, therefore, *unknown* cannot be treated as a logical value makes no sense to me. After all, it

---

[5] I think there's a muddle here. The expression in question is a tautology in 2VL *but not in 3VL*—and the system in question is supposed to be operating under 3VL. So the problem isn't that the system can't detect tautologies; rather, it's that what constitutes a tautology in the system and what does so in the real world are two different things. 3VL doesn't match reality.

is very common in mathematics to label unknown values by letters such as *m*, *n*, *x*, *y*, *z*. The fact that the letters *m*, *n* do not "look like" any of the integers does not prevent them from actually having integer values in an expression such as $m + n$, $m - n$, or an assertion that $m \times m = n$. In any event, when dealing with missing values, an RDBMS must be able to determine whether [each of] NOT A, A OR B, and A AND B is *true*, *false*, or *unknown* when A, or B, or both are *unknown*.

Date's argument that the number of distinct functions from truth values to truth values is very large, and that fact makes 3VL and four-valued logic (4VL) unusable is ridiculous. After all, the number of distinct functions from integers to integers is infinite, because the number of distinct integers is infinite. However, no one in his right mind would use that as an argument that integers are unusable.

Taking the whole of Date's article into consideration, I completely reject Date's claims:[6]

- To have inserted "more nails into the 3VL coffin";
- That it is time to drop the pretense that 3VL is a good thing.

See Date's Rebuttal IV

## DATE'S REBUTTAL I

Let me begin by making one thing crystal clear: My quarrel isn't with the relational model. On the contrary, I felt at the time when it was first introduced, and I still feel now, that the original model was a work of genius. All of us owe Dr Codd a huge debt of gratitude for his major contribution. And, as the originator and "elder statesman" of relational theory, Codd always deserves the courtesy of very close attention to his remarks on relational matters.

Actually there's something else I'd like to make "crystal clear" as well. In his remarks, Codd accuses me of "often failing to make a clear distinction

---

[6] These "claims"—characterized as such by Codd, not me—are paraphrased versions of remarks I made in my article "Nothing in Excess" (*DBP&D 6*, No. 1, January 1993); republished in my book *Relational Database Writings 1991-1994* (Addison-Wesley, 1995).

between SQL and the relational model." I utterly deny this charge![7] In fact I'm rather amazed that anyone, let alone Codd himself, would even consider making it, given my well known and well documented criticisms of SQL as such—especially since those criticisms are directed in very large part at, specifically, SQL's failure to serve as a good realization in concrete terms of the abstract concepts of the relational model. What's more, many of those documented criticisms appeared in the public domain well before 1993, the date of this debate. Some of them were even published under the auspices of our own consulting company!—the company, that is (viz., Codd & Date International), of which Codd and I were principals and founding members.

So, to say it again, my quarrel isn't with the relational model, but rather with nulls and three-valued logic (3VL), which were first discussed by Codd in detail, at least in the database context, in his 1979 paper.[8] It's true that Codd now regards 3VL as an integral part of the relational model, but I don't (and I'm not alone in taking this position). Indeed, the whole question of how to handle missing information is largely independent of whether the underlying model is relational or something else. Thus, I'd like to distinguish very carefully between what we might call "RM" (the original model, with two-valued logic) and "RM+3VL" (Codd's version, with three-valued logic). My quarrel, to repeat, is with the "3VL" portion of "RM+3VL."

Now, regarding Codd's first point (viz., that default values misrepresent the fact that information is missing): I don't dispute this! However, I'd like to make two points:

1. It's default values, not nulls, that we use in the real world, as I've pointed out on many occasions.

2. Nulls misrepresent the semantics too (see below). The fact is, I don't think we yet know how *not* to misrepresent the semantics; and given that this is so, I take the position that we shouldn't undermine the solid foundation of the relational model with something as suspect as 3VL, when it

---

[7] Especially since, with respect to the present debate specifically, I went out of my way in the first of the two *DBP&D* articles that triggered that debate—viz., "Why Three-Valued Logic Is a Mistake," *DBP&D 5*, No. 12 (December 1992), republished in my book *Relational Database Writings 1991-1994* (Addison-Wesley, 1995)—to say this: "Let me make it quite clear that my argument here is not so much with SQL per se; rather, it's with the underlying theory, namely 3VL, on which SQL is based."

[8] A slight chronological oversimplification. See Chapter 2, footnote 1.

demonstrably doesn't solve the problem anyway. In other words, I would advocate adherence to *The Principle of Cautious Design*.[9]

*Note:* When I talk about "undermining the foundations of the relational model," what I mean is that a "relation" that contains nulls, whatever else it might be, *isn't a relation.* As a consequence, the entire foundation crumbles; we can't be sure any longer of *any* aspect of the underlying theory, and all bets are off. I find it hard to believe that Codd really wants to destroy the entire edifice that he has so painstakingly constructed over the years.

Let me elaborate briefly on the foregoing paragraph. I said that a "relation" that contains a null isn't a relation, and that's true. In fact, a "type" (or "domain") that contains a null isn't a type, and a "tuple" that contains a null isn't a tuple, either. The point is, types and tuples and relations all (by definition) contain *values*, and the one thing that everyone agrees on—well, Codd and I agree on, at any rate—in connection with this topic is that nulls, whatever else they might be, certainly aren't values.[10] Thus, I repeat: If nulls are involved, then all bets are off.

As for nulls also misrepresenting the semantics, consider the following two points:

- A (Codd-style) 3VL system supports just one kind of null, viz., "value unknown." Thus, there's a strong likelihood that users will use that null for purposes for which it's not appropriate. For example, suppose employee Joe isn't a salesperson and so doesn't qualify for a commission. Then Joe's commission is quite likely to be misrepresented as "value unknown" (it should of course be "value doesn't apply"). One simple consequence of this misrepresentation error is that Joe's total compensation (salary plus commission) will incorrectly be considered to be "unknown" instead of just the salary value.

  What's more, an analogous argument will continue to apply so long as the system supports fewer kinds of nulls than are logically necessary. In other words, simply adding support for a "value doesn't apply" null might solve the specific problem mentioned in the previous paragraph, but it

---

[9] That principle can be stated as follows: Given a design choice between options *A* and *B*, where *A* is upward compatible with *B* and the full consequences of going with *B* aren't yet known, the cautious (and, I'd very much like to add, sensible) decision is to go with *A*.

[10] I say this despite the frequesnt appearance of the phrase "null values" in various early writings of my own. I do now regret my use of such a phrase.

doesn't solve the general problem. Thus, a system that supports fewer types of null than are logically necessary is just as open to misuse—perhaps even more so—than a system that doesn't support nulls at all.

- Now suppose the system supports two kinds of nulls, "value unknown" and "value doesn't apply" and *four*-valued logic (4VL)—which Codd in fact advocates—and suppose employee Joe's job is unknown. What then do we do about Joe's commission? It surely must be null—the information is surely missing—but we don't know whether that null should be "value unknown" or "value doesn't apply." Perhaps we need another kind of null, and *five*-valued logic (the new null meaning we don't know which of the first two is appropriate) ... This argument clearly goes on for ever, leading to an apparent requirement for *an infinite number of kinds of nulls*. What do we conclude from this state of affairs?

Next, regarding Codd's allegation that the default values approach lacks a "clear description of how [such] values are to be treated": Well, I've published several such descriptions over the years, the first in 1982, a more extensive one in 1992, and others since then (see, e.g., the present book's Appendix A).

Of course, Codd is quite right to warn of the dangers of *undisciplined* use of default values. That's why I've consistently advocated a *disciplined* approach. One aspect of the discipline I have in mind is that users never need to know what the default values actually are—instead, they can refer to the default value that applies to some specific column *C* by means of an operator invocation of the form DEFAULT (*C*). Thus, I reject Codd's argument that "the user [will] have to understand and cope with as many different representations and treatments of missing values as the columns that are touched" (i.e., in some given relational expression).

By the way, a system that supports nulls can still be used in an undisciplined way, as I've already shown. In fact, an argument can be made that such a system is *more* susceptible to lack of discipline, partly (a) because of the false sense of security provided by the fact that nulls are supported ("Missing information? Don't worry about it—the system can handle it"), and partly (b) because

1. The system designers assume that users are going to use nulls, and so

2. They typically don't provide explicit support for defaults, and so

3. Users who have made the (in my opinion, very sensible) decision to avoid nulls are on their own—the system doesn't help; in fact, it positively hinders.

Finally, I categorically reject Codd's allegation that the default values idea comes from prerelational systems. On the contrary, it comes from the real world, as I've already said. Indeed, let me point out that examples *in Codd's own book* all use values (e.g., dashes, question marks), not nulls as such, to represent missing information! *Question*: In the real world, when we fill out an application form or something of that nature, what do we do if some piece of information is missing? *Answer:* We leave the position blank, or we put a dash, or a question mark, or N/A, or something along those lines—and those blanks and dashes and the rest are all very definitely values. What we don't do is put a null (or "mark") in that position. There's no such thing as a null in the real world. So all the default values scheme does is this: It makes the database system behave the same way the real world behaves. That's all.

I also reject Codd's allegation that the default values scheme has anything to do with "record at a time" thinking. How we deal with missing information has nothing to do with whether the operators are record or set at a time. And on behalf of the DBMS vendors, I reject the allegation that default values appealed to them "because it placed all of the responsibility on the users." Might it not have been that the vendors had their own misgivings concerning 3VL? In any case, I know of no vendor that actually supported a proper default values scheme prior to supporting 3VL. Moreover, a proper default values scheme does *not* "place all of the responsibility on the users." To contend otherwise is to misrepresent the semantics of the default values scheme.[11]

---

[11] Mind you, I don't want to "come on too strong" regarding default values. That is, I don't mean to suggest that default values are the perfect solution to the missing information problem, because they're most certainly and obviously not. I just think that (a) in some cases, possibly only rather simple cases, they can be made to work, and (b) in all cases, they're better than nulls. I do think we need to do everything we can to avoid nulls and 3VL—and the great thing about defaults is that they do keep us firmly in the realm of 2VL. At the same time, I think there are other approaches to the missing information problem than can and sometimes, prhaps often, should be used that are better than defaults. See Chapter 8 of the present book for one specific proposal in this regard, as well as several related suggestions.

## DATE'S REBUTTAL II

First, a small point regarding Codd's claim that a certain "mild error" (as he calls it) "is just as likely to occur (and other kinds [are] much more likely)" in a default values scheme: It seems to me that there's all the difference in the world between

a. On the one hand, building a system—i.e., one based on 3VL—in which we *know* errors will occur, because the system has logical flaws in it, and

b. On the other hand, building a system that's at least logically correct but is open to misuse. *Any* system is open to misuse. That's why we have to have discipline.

Second, and more important: Contrary to Codd's claim that I've "failed to provide a single example of a severely wrong answer," I gave such an example in 1989[12]—i.e., several years before we engaged in the present debate— and repeated it in 1992,[13] and I repeat it again now. We're given a database as shown below (the question marks represent a "value unknown" null):

DEPT

| DNO |
|---|
| D2 |

EMP

| ENO | DNO |
|---|---|
| E1 | ??? |

Now consider the following SQL expression:

```
SELECT ENO
FROM   DEPT , EMP
WHERE  NOT ( DEPT.DNO = EMP.DNO AND EMP.DNO = 'D1' )
```

Let's focus for a moment on the expression ("*exp1*") in parentheses:

```
DEPT.DNO = EMP.DNO AND EMP.DNO = 'D1'
```

---

[12] In my paper "Three-Valued Logic and the Real World" (*InfoDB 4*, No. 4, Winter 1989), republished in my book *Relational Database Writings 1989-1991* (Addison-Wesley, 1990).

[13] In my paper "Why Three-Valued Logic Is a Mistake" (*DBP&D 5*, No. 12, December 1992), republished in my book *Relational Database Writings 1991-1994* (Addison-Wesley, 1995).

For the only data we have in the database, this expression becomes *unknown* AND *unknown* and thus evaluates to *unknown* overall. It follows that the original SELECT – FROM – WHERE expression returns an empty result, and thus in particular a result that doesn't contain the employee number E1. *But observe now that since employee E1 does have* **some** *(unknown) department, the question marks stand for some real value, say d.* Now, either *d* is D1 or it isn't:

- If it is, then expression *exp1* evaluates to *false,* because the term DEPT.DNO = EMP.DNO evaluates to *false*.

- Alternatively, if it isn't, then expression *exp1* again evaluates to *false*, because the term EMP.DNO = 'D1' evaluates to *false*.

In other words, expression *exp1* is always *false* in the real world, *regardless of what real value the question marks stand for*. Hence NOT (*exp1*) is *true* in the real world, and the right answer to the query in the real world should contain E1 (only).

What do we learn from this example? Well, the basic point is that the expression in the WHERE clause is "actually *unknown*" (Codd's phraseology) but is treated as *false*, with the result that—as we've seen—employee number E1 isn't returned but should be. That's a severe error by Codd's definition.

Another way to put it is: The answers that 3VL says are correct aren't always the answers that are correct in the real world. In other words, 3VL doesn't behave in accordance with the way the real world behaves; that is, it doesn't have a sensible *interpretation*.

Please note too that the error the example demonstrates isn't just an SQL error—it's intrinsic to the 3VL scheme. In fact, on page 183 of Codd's own book we find the following (slightly paraphrased here):

> Executing a query delivers only those cases in which the condition part evaluates to *true*.

But this is tantamount to treating *unknown* as *false*—which is, again, a severe error by Codd's own definition.

In case you're still not convinced, let me give another example. Consider the database shown below and the query "Does anyone in department D1 earn a salary of 100K?" This query will involve a test to see whether the literal row (D1,100K) appears in the projection of EMP on DNO and SAL. In forming that projection, however, the row (D1,???) will be thrown out as a duplicate ([*sic!*]—see Codd's book, pages 189-190).[14] Result: The 3VL answer to the query is *false*; the real world answer, by contrast, is *unknown*. This is surely also a severe error by Codd's definition.

EMP

| ENO | DNO | SAL |
|---|---|---|
| E1 | D1 | 50K |
| E2 | D1 | ??? |

Third and last (and much more important still): The whole business of "severe" vs. "mild" errors in any case is surely nonsense. It seems to me that it's nothing more than a rearguard attempt to shore up an already suspect position. After all, if we were talking about integers instead of truth values, what would we think of a system that occasionally produced the answer 2 when the correct answer was 1 or 3? And in what sense could this be any more acceptable than one that occasionally produced 1 or 3 when the correct answer was 2?

Suppose the DBMS says it *doesn't know* whether Country X is developing a nuclear weapon, whereas in fact Country X is *not* doing so; and suppose Country Y therefore decides to bomb Country X "back to the Stone Age," just in case. The error here can hardly be said to be mild. *Note:* This example is certainly not to my taste; I choose it deliberately for its shock value.

## DATE'S REBUTTAL III

Here I'd just like to ask a few questions.

1. What evidence is there that "a reasonably good algorithm can be developed"?

2. Is there a precise definition of the "simple cases" that such an algorithm will handle?

---

[14] Actually, a literal reading of the text on those pages would allow the row (D1,50K) to be thrown out instead. I'll leave you to think about that.

3. If there is, is that definition intuitively understandable? In other words, will the user be able to predict with any confidence whether or not the DBMS is going to give the right answer to a given query?

4. If the answer to the previous question is no, then why would anyone ever use the system for any purpose at all?

5. In fact, Codd is requiring the DBMS itself to "admit its inability to deduce a sound response to a user request" whenever applicable. In other words, he's asking for a *decision procedure*—a procedure, that is, regarding the decidability of formulas in three-valued logic. What evidence is there that such a procedure exists?

6. What fraction of real world queries that are "encountered in commercial activities" are "simple" in the foregoing sense?

7. What evidence exists to support the answer to the previous question?

8. If we're limited to using such "simple" queries only, exactly what incremental value is the "RM+3VL" system providing over a prerelational, record at a time system?

9. What exactly does "commercial activities" include?

I think it's time to quote Wittgenstein again: *All logical differences are big differences*. (To my regret, I don't know the source of this quote. I'd be grateful to any reader who could help.)[15]

Turning now to Codd's discussion of missing values in his book, and refutation of my views therein: Codd claims that his book "refutes my criticisms in detail." I don't think it does. The two major criticisms dealt with in his book are (1) "the alleged counterintuitive nature" (i.e., of nulls and 3VL) and (2) "the alleged breakdown of normalization."

---

[15] I'm delighted to be able to report that after I first raised this question, a reader did come through with the answer. The source is P. T. Geach, "History of the Corruptions of Logic," in his book *Logic Matters* (Basil Blackwell, 1972). The complete quote is: "As I once heard Wittgenstein say, all logical differences are big differences; in logic we are not making *subtle* distinctions, as it were between flavours that pass over into one another by delicate gradations."

- Regarding (1), Codd doesn't actually address the counterintuitive nature of 3VL at all, but simply claims that default values are counterintuitive too.[16] In doing so, incidentally, he confuses the semantics of the two very different expressions "not known" and "known not"—a trap that's all too easy to fall into, of course (indeed, this confusion is precisely one of the reasons why I claim that 3VL is counterintuitive).[17] I stand by my contention that 3VL is difficult to deal with on an intuitive level.

- Regarding (2), I originally claimed that "the fundamental theorem of normalization" breaks down in the presence of nulls, and so it does.[18] Codd's counterargument is unconvincing. Here for the record is that counterargument in its entirety (RM/V2 book, pages 200-201):

> It should be clear that because nulls—or, as they are now called, marks—are *not* ... values, the rules of [normalization] do not apply to them. Instead, they apply to all unmarked ... values.

In any case, I have several further (and serious) criticisms of 3VL that Codd's book doesn't address at all. They include (and this isn't an exhaustive list):

- The fact that we apparently need an infinite number of kinds of nulls

- The semantic overloading or "misrepresentation" that occurs if some kinds of nulls aren't supported (which is bound to be the case, given the previous point, and quite obviously is the case in SQL)

---

[16] I'm not sure how valid this claim can be, given that (as I've already said) default values are what we use to represent missing information in the real world. However, I'm prepared to let the point go for the sake of the discussion.

[17] Recall the example in Chapter 4 of a 3VL expression that Codd and I and Nat Goodman all misinterpreted. I claimed in that chapter that our misinterpretation arose from a confusion between "not" and NOT, and so it did. But that confusion in turn led to a further confusion between "not known" and "NOT known," and hence to a confusion between "not known" and "known not." Once the confusions start, who knows where they're going to stop.

[18] The theorem in question is Heath's Theorem, which can be stated thus: Let relation $r$ have heading $H$ and let $X$, $Y$, and $Z$ be such that their union is equal to $H$ (so $X$, $Y$, and $Z$ are all subsets of $H$); let $XY$ denote the union of $X$ and $Y$, and similarly for $XZ$; if $r$ satisfies the FD $X \rightarrow Y$, then $r$ is equal to the join of its projections on $XY$ and $XZ$. This theorem breaks down if $X$ can be null.

- The lack of any convincing justification for the difference in treatment between (a) equality of nulls in comparisons and (b) equality of nulls in duplicate elimination

- The fact that the (admittedly informal) argument in support of the entity integrity rule ("primary keys in base relations don't permit nulls") quite obviously extends to *every column in the database*—implying that nulls should be inadmissible *everywhere*

- If TABLE_DUM corresponds to *false* and TABLE_DEE corresponds to *true*—see Chapter 5 in the body of the book—then what corresponds to *unknown*?

## DATE'S REBUTTAL IV

Regarding my argument that there are only two truth values: Codd's counterargument here makes no sense to me. Is he suggesting that *unknown* isn't a truth value after all, but just a variable whose actual value at any given time is either *true* or *false*? So we aren't really dealing with 3VL after all?

The only way I might make sense of Codd's position here is to interpret his remarks as actually *agreeing* with what I originally said in this connection, which I'm sure wasn't what he intended. Here in essence is what I said originally (i.e., in the paper mentioned in footnote 6, but you'll immediately recognize this text as a minor paraphrase of remarks elsewhere in the present book):

> How many truth values are there? The answer, of course, is two: namely, *true* and *false*. Now, we might *say* that *unknown* is a third truth value, but that doesn't make it one. After all, I might *say* that &%$*@#!? is another integer, but that doesn't make it one; it has absolutely no effect on the set of all integers. Likewise, the set of all truth values just *is* the set {*true*, *false*}, and there's nothing more to be said.
>
> If we're given some proposition, say the proposition "Employee E1 works in department D1," then that proposition is either *true* or *false*. Of course, I might not know which it is, but it *is* one of the two (if it isn't, it isn't a proposition). Let's assume that I don't know which it is. Then I certainly might say, informally, that the truth value of the proposition is unknown to me; but that "unknown" is a very different kind of object from the truth values *true* and *false* themselves. And pretending that it's the same kind of object—in other words, pretending that we

> have three truth values—is bound to lead to problems of interpretation, and so indeed it does.

Of course, I understand that we're free to define a purely *formal* system in which there are as many "truth values" as we like. But that possibility doesn't alter the fact that, in the real world, the values *true* and *false* (on the one hand) and *unknown* (on the other) are totally different kinds of things. To spell the point out: *True* and *false* refer to actual states of affairs in the real world; *unknown* refers to someone's knowledge (or some DBMS's knowledge) of those states of affairs. They have to do with two different realms. Confusing those realms is what causes the muddle.

Finally, regarding my argument concerning truth valued functions (actually I prefer the term *operators* in this context): Here Codd both misrepresents my position and misses the point. My argument wasn't that because there were so many operators, we shouldn't support 3VL; rather, it was that if we want to support 3VL, we should be sure that we support all possible 3VL operators. Now, in the case of integers, it's true that the total number of operators is infinite—but it's also true that any such operator is expressible in terms of a small number of primitives, so all we have to do is support those primitives properly. Likewise, in two-valued logic (2VL), we know that all 2VL operators can be expressed in terms of a small (*very* small!) number of primitives, and so again all we have to do is support those primitives properly.

For 3VL, therefore, I was asking, first, for a suitable set of primitives that would guarantee that all 19,710 monadic and dyadic operators were supported. (Indeed, if any of them aren't supported, then it can't reasonably be claimed that the system we're dealing with is 3VL.) Second, I was also asking for a suitable set of *useful* operators (not necessarily the same thing as primitive operators). I was also asking for a proof of completeness. I was also raising questions of testing, debugging, and usability. And then I was asking the analogous questions all over again for 4VL, where there are over *four billion* such operators. I believe these to be serious questions, questions that I've never seen 3VL and 4VL advocates even raise, let alone answer—and yet I believe those advocates are morally obliged to address them.

Taking the whole of Codd's comments into consideration, I stand more firmly than ever by my original position.

## REBUTTING THE REBUTTALS

*Editor's comment: To close out this debate, Dr Codd offers the following comments on Date's rebuttals.*

Just about every database contains missing values scattered over numerous parts of the database. For example, an employee's birthdate might have to be marked "missing but applicable," because it is at present unknown. Or the employee's year to date commission might have to be marked as missing and inapplicable because he or she is not a salesperson.

Database management would be simpler if missing values didn't exist.[19] Unfortunately, for a variety of reasons, they do occur and need to be managed. Date's assertion that a relation containing missing values is not a relation is unacceptable. While relations that contain missing values [*sic*] are not normally encountered in mathematics, the same operators in the relational model continue to be applicable. Requests expressed in a relational language must be able to cope with missing values, without resorting to guessing.

With Date's default value approach, both the representation and treatment of missing values can be peculiar to the columns in which missing values are permitted. This might be acceptable in a single record at a time DBMS; it is clearly *not* in a multiple record at a time DBMS. The principal reason for adopting an approach that is *uniform across the entire database* is that a single relational request may involve data from numerous distinct columns of the database, and many of these columns are likely to be permitted to have missing values. Imagine a request that deals with 12 or more such columns: A significant part of formulating this request would involve detailed knowledge of the 12 or more representations and treatments of missing values, if the default value scheme were adopted.

For uniformity, one might look to support in hardware. Today's memory technology, however, can't distinguish between values to be taken seriously and those that are not—such as those left in some condition by some previous activity. Once a disk is formatted, the computer regards every bit as part of the value of something. In my relational model version 2 (RM/V2), any column in which missing values are permitted is assigned one extra byte to indicate, for each row, whether the associated value is:

---

[19] See my comments on this remark in the preface to this book.

1. To be treated seriously, or
2. Missing and applicable, or
3. Missing and inapplicable.

IBM's DB2 partially supports this representation.[20]

A basic ground rule in the relational model is that *the DBMS must NOT provide a definite response to a query when it is not certain about the response because values are missing.*[21] I remember well when I first arrived in New York City to reside in the U.S. It was the fall of 1948 and I was looking vigorously for a job. Often I would have to ask people on the street how to get to specific parts of the city. I received detailed directions, but almost invariably these directions were wrong. I stopped asking and used street maps instead. Similarly, people who use a DBMS that *guesses* the answer to a query but delivers it as if it were not guessing are likely to abandon its use.

In Date's Rebuttal I, he decries the inadequacies of three-valued logic, which I first discussed [*i.e., 3VL, not the inadequacies*] in my 1979 paper. I proposed a significant improvement [*i.e., to the 3VL scheme*] in my 1986 paper "Missing Information (Applicable and Inapplicable) in Relational Databases," *ACM SIGMOD Record 15*, No. 4 (December 1986). [*That improvement, which I subsequently incorporated into RM/V2,*] distinguished between two categories of missing database values:

1. Temporarily unknown;
2. Inapplicable, and hence unknowable.

Semantics make this distinction necessary. I also proposed four-valued logic (4VL) and *additional general purpose functions* to permit adequate handling of missing information. Date, in many of his examples, ignores both.

---

[20] It's interesting to see Codd saying here that this scheme for representing missing information is, in effect, *required* by RM/V2. It's not required in his RM/V2 book as such. All the latter has to say on the subject is this: "The representation in IBM relational products of *missing database values* in any column by means of an extra byte seems correct" (page 197, italics in the original).

[21] But that's *exactly* what Codd's "RM+3VL" does! And it's exactly what SQL does, too. Numerous examples earlier in this book illustrate these points.

This double oversight makes his examples merely cases of the incorrect use of the missing value machinery in RM/V2. [*A considerable overstatement.*]

In his Rebuttal I, Date asserts: "It is default values, not nulls, that we use in the real world." Arguments of this type can, and have, been used [*sic*] to delay every technical or scientific step forward. It could have been used to argue against the introduction of computers: "It is mental arithmetic that we use in the real world, not machines." The phrase "real world" is a serious trap, because what is real is continually changing.

Let's take one of Date's examples: A user enters data with an element missing, and he or she does not know whether the element is applicable or inapplicable. Date would claim that, as a consequence, we need a third kind of missing value. In his rebuttal, he goes on to say that we need more and more distinct types of missing values.

I reject this sequence of arguments. In RM/V2, I discontinued using "null" because the term has been so often misinterpreted. As I pointed out earlier, missing values are either *A-marked* (applicable, presently unknown) or *I-marked* (inapplicable, hence unknowable).[22] Let's assume we have an RDBMS that is faithful to RM/V2. As background, remember that:[23]

- For each column other than a primary key column, the DBA may declare that A-marks be permitted or prohibited.
- For each column other than a primary or foreign key column, the DBA can declare that I-marks be permitted or prohibited.
- A-marks are weaker and more flexible than I-marks.
- A-marks likely occur more often than I-marks in a relational database that is in conceptual normal form (*p*) because *p* is the maximum percentage of I-marked values in any column, and *p* is normally set by the DBA to be considerably less than 1.

---

[22] Despite Codd's opening words here ("As I pointed out earlier"), the terms *A-marked* and *I-marked* haven't actually been mentioned in his text at all prior to this point.

[23] This instruction of Codd's strikes this particular reader as more than a little unfair, since *none* of the items in the subsequent bullet list has previously been discussed, or even mentioned. For further information on any of them, I refer you to Codd's RM/V2 book.

- Whenever a tuple is entered with a missing value, this value is A-marked in the database, unless an integrity constraint exists that clearly indicates an I-mark must be recorded.

In this [*Date's?*] example, we must assume that both types of marking are permitted in the pertinent column, and that no declared integrity constraint resolves the issue of whether an A-mark or I-mark should be used. Then RM/V2 marks the missing value as applicable.[24] Later, if it is discovered that the value should have been I-marked, not A-marked, then the DBA or someone with suitable authorization changes the marking on this missing value. Thus, I fail to see the need for more than two kinds of markings.

Date also asserts that multivalued logic destroys the foundation upon which the Relational Model is built. I do not agree. There is no theoretical impairment and no loss of usability, whereas both scope and usability are lost if the default value scheme advocated by Date is adopted.

Date also asserts that normalization becomes invalid when multivalued logic is introduced. This is false, providing that this logic is introduced correctly (few RDBMSs do this today) and care is taken with its use. For example, if the RDBMS supported DBA-defined requests (few do), the DBA could define integrity constraints that will be stored in the catalog to enable the RDBMS to enforce the functional, multivalued, and inclusion dependencies discovered at database design time. However, the RDBMS must withhold the enforcement of these constraints from the *missing* tuple components until they are replaced by actual values. This enforcement should occur at the time of attempted replacement.

Finally, I oppose the use of default values only if it's done to represent that a value is missing. Default values might be useful in other contexts. For example, a bank teller shouldn't be required to re-enter his or her terminal identifier every time he or she enters a customer transaction. The terminal should handle this itself.

(*DBP&D gave me the opportunity to reply to Codd's additional comments, but it seemed to me that no further reply was warranted.*)

---

[24] But how can it be marked at all if isn't there? Please understand that this isn't a frivolous question—I believe it strikes at the very heart of Codd's entire scheme. What it leads to, it seems to me, is the need to draw a distinction between values as such, on the one hand, and storage positions or locations that hold such values, on the other—*a distinction that didn't previously exist in the relational model at all.*

# Index

*For alphabetization purposes, (a) differences in fonts and case are ignored; (b) quotation marks are ignored; (c) other punctuation symbols—hyphens, underscores, parentheses, etc.—are treated as blanks; (d) numerals precede letters; (e) blanks precede everything else.*

www.ingramcontent.com/pod-product-compliance
Lightning Source LLC
Chambersburg PA
CBHW080638060326
40690CB00021B/4977

*9781634624763*